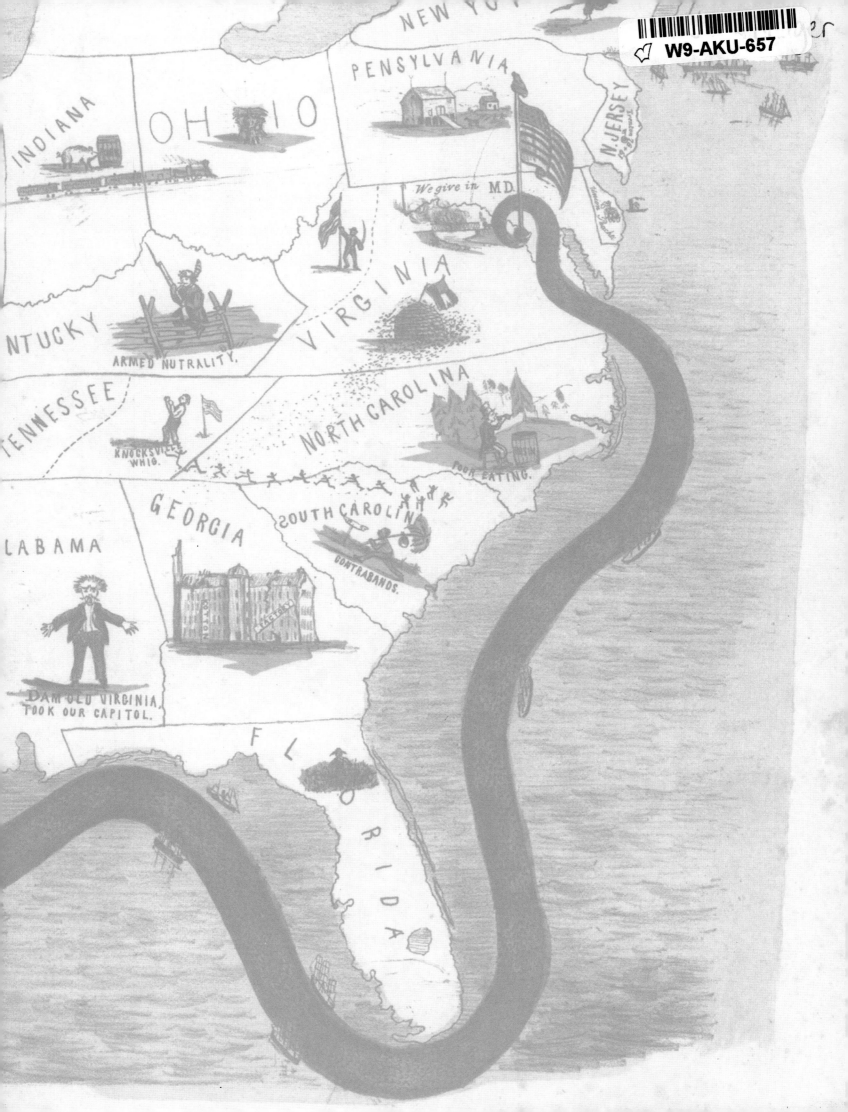

GREAT COMMANDERS
HEAD-TO-HEAD

THE BATTLES
OF THE
CIVIL
WAR

Great Commanders
Head-to-Head

The Battles of the Civil War

Thunder Bay
P·R·E·S·S

San Diego, California

Thunder Bay Press
An imprint of the Advantage Publishers Group
10350 Barnes Canyon Road, San Diego, CA 92121
www.thunderbaybooks.com

THUNDER BAY
P · R · E · S · S

Amber Books Ltd
Bradley's Close
74–77 White Lion Street
London N1 9PF, UK
www.amberbooks.co.uk

Project Editor: Michael Spilling
Design: Zoe Mellors and Hawes Design
Picture Research: Terry Forshaw

Library of Congress Cataloging-in-Publication Data

Dougherty, Kevin.
   Great commanders head-to-head : the battles of the Civil War / Kevin Dougherty.
      p. cm.
   ISBN-13: 978-1-59223-988-7
   ISBN-10: 1-59223-988-9
   1. United States--History--Civil War, 1861-1865--Campaigns. 2. Command of troops--
History--19th century--Case studies. 3. Generals--United States--History--19th century.
4. Generals--Confederate States of America. 5. Military art and science--United States--
History--19th century--Case studies. I. Title.
   E470.D67 2008
   973.7'3--dc22
                              2008053784

Printed in Thailand

1 2 3 4 5 13 12 11 10 09

CONTENTS

INTRODUCTION

Leadership is the process of influencing people by providing purpose, direction, and motivation in order to accomplish the mission and improve the organization. It is the most dynamic element of an army's combat power. *Great Commanders Head-to-Head: The Battles of the Civil War* examines the role that leadership played in some of the key battles of the Civil War.

Civil War leaders of both the North and South had many shared experiences. Many were products of the United States Military Academy at West Point, and many had first tasted combat in the Mexican War. This shared background meant many of them had been good friends and comrades in the "Old Army." They knew each other personally and professionally. They were aware of one another's strengths and weaknesses, capabilities and limitations, likes and dislikes. Perhaps in no other war have the opposing commanders been so familiar with each other.

The armies they commanded were also similar. To be sure, the Federal army was larger and better equipped, but both armies were made up of American soldiers, largely volunteers, who brought with them the typical American characteristics of independence, patriotism, and ingenuity. Molding these mass armies into disciplined fighting units would be an important leadership task for Civil War commanders.

ADJUSTING TACTICS AND OPERATIONS

Both armies had to come to grips with the impact of new technologies on the battlefield. Rifles, railroads, mines,

Below: This 1907 lithograph by George Bagby Matthews shows Robert E. Lee (1807–70) with his generals. In reality, they were never all gathered together in one place, and several of them died during the war.

balloons, ironclads, and steam-powered ships all required tactical and operational adjustments by the commanders. Some understood the impact more readily than others, and many times the soldiers in the ranks paid the price for their commander's slow learning.

The result of all these phenomena was that leadership was a critical component in determining the outcome of many Civil War battles. Superior leadership allowed Stonewall Jackson and Robert E. Lee to overcome huge disadvantages at the Battles of Kernstown and Chancellorsville. Resolute leadership allowed generals such as Ulysses S. Grant to turn defeat at Shiloh into victory. Timid leadership caused other generals such as George B. McClellan to forfeit the advantage at Antietam. Many leaders found themselves in command positions for which they were unprepared, such as John Pemberton at Vicksburg and Irvin McDowell at First Manassas, and the results of the battles reflected that situation. Other leaders, such as William Tecumseh Sherman in the Atlanta Campaign, had grown throughout the war and found themselves in situations tailor-made for their abilities. Some leaders rose to the challenge presented to them, such as George Meade at Gettysburg, while others failed, such as Braxton Bragg at Perryville. And in some cases, such as Lee at Spotsylvania, leaders won the battle but failed in the broader strategic context.

Great Commanders Head-to-Head: The Battles of the Civil War explores eleven Civil War battles. Each is examined in terms of its preliminaries, conduct, and results, but the key to each chapter is an analysis of the leadership of both principal commanders involved. In every case, the battle's results are easily understood in light of the actions of these leaders.

Below: This photograph shows President Abraham Lincoln (center) with Allan Pinkerton (left), head of the Secret Service, and Major General John McClernand (right).

BEAUREGARD VS. McDOWELL

FIRST MANASSAS, 1861

I n the Battle of First Manassas, Brigadier General Irvin McDowell and the Federal Army of Northeastern Virginia battled the Confederate Army of the Potomac, commanded by Brigadier General Pierre Gustave Toutant Beauregard. Two other armies, Major General Robert Patterson's Department of Pennsylvania and General Joseph (Joe) Johnston's Army of the Shenandoah, would also play key roles.

At this stage in the war, both the Federals and the Confederates were equally inexperienced and the battle could have gone either way. As it turned out, the Confederates dealt the Federals a humiliating defeat that showed the nation the war would not be settled

IRVIN McDOWELL

RANK: BRIGADIER GENERAL
BORN: 1818
EDUCATED: UNITED STATES MILITARY ACADEMY
MILITARY CAREER
VETERAN OF MEXICAN WAR
INSTRUCTOR AT THE UNITED STATES MILITARY ACADEMY
ADMINISTRATIVE POSITION IN ADJUTANT GENERAL'S OFFICE
ENDED WAR AS A MAJOR GENERAL IN THE DEPARTMENT OF
   THE PACIFIC
DIED: 1885

quickly. Of great military significance was the role railroads would play in the battle, a precursor to the importance they would have throughout the war.

PRELIMINARIES

On April 14, 1861, the battle at Fort Sumter, South Carolina, had confirmed that the growing sectional crisis could now only be settled by force. The day after the battle, President Abraham Lincoln declared an insurrection to be in existence and called for 75,000 volunteers with ninety-day enlistments to restore order. This proclamation compelled the border states of the South to decide between bearing arms against their fellow Southern states or joining them in secession. As a result, four additional states, Virginia, Arkansas, North Carolina, and Tennessee, all chose to side with the Confederacy.

On May 3, Lincoln called for 42,034 volunteers to serve for three years unless sooner discharged, and increased the Regular Army's strength by 22,714. In an outpouring of enthusiasm, the rush of volunteers exceeded Lincoln's request astronomically. By July 1, Secretary of War Simon Cameron reported 310,000 men under arms.

The situation was similar in the Confederacy. On March 6, 1861, two days after the inauguration of Lincoln as the sixteenth president of the United States, the Congress of the Confederate States of America voted that 100,000 volunteers be enlisted for one year. As in the North, volunteers rushed to the call.

These mobilizations took on a very decentralized and haphazard nature. Often without standardized uniforms, training, equipment, or discipline, the volunteers flooded in. The result was two armies filled with unquestionably patriotic but marginally skilled individuals. The training that did occur was at the lower levels, and training at the brigade or division level was almost nonexistent. This high level of inexperience on both the Federal and Confederate sides would be evident in the Battle of First Manassas.

THE FEDERAL PLAN

At the outbreak of the Civil War, Lieutenant General Winfield Scott had been on active duty since 1808, having performed heroically in the War of 1812 and the Mexican War. Now far too old and infirm to take the field, Scott was still

FIRST MANASSAS

Date	July 21, 1861
Location	Manassas, Virginia
Result	Confederate victory

Strength	
Union: 35,000	Confederate: 35,000

Casualties and losses	
2,706	1,981

PIERRE G. T. BEAUREGARD

RANK: BRIGADIER GENERAL
BORN: 1818
EDUCATED: UNITED STATES MILITARY ACADEMY
MILITARY CAREER
VETERAN OF MEXICAN WAR
SUPERINTENDENT OF THE UNITED STATES MILITARY ACADEMY
"HERO OF SUMTER"
ENDED WAR AS A GENERAL, SERVING AS SECOND IN COMMAND
   TO JOSEPH JOHNSTON IN THE CAROLINAS CAMPAIGN
DIED: 1893

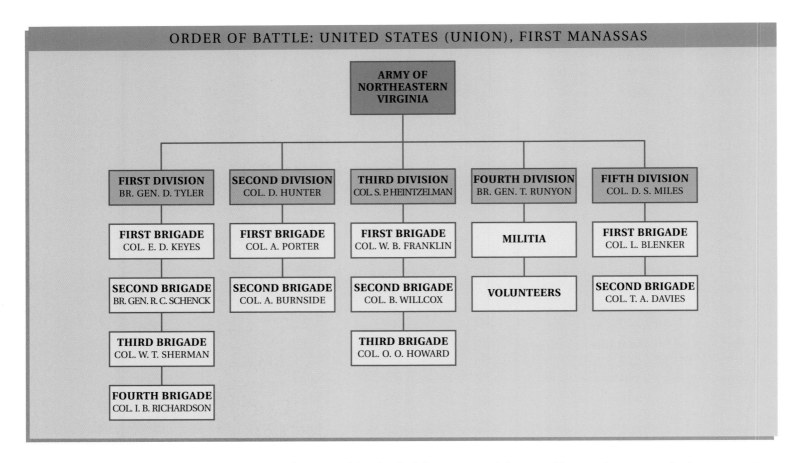

ORDER OF BATTLE: UNITED STATES (UNION), FIRST MANASSAS

ARMY OF NORTHEASTERN VIRGINIA

FIRST DIVISION BR. GEN. D. TYLER	SECOND DIVISION COL. D. HUNTER	THIRD DIVISION COL. S. P. HEINTZELMAN	FOURTH DIVISION BR. GEN. T. RUNYON	FIFTH DIVISION COL. D. S. MILES
FIRST BRIGADE COL. E. D. KEYES	FIRST BRIGADE COL. A. PORTER	FIRST BRIGADE COL. W. B. FRANKLIN	MILITIA	FIRST BRIGADE COL. L. BLENKER
SECOND BRIGADE BR. GEN. R. C. SCHENCK	SECOND BRIGADE COL. A. BURNSIDE	SECOND BRIGADE COL. B. WILLCOX	VOLUNTEERS	SECOND BRIGADE COL. T. A. DAVIES
THIRD BRIGADE COL. W. T. SHERMAN		THIRD BRIGADE COL. O. O. HOWARD		
FOURTH BRIGADE COL. I. B. RICHARDSON				

Below: One Civil War development was the use of distinctive devices to identify organizations. The trefoil on this soldier's cap identifies him as a member of the Federal Army, Second Corps, Third Division.

the general-in-chief of the army and the man to whom President Lincoln turned to develop the Federal strategy.

Scott was a strong advocate of limited war, the idea of using the minimum force necessary to achieve the war's political objective, and, as he had in Mexico, sought to avoid a bloody war as he developed the Federal strategy. His plan was to mobilize an army so big and powerful that the Confederacy would negotiate a return to the Union without a fight. In the meantime, he envisioned seizing the entire line of the Mississippi and Ohio rivers in order to split the Confederate states east of the Mississippi from those in the west. At the same time, he would impose a naval blockade of the Confederate coast. Large-scale fighting might be avoided by tightening this ring around the eastern Confederate states. Once put in place, Scott's "Anaconda Plan," like the great snake for which it was named, would strangle the Confederacy into submission.

The strategy was a sound one, but it would take time. Scott himself noted that "the greatest obstacle in the way of the plan" was "the impatience of our patriotic and loyal Union friends. They will urge instant and vigorous action, regardless, I fear, of consequences." Indeed, with the Confederate army now just outside Washington and in the wake of the recent Federal defeat at the Battle of Big Bethel in June, President Lincoln found Scott's plan too slow. Instead, Lincoln ordered Scott to mount a campaign in northern Virginia, and Scott reluctantly passed the order on to McDowell, who commanded the army at Washington. When the latter complained his men were not yet ready, Scott replied, "You are green, it is true, but they are green also; you are all green alike." With that small comfort, McDowell set to work to develop a plan.

TRIPARTITE TACTIC

It took McDowell several attempts to come up with something that met the approval of Scott, Lincoln, and his cabinet. In the plan that was finally accepted, McDowell proposed dividing his army into three columns in order to facilitate speed and maneuver. He would then advance westward on roughly parallel routes and seize the Confederate outposts at Fairfax Court House, sixteen miles from Washington, and at

Centreville, five miles past Fairfax Court House. Once these preliminary missions were complete, two of the Federal columns would move ahead and conduct a diversionary attack against what McDowell figured would be the center of the Confederate line at Bull Run, a small creek flowing into the Occoquan River. With the center thus held in check, the third column would move around the Confederates' right flank and strike southward to cut the railroad to Richmond.

To meet this threat to their rear, the Confederates would have to abandon Manassas Junction and fall back to the next defensible position, which was the Rappahannock River, about fifteen miles away. If this plan worked, Washington would have an acceptable buffer zone between it and the Confederate force, and McDowell would have won a victory largely by maneuver rather than having to expose his untrained army to a pitched battle. He would also be that much closer to his ultimate objective of Richmond.

Critical to McDowell's plan was the ability of Major General Robert Patterson and his 18,000 men of the Department of Pennsylvania to keep General Joe Johnston and his 12,000-man Army of the Shenandoah from reinforcing Beauregard. If Johnston got loose from the Shenandoah Valley, he could descend upon McDowell's right flank and disrupt the entire attack. Patterson was almost seventy years old and, like Scott, was a veteran of the War of 1812 and Mexico. His best days as a soldier, however, were behind him. McDowell told Scott he felt "very tender" about this aspect of the plan, but Scott, who was an old friend of Patterson, assured McDowell that everything would be all right. If Johnston did happen to slip by, Scott assured McDowell that "he would have Patterson on his heels."

THE CONFEDERATE PLAN

Brigadier General Pierre Gustave Toutant Beauregard, the hero of Fort Sumter, stood in McDowell's way. Beauregard anticipated McDowell would advance on

Manassas Junction by way of Centreville, and had built a defense along the south bank of Bull Run whose five-foot-high banks presented a formidable obstacle. Beauregard's line ran from his right flank near the railroad bridge at Union Mills northward more than seven miles along Bull Run to the Stone Bridge on the Warrenton Turnpike. The Stone Bridge was the only span over Bull Run that could support military wagon traffic, but the creek was fordable at many other places, and Beauregard's force was too thin to defend all the possible crossings.

The northernmost crossing was Sudley Ford, about two and a half miles upstream from the Stone Bridge. Because of the poor road network leading from Centreville to Sudley Ford, Beauregard assumed McDowell would not use this crossing and therefore left it unguarded.

Above: The Stone Bridge was the only span over Bull Run that could support military traffic. It was defended by the hard-fighting Confederate Colonel Nathan Evans.

Above: The Battle of First Manassas ruptured the quiet of the Virginia countryside and caught several civilians in its wake. Continued fighting in the area led Wilmer McLean to move his family— ironically to Appomattox, where Lee's surrender took place in his parlor.

"TODAY WILL BE KNOWN AS BLACK MONDAY. WE ARE UTTERLY AND DISGRACEFULLY ROUTED, BEATEN, WHIPPED BY SECESSIONISTS."

UNION DIARIST
GEORGE TEMPLETON STRONG

The Stone Bridge was the obvious crossing site for the Federal forces. In fact, Beauregard considered it so obvious that he was certain McDowell would try elsewhere. Thus, Beauregard assigned only part of Colonel Nathan Evans's Seventh Brigade to guard it. Evans was gruff, hard-drinking, and often insubordinate, but he was also a fighter. The next three fords crossed Bull Run in dense woods that reduced their suitability for maneuver, so Beauregard lightly defended them with Colonel Philip St. George Cocke's Fifth Brigade.

Where Beauregard expected the Federal attack to come was at Mitchell's Ford, two and a half miles from the Stone Bridge at a crescent-shaped bend in Bull Run. Mitchell's Ford was the most direct route between Centreville and Manassas Junction. On the Centreville side, a good branch road off the Warrenton Turnpike provided a speedy approach, and beyond the ford two miles of level, open plain would give the Federals an unobstructed march to Manassas Junction. Beauregard was so sure that McDowell would use this crossing that he placed more than half his army in the area of Mitchell's Ford. Brigadier General Milledge Bonham's First Brigade guarded Mitchell's Ford, and Brigadier General James Longstreet's

Fourth Brigade was half a mile downstream at Blackburn's Ford. A mile farther down, Brigadier General David Jones's Third Brigade blocked McLean's Ford. Behind these three brigades was a reserve force, the Sixth Brigade commanded by Colonel Jubal Early. Brigadier General Dick Ewell's Second Brigade anchored the Confederate right guarding Union Mills Ford and the nearby Orange and Alexandria Railroad. All told, Beauregard had five of his seven brigades on the right half of his line.

READY TO STEAL THE INITIATIVE
There was more on Beauregard's mind than just parrying the expected Federal main attack when he aligned his forces so heavily toward the right. Beauregard also planned to attack across the fords himself, outflank the Federal army, and cut it off from Washington. For the time being, President Jefferson Davis had ordered Beauregard to remain on the defensive, but if he saw an opportunity, Beauregard wanted to steal the initiative from the Federals.

He instructed Captain E. Porter Alexander to build four signal towers along Bull Run and at Manassas Junction to provide early warning of any enemy movements. Alexander would report any information with a "wigwag system" that employed five separate, numbered movements of a single flag in order to communicate messages. In addition to Alexander's reports, Beauregard had the benefit of a friendly civilian population to keep him well informed.

THE BATTLE

On July 16 McDowell got his army moving toward Manassas Junction. The excited soldiers shouted, "On to Richmond!" as they took off. Before long, Beauregard got word of the Federal advance and requested reinforcements. Brigadier General Theophilus Holmes's independent brigade in Fredericksburg and Colonel Wade Hampton's six-company Hampton Legion in Richmond were hurried north.

McDowell had hoped to reach Centreville by July 17, but the unseasoned troops were unaccustomed to hard marching and by 11:30 a.m. the head of McDowell's army was just reaching Fairfax Court House. McDowell wanted to press on, but the men were too tired, so he set up camp near Fairfax.

The next day's march was also slow and it was not until 11:00 a.m. that the lead elements of Brigadier General Daniel Tyler's First Division reached Centreville. McDowell ordered Tyler to observe the roads to Bull Run and Warrenton, but under no circumstances to bring on a general engagement. Contrary to these orders, Tyler clashed with Confederates at Blackburn's Ford. The Federals suffered eighty-three casualties compared to sixty-eight for the Confederates, but more importantly, McDowell now considered his plan to be compromised. Fearing Beauregard would now strengthen his right flank, McDowell began looking for alternatives. He assumed the Stone Bridge would be heavily mined, so he sent his engineers farther north to find another crossing.

While McDowell conducted his reconnaissance, the Blackburn's Ford skirmish had caused the Confederate War Department to order Johnston to come to Beauregard's aid. Johnston marched out of Winchester around noon with Colonel James Ewell Brown "Jeb"

Stuart's cavalry screening the movement from Patterson. The latter was so deceived that an hour after Johnston and his force had departed, Patterson sent this telegraph to Washington: "I have succeeded, in accordance with the wishes of the General-in-Chief, in keeping General Johnston's force at Winchester." McDowell's greatest fear had come to fruition.

RAIL PLAYS A PIVOTAL ROLE

At 7:30 a.m. on July 19, the first members of Johnston's command arrived at Piedmont Station, a stop on the Manassas Gap Railroad. Two hours later, Brigadier General Thomas Jackson had his men boarded on trains and heading for Manassas Junction. More brigades

Below: Brigadier General Thomas Jackson overlooks his men on Henry House Hill. High ground was especially important on Civil War battlefields because of the good observation it afforded.

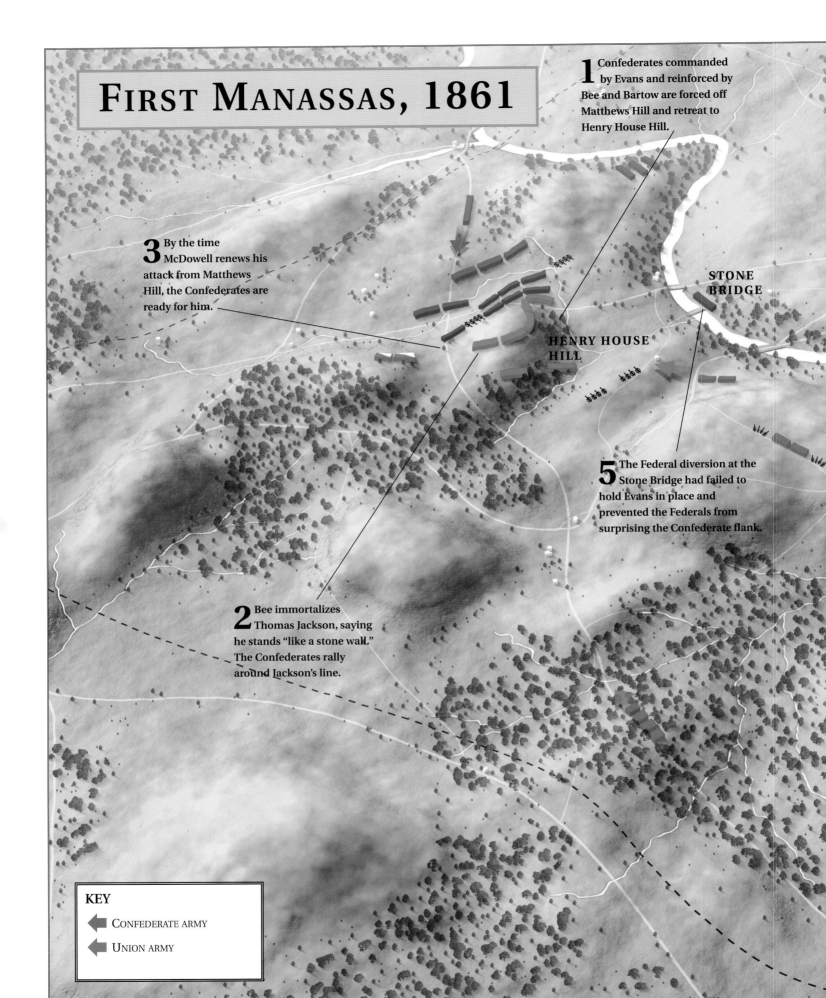

FIRST MANASSAS, 1861

1 Confederates commanded by Evans and reinforced by Bee and Bartow are forced off Matthews Hill and retreat to Henry House Hill.

3 By the time McDowell renews his attack from Matthews Hill, the Confederates are ready for him.

STONE BRIDGE

HENRY HOUSE HILL

5 The Federal diversion at the Stone Bridge had failed to hold Evans in place and prevented the Federals from surprising the Confederate flank.

2 Bee immortalizes Thomas Jackson, saying he stands "like a stone wall." The Confederates rally around Jackson's line.

KEY

← CONFEDERATE ARMY

← UNION ARMY

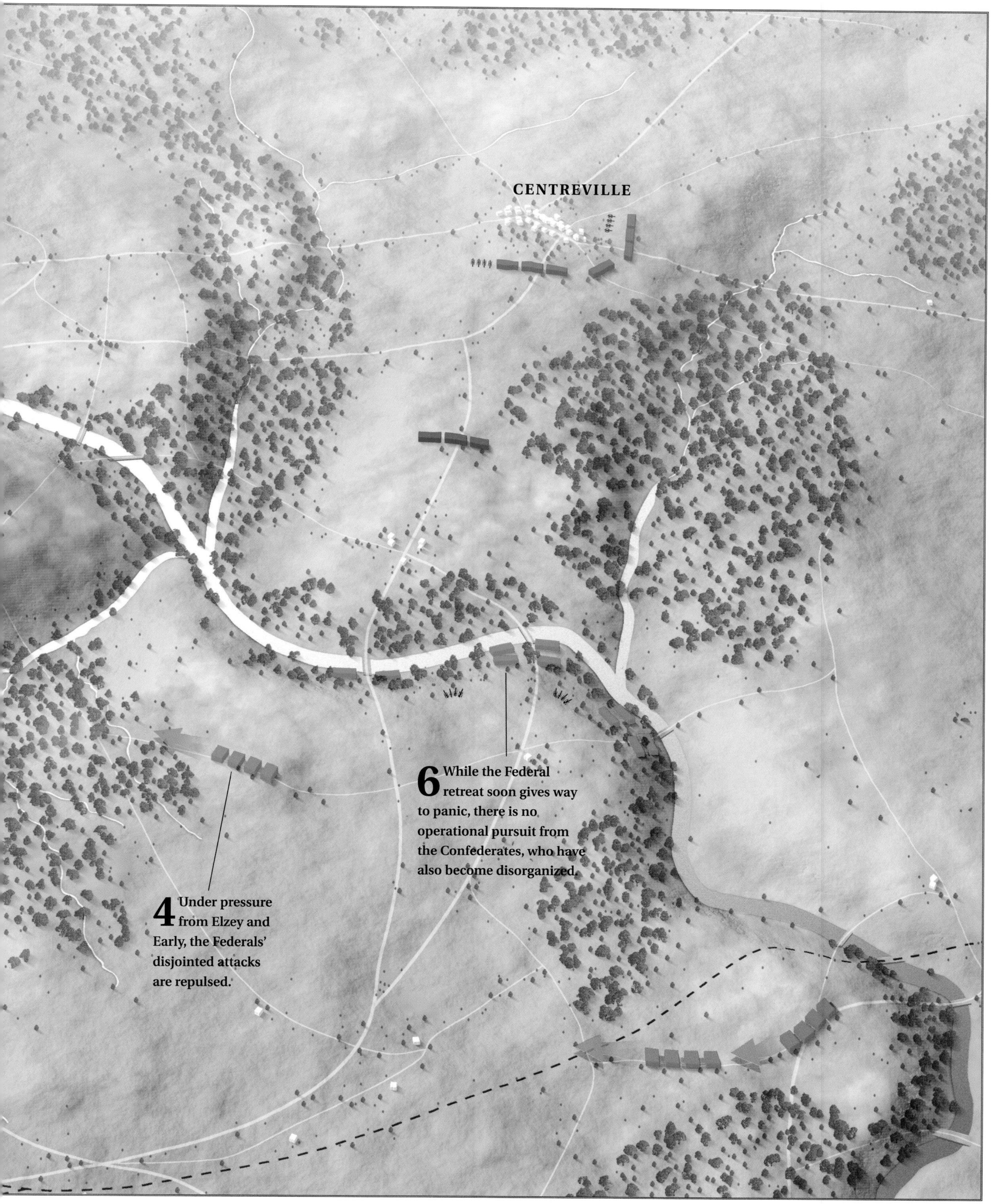

CENTREVILLE

6 While the Federal retreat soon gives way to panic, there is no operational pursuit from the Confederates, who have also become disorganized.

4 Under pressure from Elzey and Early, the Federals' disjointed attacks are repulsed.

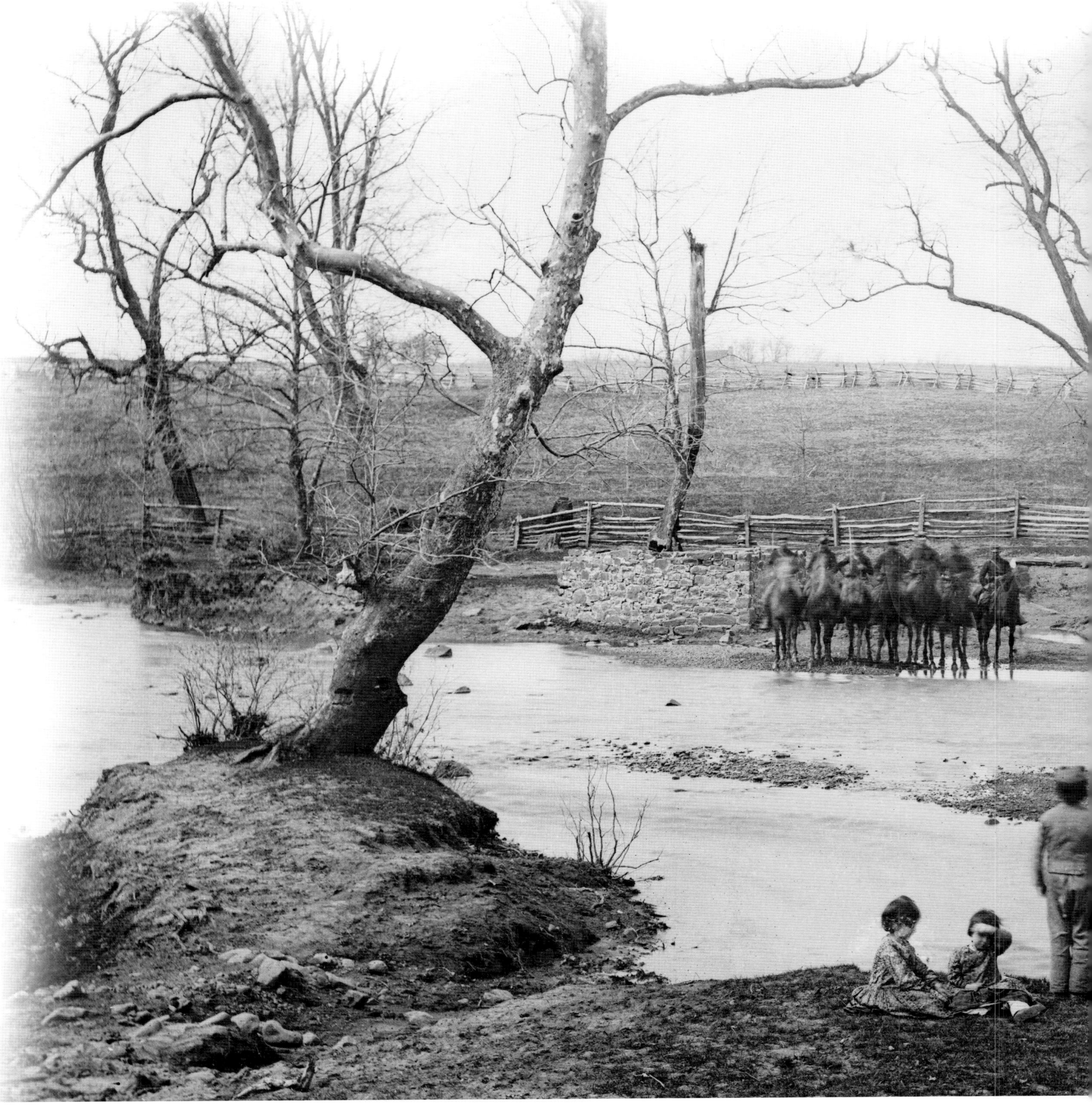

Below: Sudley Ford, shown here with a Federal cavalry patrol, was the northernmost crossing of Bull Run.

followed, and Johnston personally reached Manassas Junction around noon on July 20. Although Johnston was senior to Beauregard, he was unfamiliar with the terrain and there was insufficient daylight left for him to reconnoiter the battlefield adequately. Instead, he relinquished command to Beauregard and devoted himself to the critical role of forwarding reinforcements to the scene of the fighting throughout the battle.

The Confederate trains moved relatively slowly and lacked sufficient cars to simultaneously transport large numbers of troops, but almost all of Johnston's army arrived at Manassas in time to participate in the battle. This pivotal role of the railroad would become thematic throughout the war. Indeed, historians consider the Civil War to be "the first great railroad war."

As McDowell's troops continued to arrive at Centreville, Federal engineers located two potential fording sites north

of the Stone Bridge. The first was Poplar Ford, about a mile to the north, and the second was Sudley Ford, another mile beyond that. McDowell decided to avoid what he considered to be the strong Confederate right by conducting a feint toward Blackburn's Ford and the Stone Bridge, while his main attack turned the Confederate left. Time was not on McDowell's side. Not only had he heard rumors of Confederate reinforcements arriving from the Shenandoah Valley, but many of the Federal soldiers' ninety-day enlistments were soon to expire. McDowell had to act quickly.

The Confederates also had reasons to hurry. Johnston was concerned that Patterson may have followed him out of the Shenandoah Valley, and he urged Beauregard to attack as soon as possible. In response, Beauregard came up with a plan to attack the Federal left using crossings at Union Mills, Blackburn's Ford, and McLean's Ford. As the senior officer on the scene, Johnston approved the plan at 4:30 a.m. on July 21.

By then McDowell had his men moving. As early as 2:30 a.m., Federal troops had broken camp at Centreville, but the march was soon beset by delays. It was not until 6:00 a.m. that Tyler reached the Stone Bridge and was able to begin his demonstration against Evans's Confederate forces.

Above: Advancing through thick woods provided Civil War troops with cover but hindered command and control. Advancing through open fields made it easier to maintain formations but exposed the men to enemy fire.

AN ATTACK THAT WENT NOWHERE

Thinking this activity at the Stone Bridge was merely a small unit engagement, Beauregard proceeded with his plan to attack McDowell's left. The firing he heard in Evans's sector, however, increasingly concerned Johnston, so around 7:00 a.m. he began sending reinforcements there. Ewell inexplicably not receiving his copy of the order to advance hindered Beauregard's attack, and by 8:00 a.m. Ewell was still waiting on the south side of Bull Run while Jones and Longstreet had already crossed to the other side. Beauregard's attack was stalled before it even got started, and ultimately went nowhere.

Then at about 8:30, Alexander, positioned at his signal station, noticed the reflections of sunlight off of bayonets in the distance. The Federal troops were Colonel Samuel Heintzelman's Third Division and Colonel David Hunter's Second Division, and they were using Sudley Ford and Poplar Ford to march around the Confederate left. Instantly

assessing the danger, Alexander warned Evans, "Look out for your left. You are flanked." Evans quickly moved his forces to meet this new threat and took up a position on the southern slope of Matthews Hill to cover the Manassas–Sudley Road. Tyler's intended diversion at the Stone Bridge had failed to hold Evans in place. Thus, though McDowell's turning movement deprived the Confederates of their formidable defense along Bull Run, he lost his opportunity to surprise the Confederate flank.

At about 10:30, Colonel Ambrose Burnside's brigade of Rhode Islanders, the lead element of Hunter's division, reached Matthews Hill and came under fire from Evans. Burnside deployed his brigade, but by now the effects of Tyler's earlier demonstration had long worn off. Even so, the Federal attack gained momentum and threatened Evans's position. At about 11:00 a.m., Confederate brigades commanded by Brigadier General Barnard Bee and Colonel Francis Bartow arrived near

"IT IS MY FIRM BELIEF THAT A GREAT DEAL OF THE MISFORTUNE OF THE DAY AT BULL RUN IS DUE TO THE FACT THAT THE TROOPS KNEW VERY LITTLE OF THE PRINCIPLES AND PRACTICE OF FIRING. IN EVERY CASE I BELIEVE THAT THE FIRING OF THE REBELS WAS BETTER THAN OURS."

UNION COLONEL W. R. FRANKLIN

Left: The Eleventh New York Infantry, best known as the First Fire Zouaves, wore colorful uniforms that sometimes included bright red blouses and red fezzes. Here, the Zouaves are charged by Jeb Stuart's cavalry on Henry House Hill.

ORDER OF BATTLE: CONFEDERACY, FIRST MANASSAS

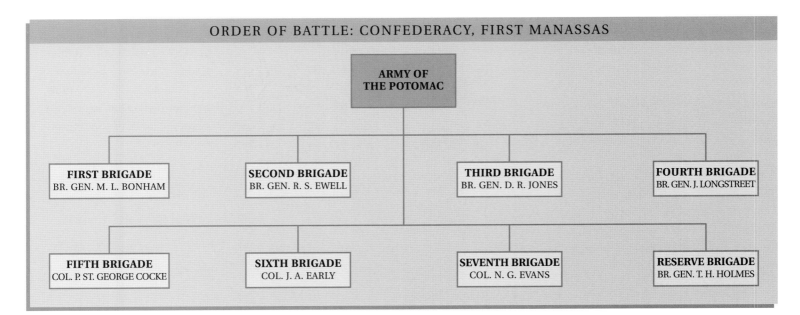

ARMY OF THE POTOMAC

FIRST BRIGADE
BR. GEN. M. L. BONHAM

SECOND BRIGADE
BR. GEN. R. S. EWELL

THIRD BRIGADE
BR. GEN. D. R. JONES

FOURTH BRIGADE
BR. GEN. J. LONGSTREET

FIFTH BRIGADE
COL. P. ST. GEORGE COCKE

SIXTH BRIGADE
COL. J. A. EARLY

SEVENTH BRIGADE
COL. N. G. EVANS

RESERVE BRIGADE
BR. GEN. T. H. HOLMES

Henry House, just across Young's Branch from Matthews Hill. Evans rode to Bee and requested reinforcements, and Bee ordered the two brigades forward. Nonetheless, the Matthews Hill position soon proved untenable, and the Confederates broke into a disorderly retreat back toward Henry House.

CRYING "VICTORY!" BEFORE
THE TURN OF THE TIDE

It was now shortly before noon and the Federal forces seemed on the verge of a great victory. One of McDowell's staff officers rode around the field shouting, "Victory, victory! We have done it!" Soldiers arriving late were genuinely worried that they had missed out on the entire war.

The tide, however, was about to turn. At about noon, Jackson's brigade had marched to the sound of the firing and taken up a position on Henry House Hill. There, Jackson met an excited Bee, who told him the Federals had driven the Confederates back. Jackson calmly deployed his men on a line that stretched north toward the Robinson House, where it joined the Hampton Legion.

The remnants of the commands of Evans, Bee, and Bartow regrouped behind Jackson. Sometime during the afternoon, Bee pointed to Jackson and said he was standing there "like a stone wall." Exactly what Bee said or meant is unclear, but the result was that after that day, Jackson was forevermore known to the world as "Stonewall."

As these developments took place, Beauregard and Johnston remained on a low hill to the rear of Mitchell's Ford awaiting maturation of the Confederate attack. Although Johnston had earlier ceded operational control of the battle to Beauregard, Johnston could remain idle no longer. Responding to the growing noise on the left, Johnston announced, "The battle is there. I am going." Beauregard joined him, and as the pair worked their way toward Henry House Hill, they brought with them guns from various batteries they had encountered along the way.

At 2:00 p.m., when McDowell finally renewed his attack after his victory at Matthews Hill, the Confederates were ready for him. Rather than launching a

Below: Manassas lay thirty miles southwest of Washington, where it blocked the Federal army's route to Richmond.

large-scale assault on Henry House Hill, McDowell frittered away his numerical advantage by piecemeal attacks. His problem had begun earlier in the day when Heintzelman's division missed the road to the crossing at Poplar Ford and ended up following Hunter across Sudley Ford.

Thus, instead of Heintzelman aligning on Hunter's left and the two divisions entering the battle abreast, they arrived one behind the other. Now McDowell exacerbated the problem by ordering brigade-sized attacks at various locations rather than massing his forces to overwhelm the defenders.

McDowell's attack in shambles

By about 4:00 p.m., the Federal attack on Henry House Hill had run out of steam and the Confederates were free to concentrate on Chinn Ridge, where Colonel Oliver Howard had earlier attacked in one of McDowell's disjointed efforts. Among the Confederates who met them was Colonel Arnold Elzey's Fourth Brigade, the last of Johnston's troops to arrive from the Shenandoah Valley that day. Under pressure from Elzey and Early, Howard's attack broke and fled back to the Warrenton Turnpike.

By now McDowell's attack was in shambles. Units were disintegrating everywhere and thousands of soldiers were fleeing in a mass exodus. Civilians who had rode out from Washington to watch the battle were caught up in the chaos, and panic took control. Unable to restore order, McDowell ordered a retreat to Fairfax and then to Washington. Hoping for news of a great victory,

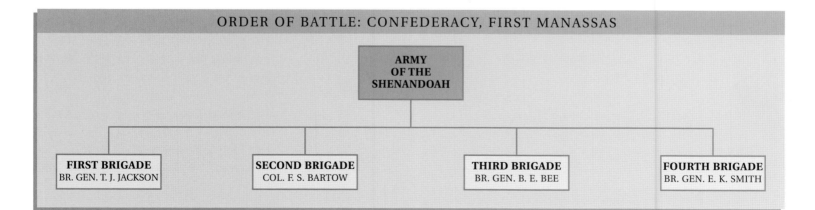

Left: Confederate cavalryman. The bulk of the fighting at First Manassas was done by infantry soldiers, although cavalry units were present on both sides, employed for both scouting and covering flanks.

President Lincoln instead received a telegraph stating, "General McDowell's army in full retreat through Centreville. The day is lost. Save Washington and the remnants of this army." By now, however, the victorious Confederate forces were almost as confused and disorganized as the Federals were. There was to be no operational pursuit.

The battle's impact

The Battle of First Manassas showed that neither of the two relatively large armies of new recruits, nor their commanders, was sufficiently trained for modern

ORDER OF BATTLE: CONFEDERACY, FIRST MANASSAS

ARMY OF THE SHENANDOAH

FIRST BRIGADE BR. GEN. T. J. JACKSON	**SECOND BRIGADE** COL. F. S. BARTOW	**THIRD BRIGADE** BR. GEN. B. E. BEE	**FOURTH BRIGADE** BR. GEN. E. K. SMITH

MCDOWELL'S LEADERSHIP

McDowell quickly became a scapegoat for the defeat at First Manassas. More blame probably rested with Patterson, who had failed to contain Johnston in the Shenandoah Valley, but Patterson's term of service expired a few days after the battle, and McDowell was left to face the nation's frustration alone. On July 25, 1861, he was relieved of command. Nonetheless, he was promoted to major general and commanded the First Corps in McClellan's Army of the Potomac, but he never escaped the blow to his reputation caused by First Manassas.

The fact of the matter is that McDowell probably never should have been in the demanding position he was in, but with thousands of volunteers streaming into Washington, someone had to lead them. Scott was physically unable to take field command, so the Lincoln administration looked for alternatives. The influential Secretary of the Treasury, Samuel Chase, championed McDowell who, like Chase, was from Ohio.

Although McDowell had served admirably in Mexico, he had spent most of his career in administrative positions with the Adjutant General's Office in Washington. It was in that capacity that he had met Chase. At the outbreak of the Civil War, McDowell was a major with limited command experience. But thanks to the support of Chase, McDowell was promoted three grades to brigadier general and on May 27 was assigned as commander of the Department of Northeastern Washington.

Those who knew McDowell well had to question his suitability for such an important command. In fact, in June, William T. Sherman and several other officers had reported in person to President Lincoln, having been told to ask for whatever positions they wanted. Sherman asked for and received the relatively low position of colonel of one of the ten new regiments of regulars that Congress had authorized.

On his way out of the White House, Sherman met McDowell, whom Sherman had known from their days at West Point. McDowell, wearing his new brigadier general's uniform, said, "Hello, Sherman. What did you ask for?"

"A colonelcy," replied Sherman.

"What?" exclaimed McDowell. "You should have asked for a brigadier general's rank. You're just as fit for it as I am."

"I know it," answered Sherman. Left unsaid was the nagging suspicion that McDowell had got himself in over his head. The Battle of First Manassas would confirm that concern.

combat. McDowell had commanded 35,000 men and, with the addition of Johnston's reinforcements, Beauregard led a similar number. Armies this size had been unimaginable in the Mexican War, where Scott had led fewer than 13,000. In the Civil War, many corps-size units would match the strength of Scott's entire army. New leadership would have to be raised to take charge of commands this large, and the soldiers would obviously need additional training. The Battle of First Manassas had made these points painfully clear.

The battle also showed that the war would not be settled in a single contest. Civil War limitations of command and control, as well as the new power of the defense made possible by rifled muskets and breastworks, would conspire to make it difficult to destroy an army. As both sides then began to prepare for a long war, President Lincoln called for an additional 500,000 volunteers with three-year enlistments to replace the ninety-day recruits, some of whom had left the service even as the battle was being fought. To rebuild the army after the disaster of First Manassas and to train the new recruits, Lincoln called upon Major General George McClellan.

In the Confederacy, meanwhile, President Jefferson Davis issued a call for 400,000 further volunteers. Beauregard, now basking in the glory of both Fort Sumter and First Manassas, was promoted to the rank of full general. However, his characteristic outspokenness, quarrelsome personality, and self-serving quest for glory soon found him in disfavor with President Davis, and Beauregard was sent west to Tennessee. Joe Johnston was left to command the army, which he entrenched around Manassas and Centreville until the spring of 1862, when, feeling vulnerable, he withdrew most of his force to the Rappahannock River, nearly half the distance to Richmond.

GOOD PLAN, FAULTY EXECUTION

McDowell's inexperience at high levels of field command led him to make several mistakes at First Manassas. Although he was active on the battlefield, he spent most of his time directing the actions of nearby regiments and brigades instead of the army as a whole.

Consequently, McDowell was unable to mount a concerted, synchronized effort. His piecemeal attacks and delays such as the one after Matthews Hill allowed the Confederates to meet each Federal challenge.

Still, given the limitations of the army at this early stage of the war and Patterson's poor performance in the Shenandoah Valley, it is hard to fault McDowell. His plan was far superior to that of Beauregard, applying the lessons of the turning movement Scott had used so effectively in Mexico. In fact, years after the war, the then-commanding general of the army, Lieutenant General William T. Sherman, would credit McDowell with having put together "one of the best-planned battles of the war" at First Manassas.

The problem lay in that plan's execution. Neither McDowell nor his men were up to that challenge. The public clamor for immediate action and McDowell's sound but overly complicated plan did not recognize the complexities of building an army and training it to fight.

A LEGACY OF LESSONS

After First Manassas, both the Federals and Confederates set about the task of absorbing its lessons. The effects on both sides were mixed. While the Federals were humiliated in defeat, many observers believe the North ultimately benefited from the loss because it shocked them into the realization that the war against the South would require increased exertion.

On the other hand, the victory may have instilled confidence in the Confederates that both encouraged them in future battles and engendered a temporary complacency that hindered mobilization. Both sides knew the conflict was far from over. In fact, one year later, many veterans of First Manassas would meet to fight again on the same battlefield.

BEAUREGARD'S LEADERSHIP

Beauregard faced some of the same command challenges that McDowell did. In fact, neither general got more than 18,000 of his men engaged in the actual fighting, but, being the defender, Beauregard suffered fewer consequences from this difficulty than did McDowell. Also, like McDowell, Beauregard generally influenced affairs only at the regimental level. For the most part, he surrendered the initiative and busied himself with reacting to Federal moves. The overall outcome of First Manassas was much more a result of the fog of war and individual action than it was of Beauregard's generalship.

Johnston perhaps acquitted himself better than Beauregard during the battle. His decision to move his men by rail to Manassas Junction was the key to the Confederate victory and, once on the scene, he made a valuable contribution by directing reinforcements to critical locations. Civil War generals called this technique "feeding the fight," and Johnston performed the task with great dispatch. By the end of the day, the Confederates had committed eight of their eleven brigades against seven of McDowell's eleven brigades. This flexibility and mobility carried the day for the Confederates.

Although sobering at the time, the casualties inflicted at First Manassas would seem small compared to the war's later battles. The Federals lost 2,706 men, or 9 percent of their force. The Confederates suffered 1,981 casualties, which represented 6.5 percent of their available strength. While these losses were relatively low, First Manassas served to temper the lust for combat that both sides had previously shown.

JACKSON VS. SHIELDS

KERNSTOWN, 1862

Virginia's Shenandoah Valley lay between the Blue Ridge and the Allegheny Mountains. It was critical to the Confederacy both as an agricultural breadbasket and as a potential invasion route into the North.

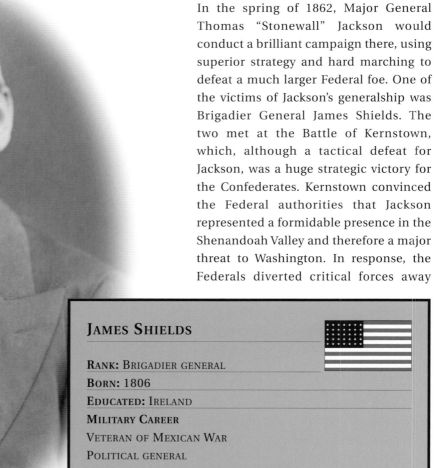

In the spring of 1862, Major General Thomas "Stonewall" Jackson would conduct a brilliant campaign there, using superior strategy and hard marching to defeat a much larger Federal foe. One of the victims of Jackson's generalship was Brigadier General James Shields. The two met at the Battle of Kernstown, which, although a tactical defeat for Jackson, was a huge strategic victory for the Confederates. Kernstown convinced the Federal authorities that Jackson represented a formidable presence in the Shenandoah Valley and therefore a major threat to Washington. In response, the Federals diverted critical forces away

JAMES SHIELDS

RANK: BRIGADIER GENERAL
BORN: 1806
EDUCATED: IRELAND
MILITARY CAREER
VETERAN OF MEXICAN WAR
POLITICAL GENERAL
RESIGNED FROM THE ARMY MARCH 1863
DIED: 1879

from the ongoing Peninsula Campaign, Major General George McClellan's offensive against Richmond, and instead used them to try to deal with Jackson.

PRELIMINARIES

On March 17, 1862, McClellan launched an enormous offensive against the Confederate capital of Richmond, Virginia. McClellan's goal was to avoid a frontal assault against General Joe Johnston's entrenched Confederate force around Manassas and Centreville. To this end, McClellan purposed a bold, amphibious move of 90,000 men and their equipment from Annapolis, Maryland, through the Chesapeake Bay to the mouth of the Rappahannock River. The landing site would be the small hamlet of Urbanna, which lay about sixty miles northeast of Richmond. From there, McClellan, having turned Johnston's defenses, would march on the Confederate capital.

From the very beginning of McClellan's planning for an operation on the Virginia peninsula, events in the Shenandoah Valley had been of great importance. Terminating on the Potomac River just thirty miles northwest of Washington, the Shenandoah Valley represented a potential Confederate avenue of approach into the Federal capital. President Lincoln had demanded that McClellan leave an adequate force behind to guarantee Washington's safety. Pursuant to this requirement, McClellan issued instructions to Major General Nathaniel Banks on March 16, 1862, to

"open your communications with the valley of the Shenandoah. As soon as the Manassas Gap Railway is in running order, intrench [sic] a brigade of infantry, say four regiments, with two batteries, at or near the point where the railway crosses the Shenandoah. Something like two regiments of cavalry should be left in the vicinity to occupy Winchester and thoroughly scour the country south of the railway and up the Shenandoah Valley. The general object is to cover the line of the Potomac and Washington."

STONEWALL STAYS PUT

In reality, the defensive-minded General Joe Johnston was certainly not intending a Confederate offensive against the Federal capital. Instead, Johnston was beginning to feel vulnerable with his position at Manassas, especially since the coming warm spring weather would

KERNSTOWN

Date	March 23, 1862
Location	Near Winchester, Virginia
Result	Union tactical victory; Confederate strategic victory

Strength	
Union: 9,000	Confederate: 5,400

Casualties and losses	
568	718

THOMAS J. JACKSON

RANK: MAJOR GENERAL

BORN: 1824

EDUCATED: UNITED STATES MILITARY ACADEMY

MILITARY CAREER

VETERAN OF MEXICAN WAR

INSTRUCTOR AT VIRGINIA MILITARY INSTITUTE

EARNED THE NICKNAME "STONEWALL" AT FIRST MANASSAS

ACCIDENTALLY SHOT BY HIS OWN MEN AT CHANCELLORSVILLE

DIED: 1863

Above: A Confederate soldier from the Lamar Rifles, Eleventh Mississippi Regiment. The horn shown on this soldier's headgear was used as a badge of light infantry. It traces its origins from Europe, where these troops were used as skirmishers and were largely men with experience as huntsmen, hence the hunting horn.

dry the roads and make it possible for McClellan to attack with superior numbers. Johnston had no intention of waiting around long enough for this development to occur, and on March 7 he ordered all of his troops east of the Blue Ridge Mountains, some 42,000 effectives, to withdraw to the Rappahannock River, nearly half the distance to Richmond. Only Stonewall Jackson's 5,400 men would stay in the Shenandoah Valley to protect Johnston's flank against a Federal advance.

Unaware of McClellan's plans to carry out an amphibious turning movement, Johnston expected the Federals to march directly south to Richmond. Accordingly, he ordered Jackson's Army of the Valley to fall back on line with the main army, protect its flank, secure the Blue Ridge passes, and slow or stop enemy progress up the Shenandoah. Of great importance was the fact that Johnston needed Jackson to stop Banks from reinforcing McClellan. At the time, Johnston could not have expected much from Jackson's small army, but as it turned out, the Shenandoah Valley Campaign would completely alter the strategic situation in Virginia in favor of the Confederates.

KERNSTOWN

After learning of Johnston's withdrawal, McClellan ordered his armies to push forward on all fronts. Cautiously, Banks and his 38,000 men moved up the valley and occupied Winchester on March 12, only to find that Jackson had departed the previous day.

In making such a decision, Jackson greatly benefited from his very capable

mapmaker, Jedediah Hotchkiss. Studying the maps of Hotchkiss, Jackson soon realized that the geography of the region would be critical to the accomplishment of his mission. He quickly recognized that his area of operations would actually be two valleys: the Luray Valley between Masanutten Mountain and the Blue Ridge, and the Shenandoah Valley between Masanutten Mountain and the Alleghenies. Jackson noticed that the only pass in the rugged mountains was the Masanutten Gap, between New Market, which lay in the Shenandoah Valley, and the village of Luray, situated in the Luray Valley. This compartmentalization of his sector greatly shaped Jackson's thinking and was a reality with which he would have to deal.

A MOBILE CAMPAIGN

Jackson could not simultaneously retreat up both corridors. Although both offered advantages and disadvantages, in the final analysis Jackson concluded that mobility was going to be the essential factor in the campaign. The roads east of the Masanutten could not support the swift operations Jackson envisioned, so he decided to fall back from Winchester to Mount Jackson, thirty-five miles to the south.

Upon arriving at Mount Jackson, Jackson learned from Colonel Turner Ashby's cavalry reports that part of Banks's army was preparing to head east to reinforce McClellan as he prepared to embark on his Peninsula Campaign. Indeed, on March 20, Brigadier General Alpheus Williams and his 7,000 men had started to Manassas while Brigadier General James Shields's division of 9,000

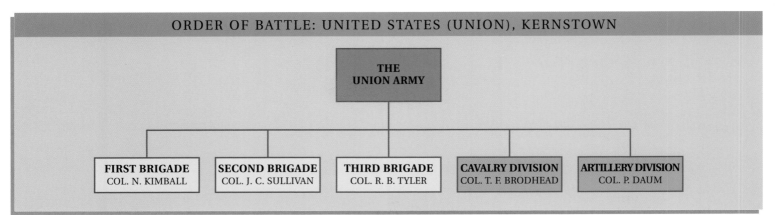

ORDER OF BATTLE: UNITED STATES (UNION), KERNSTOWN

THE UNION ARMY

FIRST BRIGADE	SECOND BRIGADE	THIRD BRIGADE	CAVALRY DIVISION	ARTILLERY DIVISION
COL. N. KIMBALL	COL. J. C. SULLIVAN	COL. R. B. TYLER	COL. T. F. BRODHEAD	COL. P. DAUM

men had dropped back from Strasburg and was preparing to follow.

Because his mission was to hold Banks in place, Jackson began hurrying his forces north. In the meantime, Ashby's troopers clashed with Shields's pickets just south of Winchester on March 22. During the fighting, Shields was struck by artillery fragments and fractured the bone just above his elbow. The painful wound forced Shields to relinquish command to Colonel Nathan Kimball. Before leaving the field, however, Shields developed a solid plan and passed the instructions on to the new commander.

In spite of his wound, Shields would remain active in directing the Federal effort throughout the battle. He ordered part of his division to move south of Winchester during the night, and another brigade to march north, to give the appearance that Winchester was being abandoned. However, that brigade would then halt and remain ready to return if Jackson approached.

The same night, Confederate loyalists from Winchester mistakenly told Ashby that Shields had left only a four-regiment rear guard, and even this scant force was thought to be under orders to depart for Harpers Ferry the next day. Ashby broke off the skirmish around sunset and sent Jackson a note about the situation. The news was exactly the opportunity for which Jackson had hoped. Crushing this exposed Federal detachment could very well keep Banks in the Shenandoah Valley. Ashby thought he could finish the job the next morning with a regiment of supporting infantry.

During the night, Shields sent Kimball instructions to move forward at first light with his brigade, its artillery battery, and one squadron of cavalry to capture Ashby's cavalry or force it to retreat. As Kimball moved forward, he found Ashby was advancing as well. The Confederates engaged the Federals and the Battle of Kernstown had begun.

As Jackson moved his army forward, he pushed four companies of the Stonewall Brigade ahead of his main body to assist Ashby. The reinforcements

arrived between 9:00 and 10:00 a.m., and Ashby fed them into what was becoming a seesaw skirmish. At first the Federals fell back, but they then returned with reinforcements and began to gain the upper hand. Seeing the odds had changed, Ashby ordered a withdrawal back to the Valley Pike, abandoning the high ground north of Kernstown.

ATTACKING ON THE SABBATH

Jackson reached Kernstown, about four miles south of Winchester, around 2:00 p.m. and received Ashby's report. Jackson was faced with a dilemma. His men were tired from marching twenty-five miles on March 22 and sixteen miles more on March 23. Around 1,500 stragglers were

Above: Alpheus Williams served as a lawyer, newspaper editor, and postmaster before the war.

Above: The Battle of Winchester in the Shenandoah Valley. Contemporary Civil War art routinely featured such themes as cavalry charges, bayonet assaults, national flags, and officers shouting commands.

already trailing behind. That left Jackson with a force of at most 3,000 tired infantrymen and Ashby's 300 cavalry. His men certainly could use some rest, but Jackson could also ill afford to give the enemy, who already controlled a knob called Pritchard's Hill and were using it to strafe Ashby with artillery fire, time to entrench or further develop their advantage. Of additional concern to Jackson was that the day was a Sunday. Traditionally, the pious Jackson rigorously adhered to the Sabbath, even considering government mail delivery on Sunday to be a violation of divine law and urging Congress to end such activity. Jackson was loath to break the commandment and violate the Lord's peace.

On the other hand, Jackson had a fleeting opportunity to defeat in detail an isolated part of the Federal army. He could not wait a day and still accomplish his mission of holding Banks in place. Although the decision distressed him, Jackson attacked Shields at Kernstown

on Sunday, March 23. He explained to his wife, Anna, who was also troubled by the action, "You appear much concerned at my attacking on Sunday. I was greatly concerned too, but I felt it my duty to do it, in consideration of the ruinous effects that might result from postponing the battle until morning. So far as I can see, my course was a wise one; the best that I could do under the circumstances, though very distasteful to my feelings; and I hope and pray to our Heavenly Father that I may never again be circumstanced on that day."

Improvising a plan for a battle he did not particularly want, Jackson surveyed the ground in front of him. Unfortunately for Jackson, the terrain favored the defenders. Kimball also knew he had an advantage, writing later, "The position I held was good for defense, and I determined to hold it."

Jackson saw that advancing on the right of the Valley Pike would expose his men to Federal fire from the guns on

Pritchard's Hill. The left, where a low ridge crested with trees ran parallel to the pike for two miles, offered better cover. Jackson decided to use this approach, mount the ridge, pivot around the Federal right, and wedge the enemy between the advancing Confederates and Winchester. It was an imperfect plan, but Jackson lacked the time or manpower for anything more elaborate.

Kimball had received orders from Shields to move forward, but before he could do so, Jackson attacked. A brigade led by Colonel Samuel Fulkerson started toward the ridge shortly after 3:30 p.m. and quickly came under fire. The Confederate attack rapidly deteriorated amid a flurry of confusing instructions. Jackson's forces became entangled and spent the better part of an hour sorting themselves out.

"SAY NOTHING . . . WE ARE IN FOR IT."

Once the attack got rolling again, the Confederates encountered unexpectedly stiff resistance. Jackson sent his aide Sandie Pendleton to reconnoiter the situation, and Pendleton returned with an estimate that the Federal strength was at least 10,000. In fact, Shields had sent Kimball the reinforcements that the Confederates

thought had abandoned Winchester. In so doing, Shields advised Kimball, "I have ordered the Thirteenth Indiana, and Thirty-ninth Illinois Infantry, and a battery, and will follow them with cavalry and other infantry . . . Tyler's brigade has been ordered within supporting distance and will communicate with you. Our whole force is now in your hands." The Confederates had fallen into Shields's trap. The stoic Jackson told Pendleton, "Say nothing about it. We are in for it."

Jackson now knew that victory was impossible. The best he could do was to hold out for another hour and retreat under the cover of darkness. Jackson called forward his reserves while Brigadier General Richard Garnett did his best to stave off the Federals with his Stonewall Brigade. Garnett soon found himself under intense pressure, and with Jackson hurrying reinforcements from the rear and therefore out of contact, Garnett had to make a decision alone. Fearing he was about to be overrun, Garnett ordered a retreat. When Jackson soon reappeared at the front and found troops falling back all around him, he

Below: The widespread use of the rifle during the Civil War posed a dangerous threat to soldiers advancing side-by-side in the Napoleonic style.

was furious. He ordered men who complained of being out of ammunition to "go back and give them the bayonet," and admonished Garnett, "Why have you not rallied your men? Halt and rally."

Garnett tried his best, but by now the retreat had gained a momentum that could not be stopped. Colonel William Harman's Fifth Virginia mounted a gallant rearguard action to allow the fleeing Confederates to reach safety. In twenty minutes, Harman lost one-fifth of his strength but bought Jackson the time he needed. Harman's men then withdrew behind a screen of Ashby's cavalry and the Battle of Kernstown was over. It had lasted just two hours. The Confederates withdrew four and half miles south along the Valley Pike to Newtown. The Federals chose not to pursue.

Left: Union troops advance at the Battle of Winchester. Winchester was the scene of much fighting in the Shenandoah Valley. According to some counts, the town changed hands more than seventy times throughout the course of the war. This illustration was sketched by artist Alfred R. Ward and was published in *Harper's Weekly* in April 1862.

Kernstown was a tactical defeat for Jackson in which he suffered 718 casualties, compared to 568 for the Federals. Jackson lost a quarter of the troops he had engaged, a figure that rivaled Confederate casualties at Gettysburg. Nonetheless, Jackson told one Confederate who had a pessimistic assessment of the battle, "I think I may say I am satisfied, sir."

Jackson's conclusion was based on the fact that, strategically, Kernstown was a huge Confederate victory. Jackson's presence and aggressive action in the Shenandoah Valley caused Federal authorities to halt plans to shift forces to McClellan. Instead Banks was held in place, Brigadier General Louis Blenker's division was withdrawn from McClellan and sent to oppose Jackson, and Major

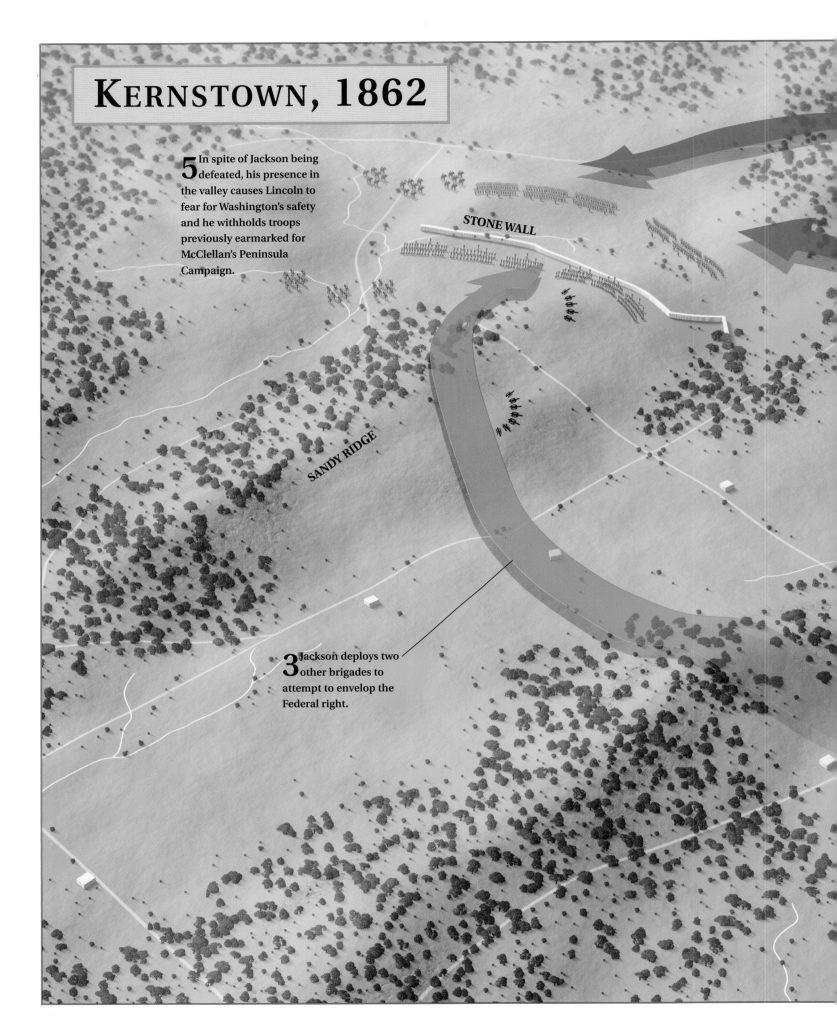

KERNSTOWN, 1862

5 In spite of Jackson being defeated, his presence in the valley causes Lincoln to fear for Washington's safety and he withholds troops previously earmarked for McClellan's Peninsula Campaign.

STONE WALL

SANDY RIDGE

3 Jackson deploys two other brigades to attempt to envelop the Federal right.

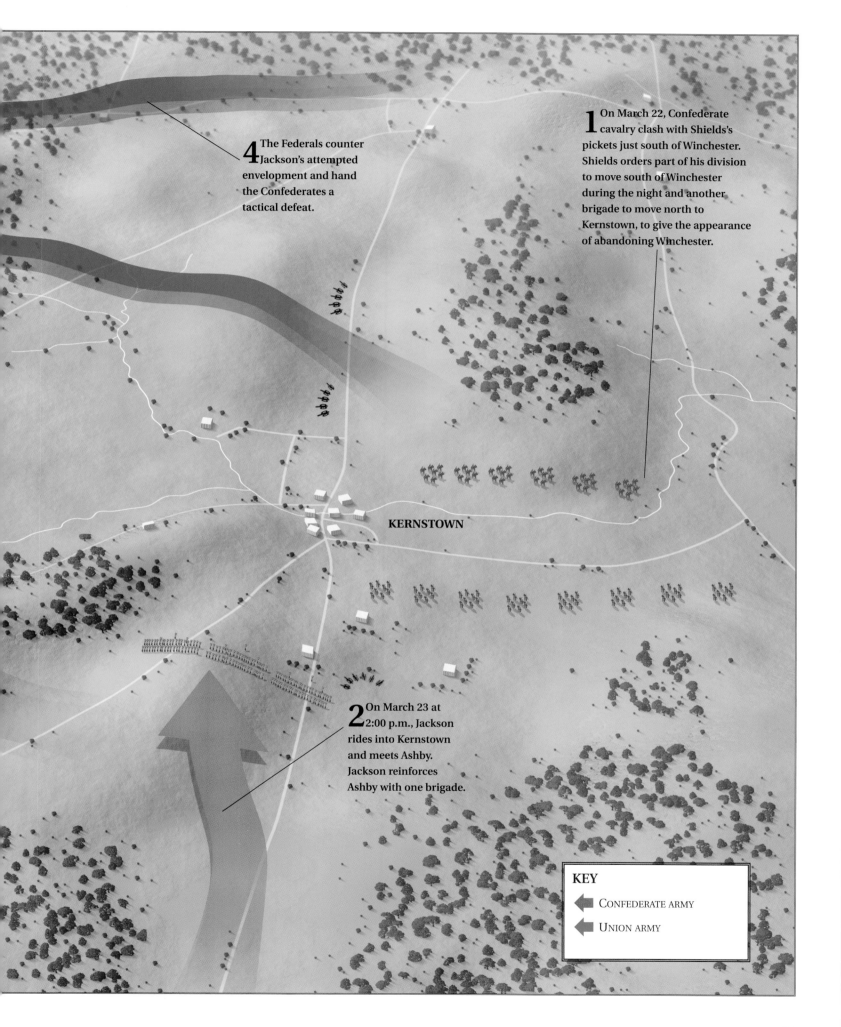

4 The Federals counter Jackson's attempted envelopment and hand the Confederates a tactical defeat.

1 On March 22, Confederate cavalry clash with Shields's pickets just south of Winchester. Shields orders part of his division to move south of Winchester during the night and another brigade to move north to Kernstown, to give the appearance of abandoning Winchester.

KERNSTOWN

2 On March 23 at 2:00 p.m., Jackson rides into Kernstown and meets Ashby. Jackson reinforces Ashby with one brigade.

KEY

← CONFEDERATE ARMY

← UNION ARMY

Above: Dick Ewell (1817–72) was known to his friends as "Baldy." He and Stonewall Jackson had different personalities, and Jackson's strict secrecy was a source of irritation for Ewell.

these developments closely and had already seen an opportunity to use Jackson in the Shenandoah Valley to threaten McClellan's plans for the peninsula. On April 21, Lee wrote Jackson, "I have no doubt an attempt will be made to occupy Fredericksburg and use it as a base of operations against Richmond. Our present force there is very small . . . If you can use General Ewell's division in an attack on General Banks and drive him back, it will prove a great relief to the pressure on Fredericksburg." While Lee was trying to buy time to concentrate forces on the peninsula, the immediate Confederate response to McClellan's offensive was actually Jackson's effort in the Shenandoah Valley.

JACKSON REINFORCED

In April, Jackson received more help when Major General Richard "Dick" Ewell arrived with 8,500 reinforcements. Jackson also received permission to use the small division commanded by Brigadier General Edward "Allegheny" Johnson, which brought Jackson's total strength to 17,000. Jackson left Ewell to hold Banks in place while Jackson, keeping his own plans secret even from his subordinates, went on the move.

Banks thought Jackson was headed for Richmond, but on May 8 Jackson suddenly appeared at McDowell, thirty-two miles west of Stanton. There he defeated the 6,000 Federals commanded by Frémont. Jackson knew Frémont's army was closing in from the Allegheny Mountains west of the Shenandoah Valley, and a junction between Frémont and Banks would have been disastrous to Jackson. Instead, the victory secured Jackson's left flank, and he then hurried back into the valley to join Ewell for a concentrated effort against Banks.

These events were occurring right as McClellan's efforts were beginning to bear fruit on the peninsula with the Confederates evacuating Yorktown on May 3, withdrawing toward Richmond, and in the process abandoning Norfolk. On May 18, McClellan had received a telegram from Secretary of War Edwin

General Irvin McDowell's First Corps was withheld from McClellan. The Federals then established three independent and separate commands: the Department of the Rappahannock under McDowell, Banks's Department of the Shenandoah, and Major General John C. Frémont's Mountain Department. These three generals reported directly to Washington, and no commander on the scene had responsibility for synchronizing the operations. This uncoordinated system of command would ultimately contribute to Jackson's success.

As President Jefferson Davis's military advisor, General Robert E. Lee watched

Stanton announcing that McDowell's First Corps would be marching from Fredericksburg, where it had been held previously for fear of Washington's safety, and would soon join him. As McClellan was eagerly awaiting McDowell's arrival, Jackson upset the Federal plans.

LINCOLN HAS CAUSE FOR CONCERN

Using a cavalry screen to make Banks think he was headed toward Strasburg, Jackson instead turned unexpectedly across the Masanutten, joined with Ewell at Luray, and with their combined 16,000 men struck the unsuspecting 1,000 Federals at Front Royal on May 23. Jackson tore through the town and the Federals fled toward Strasburg. Lincoln, who had never been comfortable with McClellan's provisions for Washington's safety, was now seriously worried. On May 24, Lincoln telegraphed McClellan, "In consequence of Gen. Banks' critical position I have been compelled to suspend Gen. McDowell's movement to join you." Jackson's local success in the Shenandoah Valley was having a much broader impact.

McClellan complained that "the object of Jackson's movement was probably to prevent reinforcements being sent to me" rather than to attack Washington. McDowell agreed, stating, "It is impossible that Jackson can have been largely reinforced. He is merely creating a diversion and the surest way to bring him from the lower valley is for me to move rapidly on Richmond." Such arguments failed to convince Lincoln, and the order stood. Disgustedly, McDowell lamented, "If the enemy can succeed so readily in disconcerting all

our plans by alarming us first at one point then at another, he will paralyze a larger force with a very small one." This disruption was exactly what Jackson had succeeded in doing.

Banks and Jackson now began a race to Winchester. On May 25, the two armies collided in what became another victory for Jackson. Enough was enough. President Lincoln and Secretary Stanton now became obsessed with the idea of trapping Jackson. They ordered McDowell and his 40,000-man corps to join Frémont's force at Strasburg and, at the beginning of June, Banks, Frémont, and Shields (who had recovered from his Kernstown wound and resumed command on April 30) all began converging on Jackson from the west, north, and east in the hopes of bagging him at Strasburg.

Above: In 1857 the U.S. Army fielded a new twelve-pounder gun-howitzer. This multipurpose piece was designed to replace existing guns and howitzers. It could fire canisters and shells like the twelve-pounder howitzer, and solid shot at an effective range of 1,680 yards like the twelve-pounder gun. Civil War artillerymen wore scarlet stripes on their pants, earning them the nickname "Redlegs."

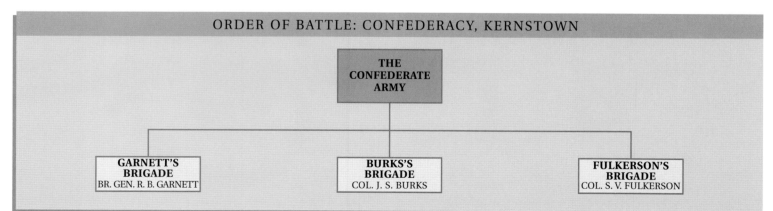

ORDER OF BATTLE: CONFEDERACY, KERNSTOWN

THE CONFEDERATE ARMY

GARNETT'S BRIGADE	BURKS'S BRIGADE	FULKERSON'S BRIGADE
BR. GEN. R. B. GARNETT	COL. J. S. BURKS	COL. S. V. FULKERSON

JACKSON'S MARCHING-ROUTINE STRATEGY

To take full advantage of his central position in the Shenandoah Valley, Jackson had developed an excellent routine for his marches. His men would march for exactly fifty minutes, halt for a ten-minute rest, and then resume the march. In the middle of the day, at noon or 1:00 p.m., they would have an hour for lunch. The role of the chain of command was also clearly articulated: "Brigade commanders will see that the foregoing rules are strictly adhered to, and for this purpose will, from time to time, allow his command to move by him, so as to verify its condition. He will also designate one of his staff officers to do the same at such times as he may deem necessary." This strict regime and the accompanying results caused Jackson's command to become known as the "foot cavalry."

Now Jackson used these techniques to march his men fifty miles in two days to escape the Federal trap closing in on Strasburg, and then fell back to Harrisonburg. Frémont and Shields pursued on parallel roads that would eventually meet at Port Republic. Jackson positioned Ewell four miles to the northwest at Cross Keys and stationed his own men on the rolling hills of Port Republic.

Ewell selected a line astride the Port Republic Road on a high, wooded ridge.

At 9:00 a.m. on June 8, Frémont's men, advancing down Port Republic Road, met Ewell's pickets. Frémont launched a weak attack against Ewell's right flank, but was easily repulsed. Casualties on both sides were light, with Ewell losing 288 and Frémont 684, but Frémont withdrew from the field. Ewell left a few men to watch Frémont and then withdrew during the night to assist Jackson at Port Republic.

At Port Republic, Jackson was in a close fight with Shields, but Ewell arrived just in time to turn the tide. Frémont could hear the fighting and took up the pursuit, but Ewell's rear guard had burned the bridge Frémont needed to cross. Frémont could only look on helplessly as Jackson and Ewell defeated Shields and forced him to withdraw.

Jackson's victory at Port Republic was the climax of the Shenandoah Valley Campaign. He had defeated portions of four Federal armies totaling more than 60,000 men. In the process, he was changing events on the peninsula as well.

CONFEDERATES ABANDON YORKTOWN

By this point, McClellan's bold turning movement had collapsed into a slow, plodding march. Instead of rapidly advancing, McClellan laid siege to Yorktown until May 3 when, as at Manassas, the Confederates abandoned Yorktown and withdrew up the peninsula

Below: A Union six-pounder artillery piece with limber. Transportation of Civil War cannon was facilitated by a limber, a two-wheeled cart that supported the trail of the artillery piece. The caisson carried ammunition and was sometimes used as a seat by the crew.

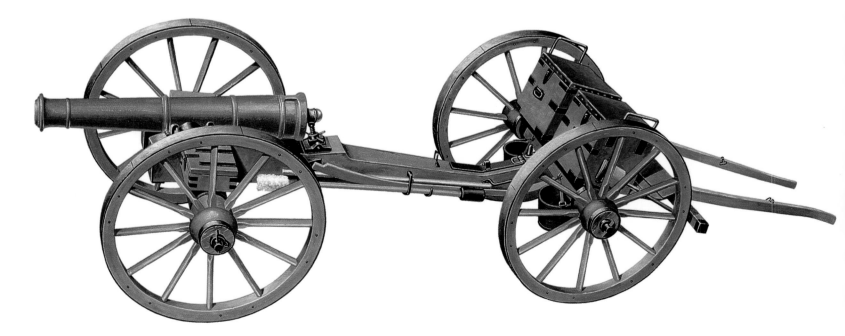

on their own terms. With the decision to evacuate Yorktown, Joe Johnston had the opportunity to pursue the strategy he had favored all along—to retreat rapidly to the immediate vicinity of Richmond and therefore remove the possibility of the Federals' outmaneuvering him by their command of the waterways and getting to Richmond first.

Thus, Johnston felt a strong desire to put as much distance between the Confederate army and Yorktown as possible. He fought an effective delaying action at Williamsburg on May 5 and continued his withdrawal. By that time, Lee had effected a "reconcentration" of troops that ultimately brought the strength of the Confederate forces opposing McClellan to 53,000. On May 31, Johnston attempted to take advantage of McClellan's force being divided by the Chickahominy River. The result was the Battle of Seven Pines. Johnston was wounded in the fighting, and he was replaced by Lee.

The new commander of the Army of Northern Virginia quickly took advantage of the opportunity created by Jackson's success in the Shenandoah Valley. On June 8, Lee wrote Jackson, "Should there

be nothing requiring your attention in the valley so as to prevent your leaving it for a few days, and you can make arrangements to deceive the enemy and impress him with the idea of your presence, please let me know, that you may unite at the decisive moment with the army near Richmond."

Three days later, Lee further explained that Jackson would "sweep down between the Chickahominy and Pamunkey, cutting up the enemy's communications, etc., while this army

Above: A sketch showing the Battle of Cross Keys, June 8, 1862. This was a decisive victory in Jackson's Valley Campaign.

Below: A sketch showing Union troops at Mechanicsville, just before the battle. The Battle of Mechanicsville, June 26, 1862, was Lee's first battle as commander of the Army of Northern Virginia.

"WE WALKED OVER A PORTION OF IT—WHERE THE FIGHT WAS THE THICKEST . . . THE TREES WERE SCARRED ALL OVER AND BRANCHES SHOT OFF BY THE BALLS—THE GROUND DISCOLORED BY THE BLOOD OF OUR MEN AND YANKS ALSO. I GOT A BULLET THAT ONE OF THE YANKS FIRED AT OUR MEN WHEN OUR MEN WERE BEHIND THE STONE WALL . . . MR. M. ASSISTED TO BURY OUR MEN— SEVENTY-NINE IN A TINY TRENCH— SIDE-BY-SIDE AND A RAIL FENCE AROUND THEM . . . IT WAS TRULY SAD TO SEE THEM."

KATE SPERRY, A YOUNG WOMAN FROM WINCHESTER, WHO VISITED SEVERAL DAYS AFTER THE BATTLE

Right: Union troops wait beside a thirty-two-pounder cannon at Seven Pines, June 1862. The Battle of Seven Pines (May 31–June 1, 1862) ended inconclusively, with both sides claiming victory despite no substantial gains.

attacks General McClellan in front. He will thus, I think, be forced to come out of his intrenchments [*sic*] where he is strongly posted on the Chickahominy and preparing to move by gradual approaches on Richmond." On June 16, Lee told Jackson, "The sooner you unite with this army the better." Jackson's Valley Campaign had been the Confederates' first response to McClellan's offensive by diverting Federal resources from the peninsula. Now Jackson's success would allow him to join Lee and give Lee the numbers he needed to go on the offensive and force McClellan to abandon his campaign.

A POLITICAL MARTYR

Because of his part in the Federal debacle in the Shenandoah Valley, Shields's reputation suffered. After Kernstown, he had been slated for promotion to major general, but the promotion was later withdrawn. A sympathetic biographer explains the fall from grace by describing Shields as "a political martyr" who fell victim to intrigue perpetrated by the likes of Secretary of War Stanton. Shields did suffer political damage when he became involved in an emotionally charged controversy over the failure to destroy a bridge used by Jackson at Port Republic, and no doubt Shields's association with the entire bungled Federal effort in the Shenandoah Valley did him no good. Shields became inconspicuous in the war's *Official Records* until March 28, 1863, when, still a brigadier general, he resigned his commission and moved to California.

NEATLY ORGANIZED WARFARE

Antoine-Henri Jomini was intellectually rooted in the eighteenth-century Enlightenment, and thus he sought to uncover the natural laws of warfare. Consequently, he found many elements of Napoleonic warfare as being chaotic and indiscriminate. In their place, he sought to use order and logic to define the principles of war in a way that formed a neatly organized system.

The result was an almost geometric approach to warfare. For Jomini, the

SHIELDS'S LEADERSHIP

The shortage of suitable professional senior officers, the need to appease valuable constituencies, and the quest to build national cohesion led both Abraham Lincoln and Jefferson Davis to appoint many political generals. James Shields was one of those appointees. Although he had commanded a brigade of volunteers in the Mexican War, Shields was at heart a politician. He had served as a senator from Illinois from 1849 to 1855 and as a senator from Minnesota from 1858 to 1859. While in Illinois, Shields had come to know Lincoln. At first the two feuded bitterly, nearly fighting a duel, but later they became friends.

In addition to his friendship with Lincoln, Shields's heritage was another political asset. He had been born in Ireland and came to America as a teenager. He was one of the more prominent Irish-Americans and this status made him useful to Lincoln in solidifying Irish support. Appointing a political general to secure an immigrant constituency was a fairly common practice and undoubtedly made sense to Lincoln in the context of the total war effort. However, on the battlefield Shields was at a severe disadvantage to a professional soldier such as Jackson.

Nonetheless, Shields held his own against Jackson at Kernstown. He developed a plan based on deception that caught Jackson—who otherwise enjoyed excellent intelligence of the enemy in the Shenandoah Valley Campaign—off guard. In so doing, Shields demonstrated the principle of war of surprise, the goal of which is to strike the enemy at a time and place for which he is unprepared. By tricking Jackson into believing the bulk of the Federal force had withdrawn, Shields was able to lure Jackson into attacking at Kernstown when Shields in fact had the numerical advantage. Thanks to this effective ruse, Shields can truly claim tactical victory over Jackson at Kernstown.

Still, Shields failed to restrict Jackson's strategic freedom of maneuver and Jackson was able to then so thwart Shields and the other Federal commanders in the Shenandoah Valley as to invoke fears of Washington's security. In fact, it was not just Shields but the entire Federal command structure that fell victim to Jackson's superior generalship.

The problem began with McClellan's failure to meet President Lincoln's demand to leave behind a sufficient force to secure Washington. As the perceived threat from Jackson increased, Lincoln ordered more and more forces to the valley. The effort, however, was ad hoc and without an overall strategy or commander. Shields, Banks, McDowell, and Frémont were all left to somehow cooperate and work together in the absence of true unity of command. This condition enabled Jackson to treat each Federal force as a separate entity, vulnerable to isolation and defeat in detail.

problem was to bring the maximum possible force to bear against an inferior enemy force at the decisive point in the theater of operations. This condition could best be achieved by properly ordering one's lines of communication relative to the enemy's so that the friendly force possessed "interior lines." Interior lines allowed the friendly commander to move parts of his army more rapidly than could an enemy operating on exterior lines. In this way, the force operating on interior lines could defeat in detail an enemy operating on exterior lines. It was this use of interior lines that allowed Jackson to defeat the larger Federal force in the Shenandoah Valley.

However, as brilliant as Jackson's actions were locally in the valley, the far greater impact was felt in disrupting McClellan's Peninsula Campaign. Jackson used his small force so effectively that it caused President Lincoln to change the entire Federal plan for the capture of Richmond. Just when the arrival of McDowell's First Corps would have given McClellan the force he needed to overwhelm the Confederate defense, Jackson temporarily paralyzed the Federal main effort. One historian concludes, "Rarely in war had so few infantry achieved such dazzling strategic results."

This result illustrates another remarkable aspect of Jackson's Valley Campaign, which is its adherence to the principle of war of economy of force. Economy of force requires that all combat power available be employed in the most effective way possible and that only the minimum essential combat power be allocated to secondary efforts. In the grand Confederate strategy, Jackson's efforts in the Shenandoah Valley were an economy of force effort designed to support Johnston and then Lee's more important operation to defend Richmond.

But this small investment, originally designed with the modest purpose of protecting the flank of Johnston's withdrawing army, developed into something much more. Lee quickly took advantage of the opportunity created by

Jackson's success in the valley, and on June 8 wrote Jackson to ask him if he could bring his forces to the peninsula. Then Major General Jeb Stuart rode completely around McClellan's army between June 12 and June 15 and returned with news that the Federal right flank near Mechanicsville did not extend far enough north to block the roads Lee planned to use to bring Jackson's troops to the battle. Moreover, the Federals' primary supply line, the Richmond and York River Railroad, was vulnerable. If Lee could turn McClellan's flank, the Confederates could threaten the Federal communications at the same time. On June 16, Lee told Jackson, "The sooner you unite with this army the better."

LOSING A BATTLE BUT WINNING THE CAMPAIGN

The result was the Battle of Mechanicsville, the first of a series of battles known as the Seven Days. At Mechanicsville, Federal forces used superior terrain around Beaver Dam Creek to inflict more than 1,500 casualties on the Confederates, compared to fewer than 400 suffered by their own side. Jackson, no doubt exhausted from the Valley Campaign, was uncharacteristically late, turning Lee's planned flanking maneuver into a costly frontal attack. But when McClellan finally ascertained that Jackson was advancing, he panicked and decided to retreat. Lee had lost the battle but, thanks to McClellan's loss of nerve, was on his way to winning the campaign.

This synergy created by the combined efforts of Jackson in the Shenandoah Valley and Lee on the Virginia peninsula was the beginning of a remarkable partnership between the two men. Jackson's initiative and ability to act independently allowed Lee to issue the type of broad, discretionary orders with which he was most comfortable. They made a powerful team, and Jackson became so indispensable to Lee's generalship that when Jackson was wounded at Chancellorsville, Lee lamented that he had "lost my right arm." The beginnings of this great command team can be traced to Jackson's Shenandoah Valley Campaign.

JACKSON'S LEADERSHIP

The fact that Shields and the rest of the Federal commanders in the Shenandoah Valley were subpar should not detract from the excellent generalship displayed by Stonewall Jackson. The Shenandoah Valley Campaign represented Jackson at his best. Later during the Seven Days' Battles, he would have difficulty coordinating his actions with others, but when operating independently in the Shenandoah Valley, Jackson was brilliant. Under such conditions, Jackson could maintain his almost fanatical need for secrecy and then use his superior marching ability to strike the enemy unexpectedly. When forced to more closely integrate his actions with the plans and movements of others, Jackson stumbled, but in the Shenandoah Valley he suffered from no such limitations.

Jackson was able to use his superior mobility and knowledge of the terrain to exploit the disjointed Federal command by employing the concept of interior lines, a strategy best articulated by Antoine-Henri, Baron de Jomini, a general in both the French and Russian armies. By the time of the Civil War, Jomini had emerged as the military theorist with the greatest influence among American soldiers. Indeed, one observer asserted, "Many a Civil War general went into battle with a sword in one hand and Jomini's *Summary of the Art of War* in the other."

GRANT VS. JOHNSTON

SHILOH, 1862

The Battle of Shiloh pitted Union Major General Ulysses S. Grant's Army of the Tennessee against Confederate General Albert Sidney Johnston's Army of the Mississippi in a struggle for control of western Tennessee.

Johnston relinquished much control of the battle to his second in command, General Pierre Gustave Toutant Beauregard, and when Johnston was killed in the afternoon of the first day of the battle, Beauregard assumed full command of the Confederate force. Although the initial Confederate attack caught the Federals off guard, Beauregard's unimaginative frontal attacks, Brigadier General Benjamin Prentiss's valiant defense, and Grant's iron will allowed the Federals to hang on until reinforcements arrived. The exhausted Confederates were little match for the reinforced Federals on the

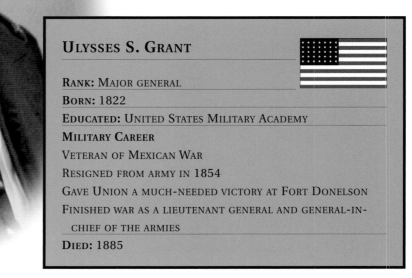

ULYSSES S. GRANT

RANK: MAJOR GENERAL
BORN: 1822
EDUCATED: UNITED STATES MILITARY ACADEMY
MILITARY CAREER
VETERAN OF MEXICAN WAR
RESIGNED FROM ARMY IN 1854
GAVE UNION A MUCH-NEEDED VICTORY AT FORT DONELSON
FINISHED WAR AS A LIEUTENANT GENERAL AND GENERAL-IN-CHIEF OF THE ARMIES
DIED: 1885

second day of the battle, and Shiloh ended up a decisive Federal victory. The deciding factor was Grant's strength of character, which withstood the panic and chaos caused by the initial Confederate advantage of surprise. While Grant was steadfastly refusing to quit, Johnston and Beauregard sapped their army's strength with uncoordinated and costly frontal attacks in what many considered a lost opportunity for the South.

PRELIMINARIES

Major General Ulysses S. Grant's victories at Fort Henry and Fort Donelson in February 1862 forced General Albert Sidney Johnston's Confederate Army of the Mississippi out of Tennessee. Johnston decided to concentrate his forces at Corinth, Mississippi, an otherwise modest town made critically important by its position as the junction of the Memphis and Charleston, and the Mobile and Ohio railroads. At the same time, Grant had assembled more than 45,000 men at Pittsburg Landing, Tennessee, about twenty miles northeast of Corinth, where he would wait for the arrival of Major General Don Carlos Buell's Army of the Ohio from Nashville.

In times of peace, one of the ways in which goods reached Corinth from the Tennessee River was along a road from the steamboat wharf at Pittsburg Landing. In the current circumstances, Pittsburg Landing offered Grant a convenient staging area for a march south to attack Corinth. Perhaps a mile

and a half southwest of Pittsburg Landing stood Shiloh Church. Home to a Methodist congregation, the log building sat overlooking the Pittsburg–Corinth Road and now some 7,300 Federal troops commanded by Brigadier General William Tecumseh Sherman camped around it.

"Camped" is exactly the right word to describe the Federal dispositions. The regiments were out of alignment with each other and all fronted different directions. They were arranged for administrative convenience rather than defense because Grant was quite sure that Corinth would be the next battlefield and that he would be the one initiating the action. He wrote one of his generals, "I am clearly of the opinion that the enemy are gathering strength at Corinth

SHILOH	
Date	April 6–7, 1862
Location	Hardin County, Tennessee
Result	Union victory

Strength	
Confederate: Army of the Tennessee (48,894); Army of the Ohio (17,918)	Union: Army of the Mississippi (44,699)

Casualties and losses	
13,047	11,694
1,754 killed	1,728 killed
8,408 wounded	8,012 wounded
2,885 captured/missing	959 captured/missing

ALBERT S. JOHNSTON

RANK: GENERAL
BORN: 1803
EDUCATED: UNITED STATES MILITARY ACADEMY
MILITARY CAREER
SECRETARY OF WAR IN THE REPUBLIC OF TEXAS
VETERAN OF MEXICAN WAR
FORCED TO WITHDRAW AFTER FORT DONELSON
KILLED AT SHILOH
DIED: 1862

Above: The Confederates' surprise attack on the first day of Shiloh wreaked havoc in the Federal lines, but Grant rallied his men for the second day.

quite as rapidly as we are here, and the sooner we attack, the easier will be the task of taking the place." Indeed, attack was all Grant had in mind. He failed to prepare any defenses and responded to suggestions that the Confederates might themselves attack by declaring, "They're all back at Corinth, and, when our transportation arrives, we have got to go there and draw them out, as you would draw a badger out of a hole."

SURPRISE: THE FIRST DAY

Unfortunately for Grant, his adversaries had other ideas. On the night of April 2, Johnston received word that Buell was fast approaching and Johnston had no desire to wait passively and let the Federal forces unite. Beauregard agreed, urging Johnston that "now is the time to go." Johnston issued the necessary orders to his corps commanders to prepare for a

movement to begin the next morning and gave Beauregard the responsibility for developing the plan of attack. Although Johnston left Beauregard to figure out the details, Johnston did lay out a broad concept for the attack. In a memorandum of April 3 to his corps commanders, Johnston specifically stated, "Every effort should be made to turn the left flank of the enemy so as to cut off his line of retreat to the Tennessee River, and throw him back on Owl Creek." Johnston expected to push rapidly with his right wing around the Federal left and drive the Federals downstream, away from their base of supplies at Pittsburg Landing. The Confederates would then envelop and defeat them in what Johnston saw as a battle of annihilation.

Beauregard, however, deviated from Johnston's intended turning movement in drafting the actual order for the attack. Instead, he developed a scheme of maneuver that would help get the attack off to a quick start but would inevitably result in units piling up into one another with no room for anything but a frontal attack. For his part, Johnston did precious little to lead his army in the direction of his original plan.

Beauregard developed a schedule for the various Confederate corps to march to Michie's (cited as Mickey's in the contemporary reports) farmhouse, about eight miles southwest of Pittsburg Landing, and from there to attack the Federal force on April 4. The movement got off to a painfully slow start, which was made even worse by heavy rains that turned the roads to mud. The attack would have to be delayed first until April 5 and later to April 6, as progress remained excruciatingly slow.

These difficulties aside, by the evening of April 5, Confederate pickets had occupied positions within half a mile of the Federal outposts. Johnston rode to meet with Beauregard and found he had already engaged in an informal council of war with First Army Corps commander Major General Leonidas Polk and the commander of the Second Army Corps, Major General Braxton Bragg. Reserve Corps commander Brigadier General John Breckinridge soon joined the group.

"ATTACK AT DAYLIGHT TOMORROW"
Johnston was surprised to learn that Beauregard now had serious misgivings about the attack. Confederates and Federals had exchanged fire during the Confederate advance, and Beauregard feared surprise had been lost. By now, he argued, the Federals would be "entrenched to the ears." Bragg sided with Beauregard in proposing the army should withdraw toward Corinth and develop a new plan. Johnston, supported by Polk, was undeterred. "Gentlemen," he announced, "we shall attack at daylight tomorrow." As he left the meeting, Johnston told an aide, "I would fight them if they were a million."

Beauregard need not have worried about the skirmishing resulting in a loss of surprise. Whereas many forward-deployed Federal soldiers spent an anxious night on April 5 as a result of the increased activity, the Federal high command remained oblivious to any danger. The Confederate contacts were attributed to mere reconnaissance patrols rather than any impending attack. When Colonel Jesse Appler of the Fifty-third Ohio tried to warn his division commander Sherman that his men had made contact with the Confederates, Sherman disparagingly told him, "Take your damned regiment back to Ohio. There is no enemy nearer than Corinth."

One of the few who took the enemy contacts seriously was Colonel Everett Peabody, who dispatched a force of 250 men led by Major James Powell before dawn on April 6 to locate the Confederates and, upon finding them, "to drive in the guards and open up on the reserve, develop the force . . . hold ground as long as possible, then fall back." At 4:55 a.m., Powell's men received fire from Confederate cavalry. Powell deployed his men in a skirmish line, but soon realized his small force was confronting around 9,000 men of Major General William Hardee's Third Army Corps. Powell beat a quick retreat as Hardee's men steadily advanced. Behind Hardee marched Bragg's corps, followed by Polk's and then Breckinridge's. Hardee's and Bragg's men were deployed in line of battle while Polk's and Breckinridge's troops came forward in column formation.

Moving this massed linear formation through the thick cover and undulating terrain was a slow, burdensome process. The force lacked room to maneuver, and the result was a frontal attack in which it appeared that the Confederates hoped to use sheer numbers to simply overpower the Federals. Beauregard had made no provision for placing a large number of troops on the Confederate right, as Johnston's plan had required. In fact, Beauregard appears to have never intended anything but a frontal attack.

The Confederate attack struck the part of the Federal line occupied by Brigadier General Benjamin Prentiss's

Above: John Breckinridge (1821–75), Confederate Reserve Corps commander at Shiloh, had been an unsuccessful candidate for president in 1860.

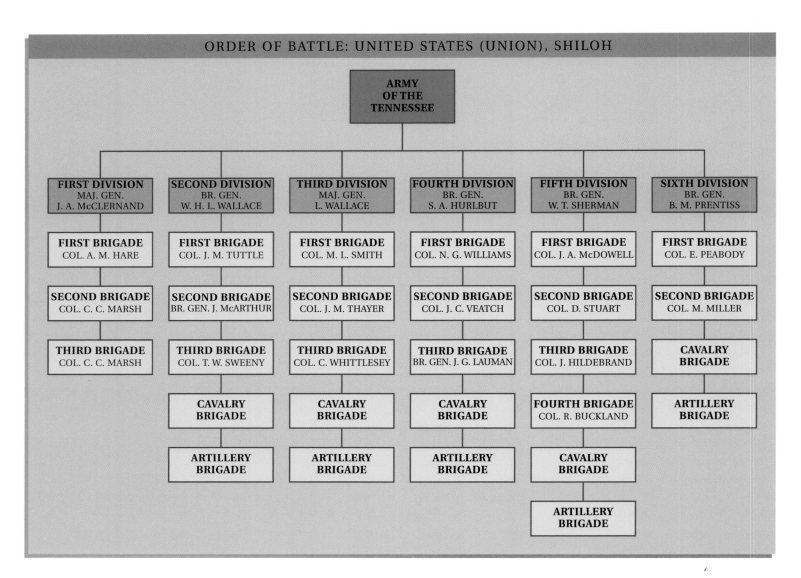

ORDER OF BATTLE: UNITED STATES (UNION), SHILOH

ARMY OF THE TENNESSEE

FIRST DIVISION MAJ. GEN. J. A. McCLERNAND	SECOND DIVISION BR. GEN. W. H. L. WALLACE	THIRD DIVISION MAJ. GEN. L. WALLACE	FOURTH DIVISION BR. GEN. S. A. HURLBUT	FIFTH DIVISION BR. GEN. W. T. SHERMAN	SIXTH DIVISION BR. GEN. B. M. PRENTISS
FIRST BRIGADE COL. A. M. HARE	FIRST BRIGADE COL. J. M. TUTTLE	FIRST BRIGADE COL. M. L. SMITH	FIRST BRIGADE COL. N. G. WILLIAMS	FIRST BRIGADE COL. J. A. McDOWELL	FIRST BRIGADE COL. E. PEABODY
SECOND BRIGADE COL. C. C. MARSH	SECOND BRIGADE BR. GEN. J. McARTHUR	SECOND BRIGADE COL. J. M. THAYER	SECOND BRIGADE COL. J. C. VEATCH	SECOND BRIGADE COL. D. STUART	SECOND BRIGADE COL. M. MILLER
THIRD BRIGADE COL. C. C. MARSH	THIRD BRIGADE COL. T. W. SWEENY	THIRD BRIGADE COL. C. WHITTLESEY	THIRD BRIGADE BR. GEN. J. G. LAUMAN	THIRD BRIGADE COL. J. HILDEBRAND	CAVALRY BRIGADE
	CAVALRY BRIGADE	CAVALRY BRIGADE	CAVALRY BRIGADE	FOURTH BRIGADE COL. R. BUCKLAND	ARTILLERY BRIGADE
	ARTILLERY BRIGADE	ARTILLERY BRIGADE	ARTILLERY BRIGADE	CAVALRY BRIGADE	
				ARTILLERY BRIGADE	

"**WE WERE ALL SPOILING FOR A FIGHT, AND THERE WAS NO LITTLE AMOUNT OF GRUMBLING DONE BY MEMBERS OF THE REGIMENT ON ACCOUNT OF THE FEAR THAT WE WOULD NOT BE THERE IN TIME TO TAKE PART IN THE BATTLE.**"

SERGEANT W. P. L. MUIR,
FIFTEENTH IOWA REGIMENT

Sixth Division of 5,400 effectives. In spite of being outnumbered, Prentiss was able to use massed artillery volleys to break the first of the uncoordinated Confederate attacks. Many more, though, would follow.

THE HORNET'S NEST

All told, the Confederates launched what most historians count as eleven assaults against Prentiss's line in a part of the battlefield that became known as the "Hornet's Nest." The attacks, under the command of Braxton Bragg, were largely piecemeal, unsupported affairs rather than efforts to probe for a weak spot and overwhelm the Federals there. Because the Confederates never massed enough forces to attack along the entire front, the Federals on either side of the line were always able to establish a deadly cross fire. Throughout the afternoon, more than 17,000 Confederate troops were thrown against the Hornet's Nest, but

never did more than 3,700 of them attack at any one time. The Federals, with barely 5,000 men defending the position, actually enjoyed a numerical advantage locally because of the Confederates' mismanagement of their overall superiority in numbers.

A major problem for the Confederates at the Hornet's Nest and elsewhere was the lack of a clear overall commander with a coherent strategy. Johnston and the Confederate corps commanders all acted as small unit commanders rather than taking responsibility for the battle as a whole. Instead of acting as army commander, Johnston, in the words of one historian, "needlessly flitted about" throughout the morning.

Much of the time, Johnston was near the front of the Confederate line. This decision undoubtedly reflected great courage on Johnston's part, but just as certainly prevented him from grasping developments outside of his immediate vicinity. After the war, Beauregard critiqued that, by leading from so far forward, Johnston reduced himself to the "part of a Corps or Division commander." Indeed, at one point in the midmorning of April 5, Johnston sent an aide to Beauregard to tell him to make decisions based on his own information. With this instruction, Johnston seemed to be acknowledging that he had ceded tactical control of the battle to his second in command. For his part, Beauregard took a position toward the Confederate rear and did little more than send couriers about the battlefield to order men toward the sound of the loudest firing. This disjointed command system created confusion and much countermanding of orders. The result was that many Confederate units spent more time marching than fighting.

As the battle unfolded, Johnston failed to exert his will over Beauregard and try to get a turning force on his right until after the battle was well begun. By then it was too late and the opportunity was lost. If a large force had been present on the Confederate right when the battle opened and when the Confederates enjoyed the advantages of surprise and momentum, chances are that the Confederates would have broken through as Johnston's original plan envisioned. Instead, the actual result was three corps attacking in line, one behind another, each of the lines feeding its components piecemeal into the line ahead. Ultimately, the frontal assault succeeded, but it proceeded so slowly that the Confederates forfeited their initial advantage of surprise and gave the Federals a chance to recover.

PLUNDER HINDERS PROGRESS

In addition to the restrictive terrain, unimaginative frontal attacks, and stiff resistance offered by Prentiss, another occurrence that slowed the Confederate advance was the fact that many Confederates stopped to plunder the overrun Federal positions. After forcing Colonel Madison Miller's Second Brigade to retreat, the Confederates found a bounty of food and supplies that the

hastily departed Federals had left behind. Many Confederates straggled to loot through the abandoned property and hungrily devour the breakfast the Federals had left uneaten. When Johnston arrived at Miller's captured camp at about 9:00 a.m., an officer who proudly showed the general an armful of loot soon greeted him. "None of that, sir; we are not here for plunder," Johnston admonished. Noticing the crestfallen look on the officer's face, Johnston softened his rebuke by picking up a small tin cup and saying, "Let this be my share of the spoils today." Still, Johnston spent thirty minutes trying to end the looting and get the advance moving again.

Interludes such as this one gave the hard-pressed Prentiss precious time to regroup, and he managed to re-form the remnants of his command on an old sunken wagon road about a mile behind their original position. Fresh Federal troops moved forward and aligned themselves on Prentiss's flanks. Two brigades commanded by Fourth Division commander Brigadier General Stephen Hurlbut moved alongside Prentiss's left, and two brigades of Major General Lew

Above: Artillery played a critical role at Shiloh when Daniel Ruggles massed sixty-two guns, at the time the largest concentration of artillery in American military history, and blasted away at the Federal artillery supporting the Hornet's Nest.

Above: William Tecumseh Sherman (1820–91) was a graduate of West Point who was superintendent of the Louisiana Military Academy at the outbreak of war. Although the state seceded, Sherman decided to fight for the Union and waged his own version of total war against the South. Like most of the Federals, Sherman did not expect the Confederate attack at Shiloh.

Wallace's Third Division anchored Prentiss's right. A third brigade from Wallace's division moved to the far left beyond Hurlbut. To Wallace's right stood Major General John McClernand's First Division and then Sherman's Fifth Division. Thus, by 10:30 a.m. the Federal line was back in a semblance of order.

Meanwhile, the renewed Confederate attack was further delayed as Johnston responded to erroneous reports of a Federal division poised to strike the Confederates' right flank. As Johnston maneuvered forces to confront what turned out to be an understrength brigade, another hour was lost to the Confederates and used to good effect by the Federals.

By 11:00 a.m., the Confederate brigades had become so hopelessly intermingled that the corps commanders were forced to improvise. Bragg told Polk, "If you take care of the center, I will go to the right." In spite of this agreement, Bragg found himself entangled in affairs in the center and never made it over to the far right, the very part of the Confederate line that was originally intended to deliver the main blow of the attack. The Confederate corps commanders continued to operate more or less independently of each other, and the work of moving troops about the battlefield fell to staff officers who acted with even less understanding of the overall situation.

FORCED TO CHARGE INTO AN AMBUSH

As Bragg was moving to his new command sector, he saw Colonel Randall Gibson's fresh brigade of about 2,350 men standing idle, waiting for orders. Bragg impetuously interpreted Gibson's inaction as a sign of cowardice and ordered the brigade to charge the Federal position at the Sunken Road. At about noon, Gibson's men blindly rushed forward into what for all purposes was an ambush. Less than 100 yards into their attack, the brigade was met by what one survivor described as "a perfect tornado of rifle fire . . . in our very faces." Gibson's men fell back, only to be ordered forward again by Bragg a second, a third, and then a fourth time. Gibson's four assaults on the Sunken Road between noon and 2:00 p.m. resulted in the brigade taking 30 percent casualties. Undeterred, Bragg then ordered Colonel R. G. Shaver's brigade into what had obviously become a meat grinder.

While Bragg was steadily bleeding his command dry in futile frontal assaults, Johnston began to focus his attention on a ten-acre peach orchard just to the right of the Hornet's Nest. The rear of the peach orchard was on the Sunken Road, and Federal troops occupied a line to its front. Johnston wanted to break that line. In the words of one historian, Johnston "became obsessed with it."

Shortly after noon, Johnston sent an order for Brigadier General John Bowen's

Second Brigade of Breckinridge's Reserve Corps to move forward. As Bowen's men arrived, Johnston personally placed them on line, assuring them, "Only a few more charges and the day is ours." Johnston positioned himself slightly to the rear of Bowen's formation. With him was Tennessee governor Isham Harris.

Johnston's leadership was hands-on, personal, and courageous. At one point, Breckinridge rode up to him and complained, "General, I have a regiment of Tennesseans that refuses to fight. I have done my utmost to rally them and get them in." Johnston turned to Harris and said, "Did you hear that, Governor?" to which Harris responded, "I will see what I can do." Shortly thereafter, Breckinridge rode up once more and said, "General Johnston, I cannot get my men to make the charge." Calmly, Johnston answered, "Then I will help you." Johnston rode to the recalcitrant troops and encouraged them by saying,

"Men of Missouri and Arkansas, the enemy is stubborn. I want you to show General Beauregard and General Bragg what you can do with your bayonets and toothpicks [Bowie knives]." To Harris, Johnston added, "Those fellows are making a stubborn stand here. I'll have to put the bayonet to them."

By 2:00 p.m., Johnston had collected a force of 4,000 men from Breckinridge's corps as well as just under 1,000 of Colonel William Stephens's who had already seen costly fighting earlier at the Hornet's Nest. Johnston's oratory had raised Confederate morale. Now he promised, "I will lead you," and the charge began. At one point, Johnston was seen riding forty paces in front of Breckinridge's line.

In the face of the Confederate onslaught, the Federal line broke back through the peach orchard and took cover in the Sunken Road. The Confederate success was a costly one,

Below: Fire from Federal gunboats on the Tennessee River helped the Federals reorganize and establish a defensive line in the face of concerted Confederate attacks.

however. Johnston's uniform was ripped by minié balls in several places and one round had hit him behind his right knee, severing an artery. Nevertheless, the injury was masked by Johnston's high-top boot. When Harris reached the general's side, Johnston calmly reported, "Governor, they came very near putting me hors de combat in that charge," but made no further complaint. In

the event, the Confederate commander was unknowingly bleeding to death.

GENERAL JOHNSTON MEETS HIS END

When Harris returned from delivering a message, he found Johnston about to fall out of his saddle. "General, are you wounded?" Harris asked anxiously. "Yes, and I fear seriously," Johnston answered. A simple tourniquet could have saved

Johnston's life, but the boot continued to hide the wound. By 2:30 Johnston was dead, and at about 3:00 Harris reached Beauregard with the news of Johnston's passing. Beauregard notified the corps commanders of the situation but cautioned them to keep the information of Johnston's death from the troops in order to preserve morale. Beauregard also ordered that the battle be pushed forward. As the new commander of the Confederate force, Beauregard continued its fixation with the Hornet's Nest. Rather than turning the crumbling Federal flanks and driving on to Pittsburg Landing, Beauregard remained focused on the Federal center. However, rather than repeat the ineffective infantry charges of previous efforts, Brigadier General Daniel Ruggles, commander of Bragg's First Division, now began gathering cannons. Before long, Ruggles had massed sixty-two guns—at the time the largest concentration of artillery in American military history—in an irregular line facing the Sunken Road. At 4:00 p.m., the Confederates began bombarding Prentiss's line, firing at a rate of two or three rounds a minute.

The shelling lasted for at least half an hour and drove off the Federal artillery. Thus, when the Confederate infantry began its assault, the Federal troops were unsupported. They were also running low on ammunition. One Mississippi major described the Confederate advantage as "like shooting into a flock of sheep. I never saw such cruel work during the war." Soon the Illinois regiment defending the Federal left was forced to withdraw to form a new line around Pittsburg Landing.

"Hold at all hazards"

This opening of the Federal left was exactly what Johnston had envisioned in his initial attack plan, and a massive Confederate push there may have successfully turned the Federal position. Instead, the attackers moved to their left, back toward the Hornet's Nest. With attacks now coming from the front and both sides, Prentiss's gallant defense had taken all it could stand and the Federal line began to give way. By 5:30 the Hornet's Nest was surrounded and Prentiss was compelled to surrender, but not before he had halted the Confederate advance for several critical hours while the Federal line elsewhere was given a chance to stabilize. Earlier in the morning, Grant had told Prentiss to "hold at all hazards." Prentiss and his men had more than done their duty.

"HERE BESIDE A GREAT OAK TREE I COUNTED THE CORPSES OF FIFTEEN MEN . . . THE BLUE AND THE GRAY WERE MINGLED TOGETHER . . . IT WAS NO UNCOMMON THING TO SEE THE BODIES OF FEDERAL AND CONFEDERATE LYING SIDE-BY-SIDE AS THOUGH THEY HAD BLED TO DEATH WHILE TRYING TO AID EACH OTHER."

SIXTEEN-YEAR-OLD UNION REGIMENTAL MUSICIAN JOHN A. COCKERILL, RECOUNTING THE BATTLE OF SHILOH

Left: Amid the closely wooded terrain of the Tennessee River, General Albert Sidney Johnston rallies the Thirteenth Arkansas Regiment at the Battle of Shiloh. Johnston tried to halt the Confederates' plundering of overrun Federal positions by claiming that a small tin cup would be his "share of the spoils today."

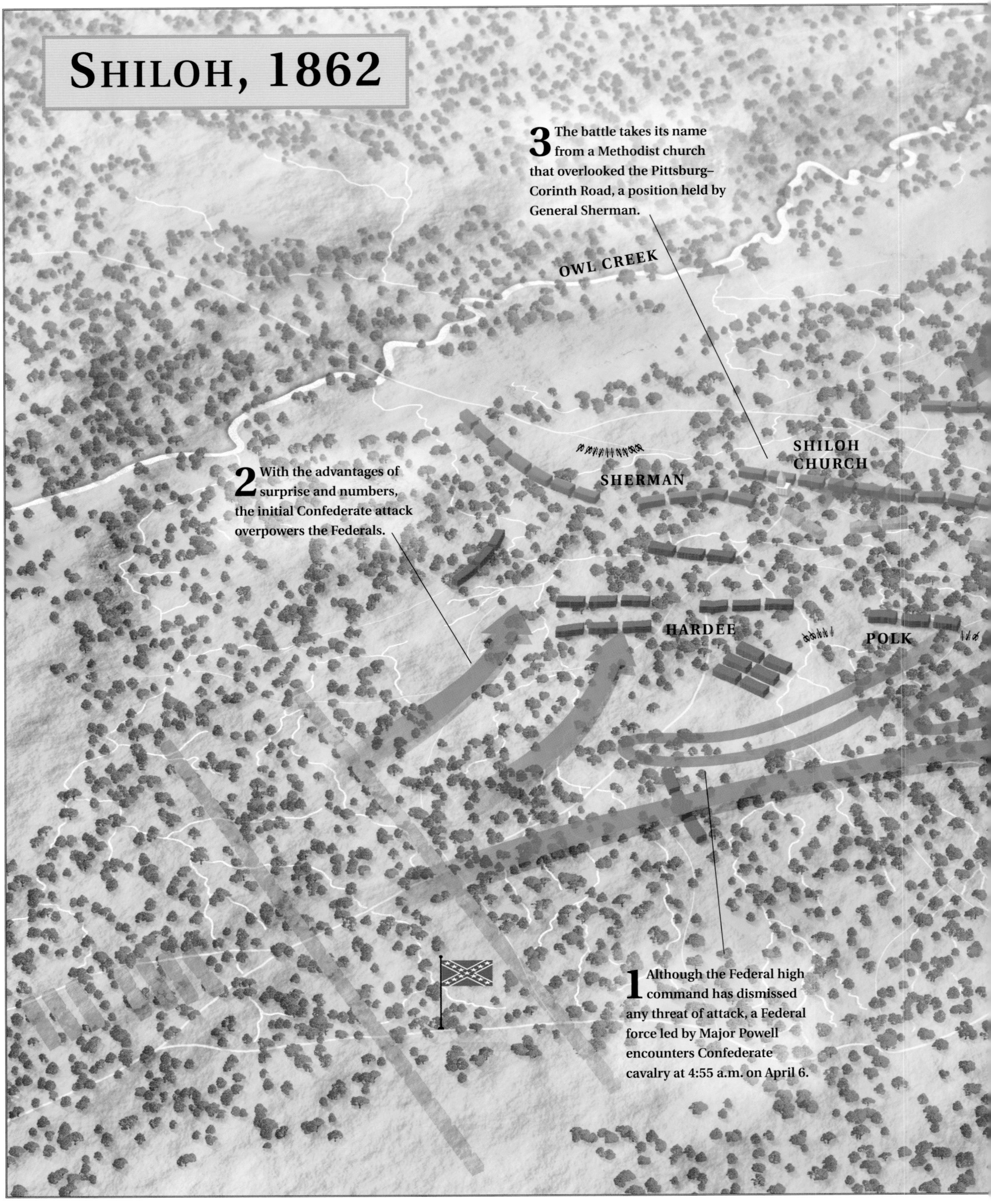

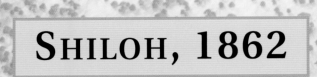

SHILOH, 1862

3 The battle takes its name from a Methodist church that overlooked the Pittsburg–Corinth Road, a position held by General Sherman.

OWL CREEK

SHILOH CHURCH

SHERMAN

2 With the advantages of surprise and numbers, the initial Confederate attack overpowers the Federals.

HARDEE

POLK

1 Although the Federal high command has dismissed any threat of attack, a Federal force led by Major Powell encounters Confederate cavalry at 4:55 a.m. on April 6.

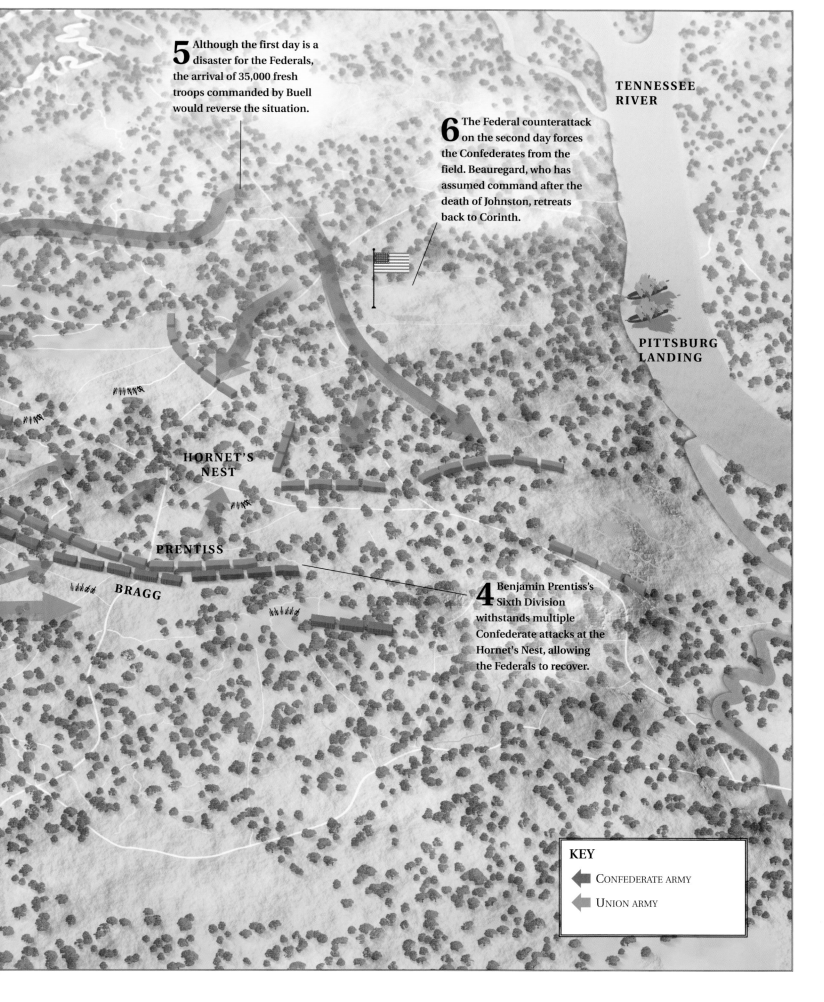

5 Although the first day is a disaster for the Federals, the arrival of 35,000 fresh troops commanded by Buell would reverse the situation.

6 The Federal counterattack on the second day forces the Confederates from the field. Beauregard, who has assumed command after the death of Johnston, retreats back to Corinth.

TENNESSEE RIVER

PITTSBURG LANDING

HORNET'S NEST

PRENTISS

BRAGG

4 Benjamin Prentiss's Sixth Division withstands multiple Confederate attacks at the Hornet's Nest, allowing the Federals to recover.

KEY

CONFEDERATE ARMY

UNION ARMY

Above: General Sherman (seated, center) with Generals Howard, Logan, Hazen, Davis, Slocum, and Mower, photographed by Mathew Brady. Wars in Europe had demonstrated the value of a well-trained, trusted, and reliable staff to support a general officer. Good staff work tended to be the exception rather than the rule in the inexperienced armies of 1862.

While Prentiss had been delaying the Confederate attack, much of the rest of Grant's army was falling back to Pittsburg Landing. Some units withdrew slowly and in good order, making the Confederates pay for the ground they gained. Others broke and ran for their lives. Initially caught off guard, Grant rallied and began organizing the stragglers into units and forming a new defensive line. Eventually, he built a line three miles long that ran inland at a right angle from the Tennessee River above Pittsburg Landing, northwest toward Owl Creek. There he held on until reinforcements from Buell's army arrived.

By 7:00 p.m., the first of Buell's troops, Colonel Jacob Ammen's brigade, began to arrive. Ammen's men were met by a chaotic scene of fugitive soldiers running from the battlefield in panic. Some were huddled under the steep bluffs, while others were swimming across the river in the opposite direction of Ammen's troops, who were being ferried over. One of the newly arrived reinforcements reported "such looks of terror and confusion I have never saw before and do not wish to see again."

Ammen's division commander, the heavyweight Brigadier General William "Bull" Nelson, was livid at the sight. On crossing the river, Nelson rode his horse right into a mob along the riverbank and bellowed, "Damn your souls, if you won't fight, get out of the way of men who will!" Nelson began assigning his men to positions along Grant's new line.

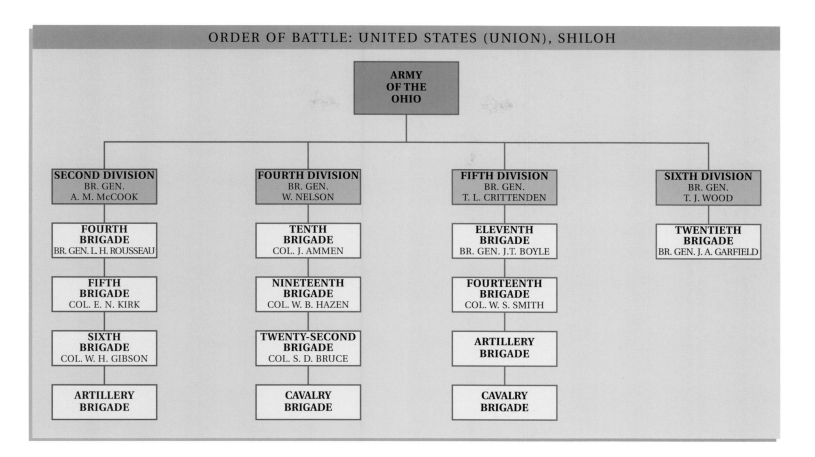

ORDER OF BATTLE: UNITED STATES (UNION), SHILOH

ARMY OF THE OHIO

SECOND DIVISION
BR. GEN.
A. M. McCOOK

FOURTH DIVISION
BR. GEN.
W. NELSON

FIFTH DIVISION
BR. GEN.
T. L. CRITTENDEN

SIXTH DIVISION
BR. GEN.
T. J. WOOD

FOURTH BRIGADE
BR. GEN. L. H. ROUSSEAU

TENTH BRIGADE
COL. J. AMMEN

ELEVENTH BRIGADE
BR. GEN. J.T. BOYLE

TWENTIETH BRIGADE
BR. GEN. J. A. GARFIELD

FIFTH BRIGADE
COL. E. N. KIRK

NINETEENTH BRIGADE
COL. W. B. HAZEN

FOURTEENTH BRIGADE
COL. W. S. SMITH

SIXTH BRIGADE
COL. W. H. GIBSON

TWENTY-SECOND BRIGADE
COL. S. D. BRUCE

ARTILLERY BRIGADE

ARTILLERY BRIGADE

CAVALRY BRIGADE

CAVALRY BRIGADE

Below: By the second day of Shiloh, reinforcements allowed the Federals to launch a decisive attack and reverse the first day's losses.

Pages 56–57: Both the Federal and Confederate commanders made serious mistakes at Shiloh. The horrific losses brought a new magnitude of suffering to the Civil War battlefield.

Above: A soldier from the Confederate Jeff David Rifles, Ninth Mississippi Regiment. Epaulets were worn as part of the dress uniform. They indicated grade, branch of service, and regimental number.

By now Grant was beginning to sense that the tide was turning in the Federals' favor. While the Federals were getting stronger with the arrival of every one of the 35,000 troops of Buell's Army of the Ohio, the Confederate attack clearly had culminated. After twelve hours of fighting on almost empty stomachs, the Confederates were exhausted. Fresh units may have been able to press the attack, but Breckinridge's Reserve Corps had already been committed and there were no new troops available. Furthermore, two Federal gunboats, the *Lexington* and the *Tyler*, were now lobbing shells inland to discourage any further advance by the Confederates.

Bragg put together two damaged brigades to make one last effort to attack across Dill's Branch, but Federal artillery cut them to pieces. Then one of Beauregard's aides rode up to Bragg with an order: "The general directs that the pursuit be stopped; the victory is complete; it is needless to expose our men to the fire of the gunboats." Bragg protested, and many others have likewise decried Beauregard's decision as a lost opportunity to press on to decisive victory.

Enough for One Day

Beauregard's critics argue that he was two miles from the front and failed to consult his subordinate commanders before calling off the battle. They point out that the entire purpose of the Confederate attack was to destroy or capture Grant's army, and anything short of that would be a failure. Beauregard's defenders counter that darkness was fast approaching, and the Confederate attack had already run its course and would have been no match for the tightened Federal line reinforced by Buell's fresh troops. Whether or not a continued Confederate attack would have been successful will never be known, but at the time Beauregard felt enough had been done for the day. He sent what proved to be a rash telegram to Richmond, declaring, "We this morning attacked the enemy in strong position . . . and after a severe battle of ten hours . . . gained a complete victory, driving the enemy from every position."

Beauregard's exaggerated assessment notwithstanding, both sides then commenced to suffer through a miserable night in preparation for renewed fighting the next day. What started as a drizzle around 10:00 p.m. was by midnight a downpour accompanied by a cold, hard wind. Many of the wounded were left to die that night because of the lack of organized evacuation systems on either side. One Confederate wrote, "This night of horrors will haunt me to my grave."

Recovery: The Second Day

Sherman had considered the damage inflicted on the Federal forces during the first day of Shiloh and concluded that, even with the arrival of Buell's reinforcements, it would be best "to put the river between us and the enemy, and recuperate." In the rain-soaked night, he sought out Grant to discuss the best way to withdraw.

Sherman found Grant standing under a tree, supporting himself by a crutch to ease the weight on an ankle he had injured earlier by falling off his horse. With his collar turned up against the weather, clenching a cigar between his teeth, Grant was the picture of determination and resolve. Upon seeing Grant, Sherman decided not to mention any plans for a retreat and instead began the conversation saying, "Well, Grant, we've had the devil's own day of it, haven't we?" "Yes," Grant replied, and after a pause added, "Lick 'em tomorrow, though." Such was the essence of Grant's generalship and approach to modern war. It was the deciding factor at Shiloh.

Grant told Sherman he planned to attack at dawn. As at Fort Donelson, Grant believed the situation was such that "either side was ready to give way if the other showed a bold front." Grant resolved to be the one to strike first, noting, "Beauregard will be mighty smart if he attacks before I do." Grant would make sure Beauregard would not have that chance.

At dawn, skirmishers moved forward all along the Federal line. Larger

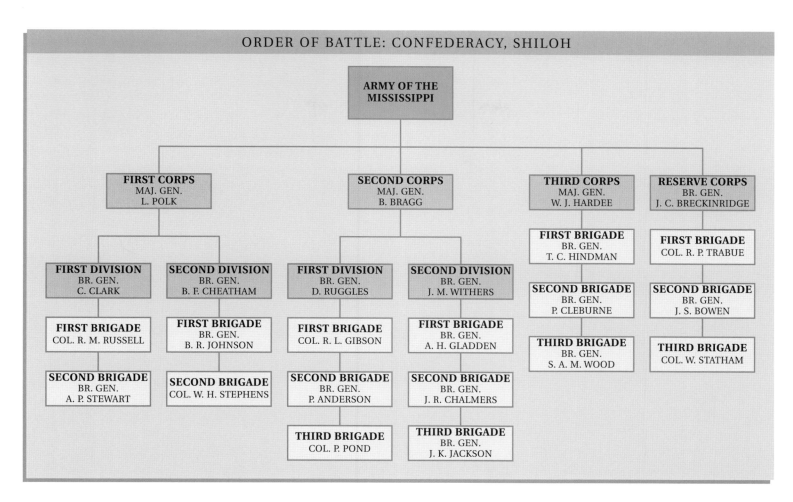

ORDER OF BATTLE: CONFEDERACY, SHILOH

ARMY OF THE MISSISSIPPI

FIRST CORPS
MAJ. GEN.
L. POLK

SECOND CORPS
MAJ. GEN.
B. BRAGG

THIRD CORPS
MAJ. GEN.
W. J. HARDEE

RESERVE CORPS
BR. GEN.
J. C. BRECKINRIDGE

FIRST DIVISION
BR. GEN.
C. CLARK

SECOND DIVISION
BR. GEN.
B. F. CHEATHAM

FIRST DIVISION
BR. GEN.
D. RUGGLES

SECOND DIVISION
BR. GEN.
J. M. WITHERS

FIRST BRIGADE
BR. GEN.
T. C. HINDMAN

FIRST BRIGADE
COL. R. P. TRABUE

FIRST BRIGADE
COL. R. M. RUSSELL

FIRST BRIGADE
BR. GEN.
B. R. JOHNSON

FIRST BRIGADE
COL. R. L. GIBSON

FIRST BRIGADE
BR. GEN.
A. H. GLADDEN

SECOND BRIGADE
BR. GEN.
P. CLEBURNE

SECOND BRIGADE
BR. GEN.
J. S. BOWEN

SECOND BRIGADE
BR. GEN.
A. P. STEWART

SECOND BRIGADE
COL. W. H. STEPHENS

SECOND BRIGADE
BR. GEN.
P. ANDERSON

SECOND BRIGADE
BR. GEN.
J. R. CHALMERS

THIRD BRIGADE
BR. GEN.
S. A. M. WOOD

THIRD BRIGADE
COL. W. STATHAM

THIRD BRIGADE
COL. P. POND

THIRD BRIGADE
BR. GEN.
J. K. JACKSON

formations of troops followed with instructions "to engage the enemy as soon as found." Neither Grant nor Buell had laid out a formal plan of attack, but as the Federals crashed into the Confederate line, they enjoyed quick success. A Confederate soldier of the

Thirty-eighth Tennessee recalled, "At daybreak our pickets came rushing in under a murderous fire. The first thing we knew we were almost surrounded by six or seven regiments of Yankees."

The numbers were clearly on the Federal side. Buell's reinforcements had

Left: Union troops and an artillery battery defend the Hornet's Nest—they repelled eleven Confederate charges before being encircled and forced to surrender. Federal artillery batteries usually consisted of six guns.

as the sheer weight of the Federal numbers crushed every Confederate effort to resist. Sensing the change of fortune from the first day's fighting, one Confederate officer noted, "The fire and animation had left our troops."

BEAUREGARD ORDERS WITHDRAWAL

By 2:30 p.m., the situation was painfully apparent to the Confederates. Colonel Thomas Jordan, Beauregard's adjutant, delicately suggested to his commander, "General, do you not think our troops are very much in the condition of a lump of sugar, thoroughly soaked with water, but yet preserving its original shape, though ready to dissolve? Would it not be judicious to get away with what we have?" Beauregard appeared to have reached the same conclusion and announced, "I intend to withdraw in a few minutes."

Beauregard ordered Jordan to round up what soldiers he could and form a rear guard. The staff officer succeeded in collecting about 2,000 soldiers and twelve artillery pieces, and positioned them on a ridge just south of Shiloh Church along the road to Corinth. Behind this protective screen, the Confederates began withdrawing at about 3:30 p.m.

The exhausted soldiers did not move far before pitching camp. They would have been easy targets for a Federal attack, but Grant's men were also spent. Grant ordered his troops to return to their original camps, explaining, "My force was too much fatigued to pursue. Night closed in cloudy and with heavy rain, making the roads impracticable for artillery by the next morning."

Above: Major General Henry Halleck (1815–72) assumed command of the Union army after Shiloh and relegated Grant to a frustrating role as assistant.

brought Grant's strength back up to where it had been the first day, while the previous fighting had reduced Beauregard's numbers by half. The battle followed the odds, with Grant easily retaking most of the ground he had earlier lost. For his part, Bragg ordered several counterattacks that resembled the piecemeal attacks that were so costly the previous day. All were unsuccessful,

RESULTS

The Battle of Shiloh had taken American warfare to a new level of magnitude and lethality. It was the biggest battle fought in North America to that date. Of the 62,000 Federals engaged, 13,047 were killed, wounded, or missing. The Confederates suffered 11,694 casualties from their 44,000-man force. After such losses, neither side was much interested in renewing the fighting.

On April 8, Beauregard began his retreat back to Corinth, with Colonel Nathan Bedford Forrest and 350 cavalrymen providing the rear guard. The Federals offered a perfunctory pursuit, but when Forrest's men clashed with the Seventy-seventh Ohio in the Battle of Fallen Timbers, a skirmish in which Sherman was nearly captured and Forrest almost killed, the Federals were content to let the Confederates withdraw. Once safely back in Corinth, Beauregard began building heavy fortifications.

The Federal victory at Shiloh was decisive and significant. The Confederate hope of recovering the initiative in western and middle Tennessee, and with it regaining control of Nashville and the state's iron-producing areas, was checkmated. Furthermore, Corinth and its critical rail links were now in serious danger. Shiloh had been a must-win for the South. By not destroying Grant's army, the Confederate forces in the west were now committed to a war of attrition that the South simply lacked the resources to win. For generations of Confederate sympathizers, the Battle of Shiloh was a missed opportunity to have created a different outcome.

Yet, in spite of the overall Federal victory, Grant's poor showing on the first day of Shiloh damaged his credibility. He was roundly criticized in the press and by Congress for allowing his army to be surprised and vulnerable. Rumors began to resurface of Grant's drinking, and many critics called for his removal. In spite of the outcry, President Lincoln continued to support Grant, explaining, "I can't spare this man; he fights."

Then, on April 11, Major General Henry Halleck arrived at Shiloh. As commander of the Department of the Mississippi, Halleck was Grant's senior. Halleck had long been distrustful of Grant, bringing unofficial charges of insubordination and neglect of duty against Grant for allegedly failing to maintain proper communications with Halleck's headquarters after Grant's victory at Fort Donelson. Now Grant's weak showing on the first day of the Battle of Shiloh reinforced Halleck's opinion that Grant lacked the capacity to administer and direct complex military operations. Accordingly, Halleck took over command of Grant's army and relegated Grant to the meaningless role of assistant commander.

Halleck then began a slow and deliberate approach toward Corinth. Every night he stopped the march and had his men dig in. After the horrific losses at Shiloh, Halleck was in no mood to risk additional heavy combat, but the failure to exploit the victory dismayed and frustrated Grant, who had no authority but to stand by and watch. At one point, Grant wrote a formal request to Halleck asking either to be given a real field command or relieved from duty. Later, Grant asked Halleck for a thirty-day leave, which Halleck granted.

"I AM IN THE WAY HERE"

It appeared now as if the North was on the verge of losing the general that would ultimately lead its armies to victory, and such might have been the case had not Halleck casually mentioned to Sherman that "Grant was going away the next morning." Sherman then sought out Grant and asked him why he was leaving. Grant replied, "Sherman, you know. You know that I am in the way here." Sherman encouraged Grant to stick it out, arguing that his own fortunes had changed, and Grant's would too. That night Grant wrote his wife Julia that he would not be coming home on leave, and the next day he notified Sherman of his decision to remain with the army. Narrowly, Grant avoided becoming a casualty of Shiloh himself—and the Union cause was much better for it.

LACK OF IMAGINATION IN WARFARE

With Beauregard thus serving as the de facto army commander, the Confederate effort was influenced profoundly by Beauregard's limitations as a general. In the Mexican War, Beauregard had had the opportunity to witness the brilliant turning movements executed by General Winfield Scott during his campaign from Veracruz to Mexico City. Time and again at places

"BUT BEFORE INSENSIBILITY, THE OPERATION WOULD BEGIN, AND IN THE MIDST OF SHRIEKS, CURSES, AND WILD LAUGHS, THE SURGEON WOULD WIELD OVER HIS WRETCHED VICTIM THE GLITTERING KNIFE AND SAW . . ."

BELLE REYNOLDS, A HOUSEWIFE FROM PEORIA, ILLINOIS, WHO HAD FOLLOWED HER HUSBAND INTO THE FIELD AT SHILOH AND WHO BECAME A BATTLEFIELD NURSE AND AN EYEWITNESS TO THE CARNAGE

Below: Shiloh damaged the high reputation Beauregard had gained at Fort Sumter and First Manassas.

JOHNSTON'S LEADERSHIP

At the onset of the Civil War, many considered Albert Sidney Johnston to be the Confederacy's best general. President Jefferson Davis was particularly supportive of Johnston, writing, "I hoped and expected that I had others who would prove generals; but I knew I had one, and that was Sidney Johnston." Such sentiments were not confined to the South alone. General Sherman described Johnston as "a real general," and General Grant said that officers who knew Johnston "expected him to prove the most formidable man that the Confederacy would produce."

In spite of these high expectations, Johnston's wartime performance thus far had been less than spectacular. The loss of Fort Donelson had forced Johnston to withdraw his Army of the Mississippi out of Tennessee, abandoning the industrial and logistical base of Nashville, and concentrate it at the rail junction at Corinth, Mississippi. This retreat damaged Johnston's popularity and credibility and seems to have left him shaken and weakened, at least temporarily. Some historians have suggested that in this dazed state of mind, Johnston began ceding more and more power to his second in command, Beauregard. Whether that was the case or not, it was becoming apparent that Johnston was not without his weaknesses.

At Shiloh, Johnston clearly failed to exert his command authority. His original intent for a turning movement was nowhere present in the plans drawn up by Beauregard, and Johnston did little to correct the situation either before or after the battle was joined. While Johnston's personal bravery is beyond question, his decision to lead from the front clearly limited his ability to influence the battle beyond his immediate vicinity, and the Confederate effort suffered from this lack of overall direction. Indeed, Johnston tacitly relinquished command to his subordinate Beauregard during the battle.

like Cerro Gordo, Scott bypassed strong Mexican positions and threatened the enemy rear. Most observers learned the utility of the turning movement from the American victory, but Beauregard was not overly impressed by Scott's performance. In fact, Beauregard attributed much of the American success to Mexican weakness rather than to Scott's generalship, and specifically felt that Scott's turning movements were dangerous deviations from "the true principles of the art of war." Beauregard was especially apprehensive of the requirement of dividing the army necessitated by a turning movement, cautioning that "the enemy occupying a central position to our line of operations might then concentrate all his means" against one or the other part.

THE TURNING MOVEMENT SPURNED

As a result of this opinion, Beauregard, in contrast to nearly every other important Civil War general, would not typically employ the turning movement. Shiloh is the most notable example of this characteristic, as was demonstrated by Beauregard's plan to attack the Federals frontally rather than following Johnston's guidance to turn the enemy's left. As Grant recalled, "The endeavor of the enemy on the first day was simply to hurl their men against ours—first at one point, then at another, sometimes at several points at once." A flanking movement would probably have produced the desired results, but Beauregard dismissed such an option.

In addition to the negative conclusions he had drawn from the Mexican War about the turning movement, Beauregard's generalship at Shiloh was also shaped by his characteristic lack of imagination. For Beauregard, warfare was to be waged according to a fairly rigid set of rules in conformity to a fixed pattern. He could not accept the risks associated with audacity, finesse, and innovation.

Beauregard's greatest weakness as a commander was his inability to adjust and improvise to meet the needs of the situation. Thus, at Shiloh he could offer no alternative to Braxton Bragg's repeated frontal assaults on the Hornet's Nest. The inflated reputation Beauregard had acquired at Fort Sumter and First Manassas was certainly not sustained at Shiloh.

THE FRIENDSHIP THAT WON THE CIVIL WAR

Sherman was one who observed and appreciated this aspect of Grant's character at Shiloh. When Ohio lieutenant governor Benjamin Stanton criticized Grant's performance, Sherman rushed to his commander's defense, telling Stanton, "The accusatory part of your statement is all false, false in general, false in every particular," and praising Grant as being "just fresh from the victory of Donelson, more rich in fruits than was Saratoga, Yorktown, or any other fought on this Continent." Sherman equally impressed Grant, who stated that while moving up and down the Federal line during the nip-and-tuck movements of the first day, Grant "never deemed it important to stay long with Sherman. Although his troops were under fire for the first time, their commander, by his constant presence with them, inspired a confidence in officers and men that enabled them to render services on that bloody battlefield worthy of the best veterans." Indeed, a certain bond was forged between Grant and Sherman at Shiloh, a bond so strong that one author credits it with being "the friendship that won the Civil War."

In the final analysis, generalship played a key role in the end result at Shiloh. Johnston's failure to provide overall direction and Beauregard's unimaginative frontal attacks served to negate the initial advantage the Confederates gained by surprise. On the Federal side, resolve and strength of character, displayed by Prentiss at the Hornet's Nest and by Grant in refusing to quit, overcame tactical errors. Both Billy Yank and Johnny Reb fought heroically. The difference was that the Federal generals better served their troops.

GRANT'S LEADERSHIP

Many observers consider Ulysses S. Grant's persistence and determination to be the key to the Union victory in the Civil War. Grant is most famous for these characteristics during his Virginia Campaign against General Robert E. Lee, but he first truly demonstrated them at Shiloh.

While Grant's failure to secure his force encamped at Pittsburg Landing and his being caught by surprise by the Confederate attack on April 6 are inexcusable, his subsequent recovery and moral courage are exemplary. Everywhere around him, Grant saw the refuse of units that had broken and run. Piles of amputated limbs and the screams of the wounded surrounded him. Throughout the first day, subordinates had asked him to retreat, or recommended he do so. It was a chaotic and depressing environment that would have broken the spirit of a lesser man.

Instead, Grant summoned his courage and refused to let the disaster of the first day shake his will. Alone in the rain under the tree where Sherman found him on that first night, Grant resolved to stay the course. Sherman could sense it immediately upon approaching Grant's presence. There would be no retreat. There would be no looking back. Tomorrow would bring attack and victory. Such was the essence of Grant's generalship.

In fact, Grant's tactical contributions at Shiloh were fairly insignificant. He failed to entrench his troops or provide adequate security on the first day. Even on the second day, Grant provided little tactical direction, instead leaving his division commanders great flexibility in developing their attack plans. When Major General Lew Wallace reported to Grant with a division of fresh reinforcements and asked him for instructions, Grant merely pointed toward Sherman's end of the Federal line and said, "Move out that way." When Wallace pressed Grant about what formation to adopt, Grant replied, "I leave that to your discretion." Grant's contribution at Shiloh was not in tactical detail. Instead it lay in strategic leadership and strength of character.

FARRAGUT VS. LOVELL

NEW ORLEANS, 1862

Although Major General Mansfield Lovell was responsible for the defense of New Orleans, the overall Confederate effort would suffer from an almost comic lack of unity. Threatening Lovell was a Federal naval force commanded by Admiral David Farragut and supported by a land force led by Major General Benjamin Butler.

At stake was the South's biggest city and one of its most important economic and shipbuilding centers. In spite of this significance, the Confederacy seemed to take an almost cavalier approach to the defense of New Orleans that certainly would prove no match for Farragut's superior force and leadership.

PRELIMINARIES

On September 17, 1861, the meager Confederate defense force at Ship Island off the coast of Biloxi, Mississippi, in the

DAVID G. FARRAGUT	
RANK: FLAG OFFICER	
BORN: 1801	
EDUCATED: AT SEA AND IN VARIOUS PLACES SUCH AS TUNIS	
MILITARY CAREER	
ENTERED NAVY AS A MIDSHIPMAN AT NINE YEARS OF AGE	
SERVED AS PRIZEMASTER AT AGE TWELVE	
FIRST MADE AN OFFICER IN 1821	
VETERAN OF MEXICAN WAR	
DIED: 1870	

Mississippi Sound abandoned the island practically without a fight. The Federals promptly began garrisoning their new possession to use as a jumping-off point for an attack on New Orleans, and by April 1862 Federal troop strength on Ship Island peaked with more than 15,000 men. One historian would later write that the loss of Ship Island exposed the Confederacy's "tender underbelly to assault," but at the time the Federal buildup caused remarkably little concern among the Confederate high command. Major General Mansfield Lovell, the man charged with the defense of New Orleans, viewed any activity on Ship Island with skepticism, writing Richmond in late February that he regarded the Federal expedition there "as a harmless menace so far as New Orleans is concerned."

The general consensus was that the strong Fort Jackson and Fort St. Philip would negate any attack on New Orleans from the south. If the city was to be attacked, the Confederates reasoned, it would be by a land assault from the north. Time would prove such thinking to be dangerously wrong, and the Confederates' false sense of security for New Orleans would soon come back to haunt them.

If the Confederates were somewhat complacent about the threat from Ship Island, the Federals clearly considered it a preliminary step toward attacking New Orleans. New Orleans, by far the South's biggest city with a population of 168,000, was a lucrative target. Lieutenant General Winfield Scott was so impressed by the importance of New Orleans that he considered it decisive to a Federal victory. He told President Lincoln that the Federals must "fight all the battles that were necessary, take all the positions we could find and garrison them, fight a battle at New Orleans and win it, and thus end the war." Likewise, Brigadier General John Barnard felt "failure [of an operation against New Orleans] would be a terrible blow; its success would bring us almost to the close of the war."

KINGS OF COTTON AND SHIPBUILDING

One of the reasons for New Orleans' importance was the wealth it had built through the cotton trade. In 1860 its port receipts exceeded $185 million, of which cotton accounted for 60 percent, and in that same year New Orleans handled

NEW ORLEANS

Date	April 25–May 1, 1862
Location	New Orleans and St. Bernard Parish, Louisiana
Result	Union victory

Strength

Union:	Confederate:
Department of the Gulf	Department No. 1
24 wooden vessels	14 vessels,
19 mortar boats	including 2 ironclads
15,000 troops	4,000 troops

Casualties and losses

229	782

MANSFIELD LOVELL

RANK: MAJOR GENERAL

BORN: 1822

EDUCATED: UNITED STATES MILITARY ACADEMY

MILITARY CAREER

VETERAN OF MEXICAN WAR

RESIGNED FROM THE ARMY IN 1849

SERVED AS A VOLUNTEER STAFF OFFICER FOR JOSEPH JOHNSTON IN 1864

DIED: 1884

two million bales of cotton. The Confederate government itself never held title to more than 400,000 bales. If cotton were indeed king, then New Orleans was a key member of its court.

New Orleans was also one of the South's most important shipbuilding centers, and by 1861, every shipyard in New Orleans was busy building, converting, or repairing some type of war-related vessel. It was a largely decentralized effort, with few of the ships actually earmarked for the fledgling Confederate navy, but three ironclads were under construction. The *Manassas* was a private enterprise built to be a profit-making privateer. The *Louisiana* and *Mississippi* were being built under separate contracts authorized by Confederate Secretary of the Navy Stephen Mallory. It was, in most cases, a confused and competing effort that did not use the scarce Confederate resources efficiently. Nonetheless, New Orleans was a hubbub of shipbuilding activity, and rumors of the presence of Confederate ironclads in New Orleans raised serious concerns in Washington.

INITIAL DEFENSES

New Orleans' original commander was Major General David Twiggs, who arrived on May 31 as commander of Department No. 1, consisting of Louisiana and the southern parts of Mississippi and Alabama. At the time of his appointment, Twiggs was the ranking officer in the Confederacy, but he was hardly a universally popular choice for commander. The people of New Orleans would have preferred native son Pierre Gustave Toutant Beauregard or perhaps Braxton Bragg. Even when Twiggs was in his prime, Winfield Scott had considered him one of his worst officers in Mexico. Now, at seventy-one years of age, Twiggs was physically infirm and often unable to leave his quarters.

Still, Twiggs was loyal to the cause and he began organizing his defenses. By the summer, he had 5,000 men camped around New Orleans, 4,000 being trained at nearby Camp Moore, and new companies still assembling. Significantly,

and perhaps reflecting the relative lack of concern for New Orleans, 8,000 Louisiana soldiers were serving outside the state.

DANGER WILL COME FROM THE SEA

At this early point in the war, the Confederacy was most concerned with an attack on New Orleans from the south. On January 10, Louisiana senators Judah Benjamin and John Slidell sent messages to New Orleans, warning, "Secret attempts continue to be made to garrison Southern ports. We think there is special reason to fear surprise from the Gulf Squadron." Likewise, the governor was warned, "The danger is not from St. Louis, but from the sea." Commodore George Hollins, the man Secretary Mallory had dispatched to New Orleans on July 31 to tend to its naval defenses, shared this opinion. These assessments were in fact consistent with the Federal strategy. Indeed, Scott's original Anaconda Plan had envisioned an amphibious attack on New Orleans from the Gulf.

By the time of Hollins's arrival, however, an alternate viewpoint had gained ascendancy in the Confederacy. Forts Jackson and St. Philip, as well as the broad inland bayous and a string of fortifications known as the Chalmette defense line, were considered so strong that observers like local resident George Cable said, "Nothing afloat could pass the forts. Nothing that walked could get through the swamps." Instead, Federal ironclad construction upriver at places like Cincinnati, Carondelet (near St. Louis), and Mound City caused many to think the attack would come from the north. Twiggs shared this view, and he developed a plan to convert six large floating docks into floating batteries that he then would have towed to a point upriver "where the channel is narrow and [could] be made an impassable barrier to the vessels of the enemy." On August 24, Secretary of War Leroy Walker approved Twiggs's project. As for the southern approach, Twiggs anticipated the Federal navy would use only wooden warships, which would be no match for the

Above: This Federal petty officer is armed with an M1851 Colt Navy revolver, which was standard issue for officers and noncommissioned officers throughout the U.S. Navy. The M1851 was a .36-caliber pistol that weighed just forty-two ounces. Officers and men would also be issued an M1841 cutlass, and some ratings would also be armed with the M1861 Whitney Navy rifle for boarding actions and shore operations.

powerful Forts Jackson and St. Philip. This trust in New Orleans' ability to thwart an attack from the south was reinforced on October 12 when Hollins, with a force consisting of the *Manassas* and six lightly armed riverboats, routed four Federal vessels commanded by Captain John Pope in a debacle that Secretary of the Navy Gideon Welles derisively dubbed "Pope's Run."

FARRAGUT ASSUMES COMMAND

Much of the Confederate confidence in New Orleans' defense was based on the notion that wooden ships were no match for heavy fortifications. While this idea had been true in the past, recent events at Hatteras Inlet, North Carolina, and Port Royal, South Carolina, had changed things. There the Federal navy had demonstrated how much the steam engine had altered the historic balance between the ship and the fort. Twiggs may have missed this lesson, but Assistant Secretary of the Navy Gustavus Fox and Commander David Porter had not. Porter saw no reason that the success at Port Royal could not be repeated on the lower Mississippi, and he thought he should be the man to give it a try. It all made sense to Fox, who had likewise begun thinking of a plan to attack New Orleans from the south.

After first seeing Fox, Porter obtained an audience with Secretary Welles and briefed him on a plan to precede the attack with a forty-eight-hour bombardment of Forts Jackson and St. Philip using mortars mounted on modified schooners. Porter argued that with the navy providing most of the firepower, the only support required from the army would be a few thousand soldiers to garrison the captured forts and occupy the city. Welles was convinced, and together with Porter, he obtained President Lincoln's approval.

But holding only the rank of commander, Porter was far too junior to lead such an expedition. Instead Welles dispatched Porter to meet with Captain David Farragut, Porter's foster brother, to determine Farragut's views on the New Orleans plan. Farragut had a positive opinion, and on January 9, 1862,

Secretary Welles gave Farragut command of the newly constituted West Gulf Blockading Squadron, whose jurisdiction stretched from western Florida to the Rio Grande.

The West Gulf Blockading Squadron was carved out of Flag Officer William McKean's Gulf Blockading Squadron, and McKean now became commander of the new East Gulf Blockading Squadron. Dividing the command meant that McKean and Farragut each would be able to concentrate on a smaller area. It also

Above: A photograph of Farragut in dress uniform taken after the war. Farragut's birth in Tennessee and marriage to a Virginian caused some to question his loyalty, but he proved to be an excellent Federal commander.

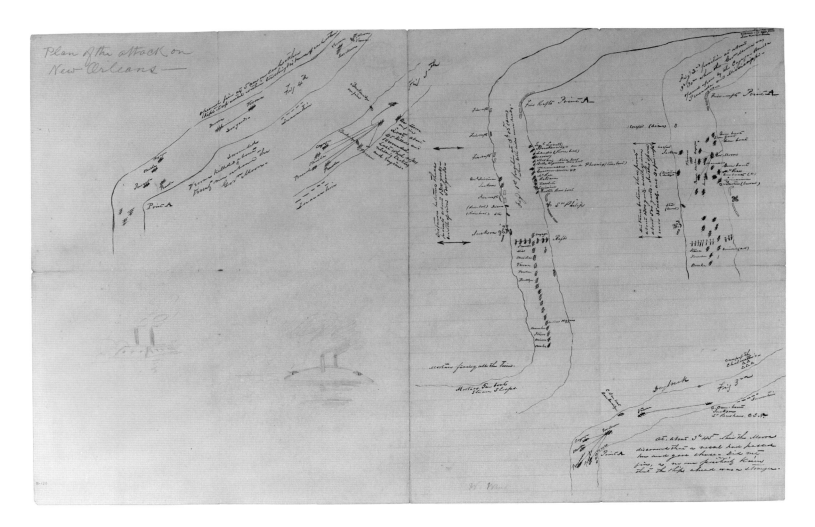

Above: Farragut was a meticulous planner and a great stickler for details. These drawings show his plan of attack for capturing New Orleans from the Confederacy.

gave Welles a cover for sending Farragut to the Gulf without telegraphing his plans to attack New Orleans. On March 19, the Senate confirmed Farragut's appointment to flag officer.

As the Federal plans and command arrangements were solidifying, those of the Confederates were moving in the opposite direction. At this time, the prevailing opinion in the Confederate high command was still that an attack would come from upriver. Thus, Secretary Mallory sent Hollins, his Mosquito Fleet, and the floating battery *New Orleans* north to join Major General Leonidas Polk in the defense of Columbus, Kentucky, a move that left New Orleans without naval protection. Perhaps Mallory felt that the army had so improved Forts Jackson and St. Philip as to warrant the removal of Hollins's fleet, but coordination between the navy and the War Department was so weak, he really had no way of knowing for sure. If such work actually was being done, it would have been the responsibility of

army commander Twiggs, but Twiggs was not doing it. In fact, on October 5, he had asked to be relieved of his command.

LOVELL'S ARRIVAL

Even before Twiggs tendered his resignation, the War Department had dispatched Mansfield Lovell to New Orleans to act as Twiggs's assistant. When Lovell arrived on October 17, he learned that he had replaced Twiggs as commander of Department No. 1 and had been promoted to major general. Lovell had already studied the department and, prior to leaving Richmond, he had spoken with both President Jefferson Davis and Secretary of War Judah Benjamin and argued that the only way to properly defend New Orleans was to unify the land and naval commands. Davis disagreed, and wrote Lovell on October 17, "The fleet maintained at the port of New Orleans and its vicinity is not part of your command; and the purpose of which it is sent there, or removed from there, are communicated in orders and letters of a department with which you have no direct communication. It must . . . be obvious to you that you could not assume command of these officers and vessels coming with your geographical department, but not placed on duty with you, without serious detriment to discipline and probably injury to the public service." Davis added that he encouraged Lovell to maintain "unrestrained intercourse and cordial fraternization" with the navy, but failed to send a similar note to Mallory or Hollins imploring them to cooperate with Lovell. What one historian calls a "Southern-style farce of divided command" had developed to plague the defense of New Orleans.

At first Lovell appeared to display the energy the residents of New Orleans had sought. He set out on an inspection tour and "found matters generally so deficient and incomplete that I was unwilling to commit their condition to writing for fear of their falling into the wrong hands." Among the discrepancies he found were manpower shortages, incompetent officers, antiquated cannons, inferior ammunition, dilapidated fortifications, unimpeded river approaches, and unfinished lines.

Lovell worked diligently to correct these problems and made progress. By January 1862 he had replaced many of the unsuitable guns, expanding local foundries and establishing his own ammunition factory in the process. He laid track to connect New Orleans with the Pontchartrain and Mexican Gulf Railroad in order to facilitate the movement of supplies and men. He also scavenged loose chains and anchors from across the South to strengthen the defensive log boom across the Mississippi. Lovell now had a barrier securely chained to both banks, held by fifteen anchors weighing from 2,500 to 4,000 pounds, and laid in twenty-five fathoms of water by sixty fathoms of strong chain. Obviously proud, Lovell wrote, "This raft is a complete obstruction, and has enfilading fire from Fort Jackson and direct fire from Saint Philip." By the end of December, Lovell had 3,500 effectives manning his entrenchments and another 6,000 well-armed volunteers in the city. Including his exterior lines, Lovell commanded a force of about 15,000 men.

DISMANTLING LOVELL'S
IMPROVEMENTS

But as fast as Lovell could improve things, the War Department seemed to stymie them. Part of this problem was the low priority New Orleans received from Richmond. Clothing, medical supplies, rifles, and even some of the big naval guns were siphoned off for service in Virginia and elsewhere because neither Davis nor Benjamin considered New Orleans to be in imminent danger of attack. Even after Lovell raised and trained a force of 10,000 infantry, Benjamin sent half of them to reinforce General Albert Sidney Johnston at Corinth, Mississippi, after the loss of Forts Henry and Donelson.

Lovell knew there was a threat much closer to home. He could see the Federal force unloading troops on Ship Island, and with Hollins's Mosquito Fleet still upriver, Lovell had only two small naval vessels operating on Lake Pontchartrain

Below: Admiral David Dixon Porter (1813–91), seen here in the center (with beard), was a capable naval officer but also had a healthy dose of self-serving ambition.

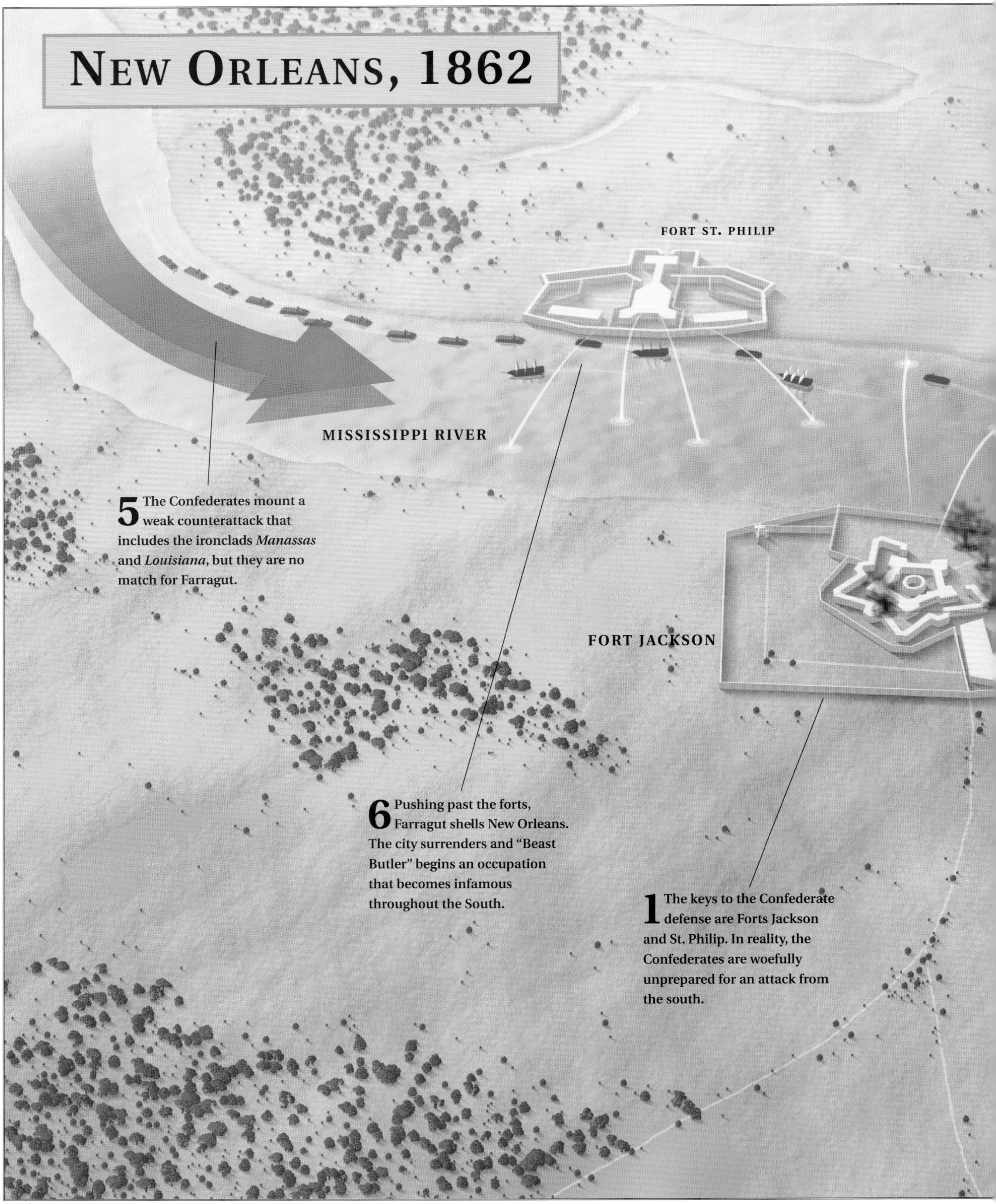

NEW ORLEANS, 1862

FORT ST. PHILIP

MISSISSIPPI RIVER

5 The Confederates mount a weak counterattack that includes the ironclads *Manassas* and *Louisiana*, but they are no match for Farragut.

FORT JACKSON

6 Pushing past the forts, Farragut shells New Orleans. The city surrenders and "Beast Butler" begins an occupation that becomes infamous throughout the South.

1 The keys to the Confederate defense are Forts Jackson and St. Philip. In reality, the Confederates are woefully unprepared for an attack from the south.

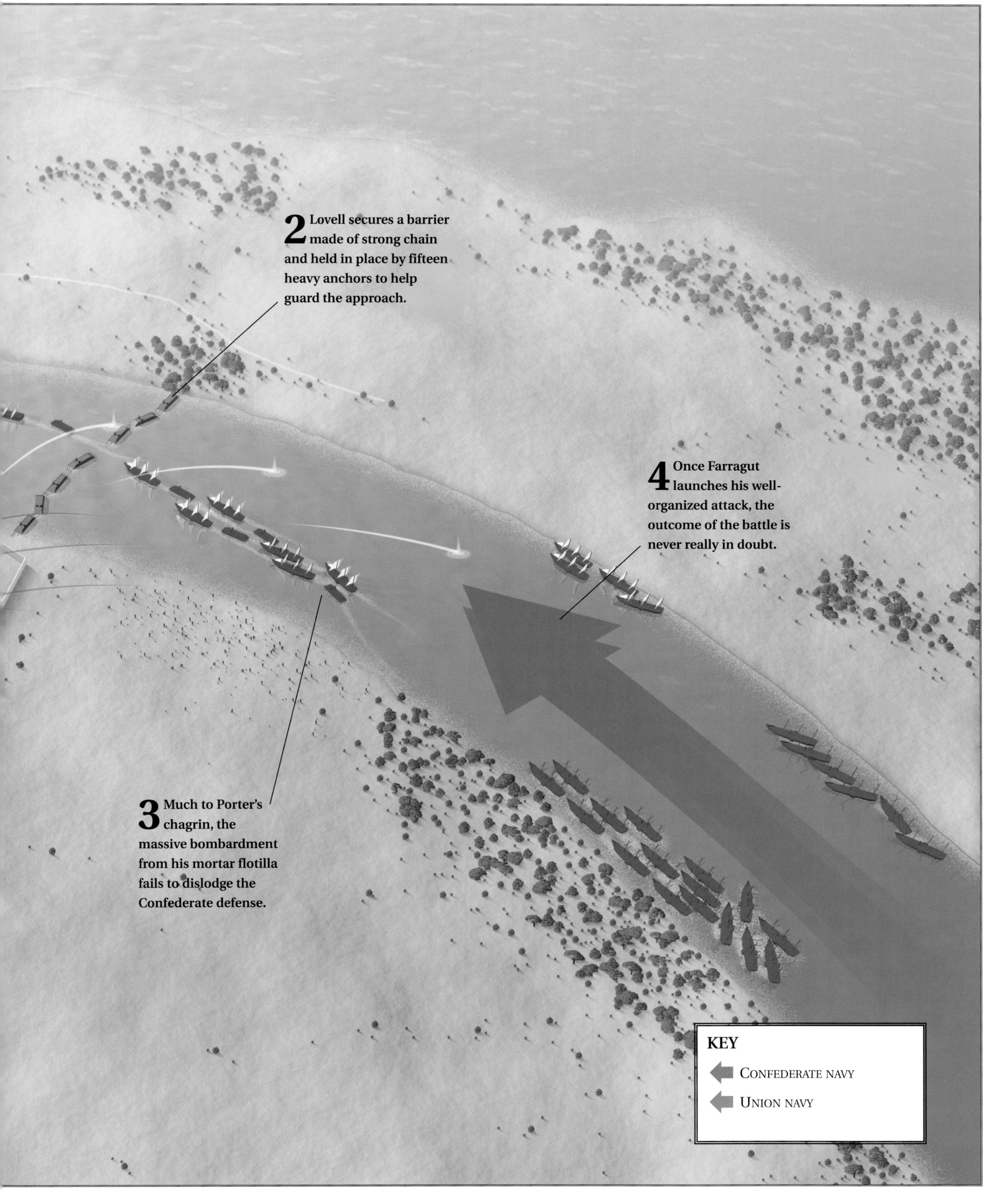

2 Lovell secures a barrier made of strong chain and held in place by fifteen heavy anchors to help guard the approach.

4 Once Farragut launches his well-organized attack, the outcome of the battle is never really in doubt.

3 Much to Porter's chagrin, the massive bombardment from his mortar flotilla fails to dislodge the Confederate defense.

KEY

← CONFEDERATE NAVY

← UNION NAVY

Above: New Orleans, 1862. One of the important characteristics of New Orleans was its status as a shipbuilding center. Especially threatening to the Federals were the ironclads being built there. The Confederate defenses for such an important city as New Orleans were surprisingly modest.

Opposite: Porter hoped to use his mortar flotilla of nineteen mortar boats to shell the Confederates at New Orleans into submission. Porter fired 2,997 shells at Fort Jackson, but was unable to compel the fort to surrender by this bombardment alone.

to help defend against a landing. Lovell took his concerns about the lack of naval cooperation to Benjamin, who promptly ordered Lovell to impress fourteen ships into public service to form what became known as the River Defense Fleet. This ragtag assembly was not quite what Lovell had in mind when he requested gunboats, and the River Defense Fleet became an ongoing headache for him.

In an effort to get rid of the burden, Lovell offered the fleet to Hollins, but Hollins wanted nothing to do with vessels belonging to the War Department. When Commander John Mitchell replaced Hollins on February 1, 1862, problems with the unity of effort continued. Mitchell showed little inclination to assume command of all the various naval components, but even if he had, Captain John Stevenson of the River Defense Fleet claimed his men had entered the service "with the condition that [the River Defense Fleet] was to be independent of the Navy, and that it would not be governed by the regulations of the Navy, or be commanded by naval officers." He said he would cooperate, but was under no obligation to obey

orders from Mitchell, and he specifically refused to station his rams along the chain barrier. Like so many other aspects of New Orleans, the River Defense Fleet had become a distraction. Lovell had to divert scarce resources, including his attention, to man, arm, and clad it. By now the defense of New Orleans was suffering from disunity between the Louisiana and Confederate governments as well as among the army, the navy, and the independently minded river steamboat captains. The whole situation was becoming a complete mess.

On March 13, 1862, Major General Benjamin Butler arrived at Ship Island with the final installment of his 15,255 men while Farragut continued building his fleet and preparing for the attack. The *Brooklyn* occupied the Head of Passes, light draft steamers moved upriver to reconnoiter the forts, and Porter positioned his mortar schooners. The Federals were obviously up to something, but Confederate defensive preparations hardly kept apace. The competing— and incompetent—shipbuilding efforts maintained a flurry of activity, but no real progress was made thanks to shortages in materials and money, strikes, poor leadership, and myriad other problems. The River Defense Fleet was sapping Lovell's energy, and he predicted, "Unless some competent person, of education, system, and brains, is put over each division of this fleet, it will, in my judgment, prove an utter failure." To make matters worse, George Randolph had replaced Benjamin as secretary of war, creating additional difficulties in the transition. As if all this was not enough, the swollen Mississippi River ripped away the raft and chain barrier that was designed to obstruct a naval advance. Lovell replaced it with a second raft, but it was just one more thing he had to worry about. In the midst of this impending chaos, Davis ordered Lovell to impose martial law.

Farragut was also experiencing some difficulties. He was having trouble getting his fleet across the mud-filled bar, and by the middle of March he had half his ships in the river and the other half

still outside. Furthermore, continued rumors of Confederate ironclad production masked the true state of confused affairs and worried Farragut about the vulnerability of his wooden ships. To make matters worse, he had to contend with disloyal communications sent from Porter to the Navy Department, delays as vessels were lightened and then resupplied, and coal shortages. It was not until April 8 that Farragut lay full strength in the river, and not until April 14 that he could report being "nearly all coaled." Remarkably, with Richmond still insisting upon retaining Hollins and

his Mosquito Fleet upriver, the Confederates had left Farragut unmolested to work out his problems. Even Lovell appeared to be ambivalent, writing Secretary Randolph on April 15 that he saw "no harm done . . . twenty-seven vessels in sight from forts." Like Nero, the Confederate command fiddled while New Orleans was about to burn.

PORTER'S "BUMMERS"

The vessels that Lovell had observed belonged to Porter's mortar flotilla. On April 16, Porter towed three schooners to a marker 3,000 yards from Fort Jackson and lobbed a few shells to test the range. The next day, all twenty-one of Porter's vessels, derisively called "bummers" by the "real" sailors in the fleet, were at anchor in carefully determined positions. Then on April 18 at 9:00 a.m., Porter began his huge bombardment. For ten straight hours, each schooner fired a round every ten minutes for a total of nearly 3,000 shells. At nightfall, Porter ceased firing and rowed forward to assess the damage. He "convinced [himself] that the fort itself was in flames," but also realized he would have to slow the pace of the next day's bombardment to conserve his ammunition as well as to save his men from exhaustion. Porter knew now that his boast of being able to reduce the forts in two days was a miscalculation. Still, Farragut let Porter continue his efforts until the morning of April 20, when Farragut summoned his officers to announce a new plan. Farragut was convinced that mortars alone would not cause the forts to surrender, and now with Butler and 7,000 of his men across the bar, Farragut had other options. He planned to destroy the chain barrier, run past the forts with his warships, and, once above the forts, land Butler's troops to seize them. Porter's mortars, much to their commander's chagrin, would remain in position.

The first part of Farragut's plan began on the night of April 20 when a force under Captain Henry Bell departed on a mission to break the chain. The Confederates attempted to disrupt the operation by launching a fire raft, but

Below: Benjamin Butler's heavy-handed occupation of New Orleans earned him the nickname "Beast."

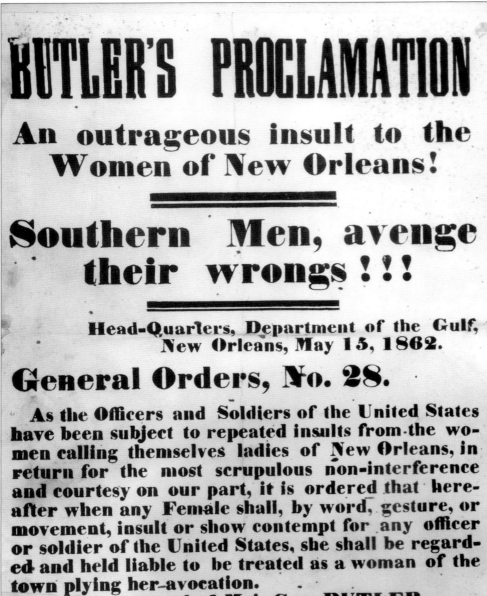

BUTLER'S PROCLAMATION

An outrageous insult to the Women of New Orleans!

Southern Men, avenge their wrongs !!!

Head-Quarters, Department of the Gulf, New Orleans, May 15, 1862.

General Orders, No. 28.

As the Officers and Soldiers of the United States have been subject to repeated insults from the women calling themselves ladies of New Orleans, in return for the most scrupulous non-interference and courtesy on our part, it is ordered that hereafter when any Female shall, by word, gesture, or movement, insult or show contempt for any officer or soldier of the United States, she shall be regarded and held liable to be treated as a woman of the town plying her avocation.

By command of Maj.-Gen. BUTLER,
GEORGE C. STRONG,
A. A. G. Chief of Staff

Bell and his men were ultimately successful in clearing the obstacle. For the present, Farragut allowed Porter to continue his bombardment, but by April 23 the promised results had not yet come. When Porter asked for still more time, Farragut replied, "Look here, David. We'll demonstrate the practical value of mortar work."

Farragut then ordered his signal officer to wave a red pennant every time a shell landed inside of Fort Jackson and a white one for every shell that missed its target. The results were indisputable as time after time the white flag was unfurled. Farragut summarized the results by saying, "There's the score. I guess we'll go up the river tonight." Opposing his advance, the Confederates had eleven vessels and some tugs along the Mississippi above the chain barrier.

FARRAGUT'S ATTACK

Throughout that evening Farragut finalized his preparations, displaying his characteristic energy, hands-on approach to leadership, and attention to detail. He had his sailors remove extra spars, rigging, boats, and all but a few sails. Heavy iron cable chains were draped on the outside of the vessels like chain-mail armor to provide additional protection to the engines and boilers. Vulnerable boilers were also protected by bags of ashes, clothing, sand, and whatever else was handy. Weight was redistributed aboard the ships so they would draw less water aft than forward, ensuring that if a ship was grounded while heading upstream, the bow would strike the bottom first and the swift current would be unable to turn the ship around. Hulls were coated with oil and mud to help conceal them from enemy observation while decks were whitewashed to help gunners find their tools in the dark. Once everything was ready, Farragut began his attack shortly after midnight on April 24.

As the fleet advanced, it took fire from both the forts and from the *Manassas*, but the passage never really was in doubt. Farragut had organized his ships into three divisions for the run. Singly or

Above: Farragut organized his attack into three divisions and ran his fleet past the powerful Confederate Forts Jackson and St. Philip, pressing on to New Orleans. Once the men in the forts realized New Orleans had been captured, they surrendered as well.

"HERE AND THERE
THE SLAVES
SWARMED UP TO THE
LEVEE, HOE IN HAND,
WAVING THEIR
BATTERED HATS, AND
SHOUTING WELCOME
TO THOSE WHO, THEY
HAD LEARNED FROM
A STRANGE SYSTEM
OF FREE-MASONRY
PECULIAR TO THE
NEGROES, HAD COME
TO BE THEIR
DELIVERERS."

HARPER'S PICTORIAL HISTORY OF THE CIVIL WAR, DESCRIBING SCENES AFTER THE CAPTURE OF NEW ORLEANS

Right: Confederate and Federal ships fight it out on the Mississippi River, April 1, 1862. The Confederate ironclads *Louisiana* and *Mississippi* (left) caused much anxiety but were little match for Farragut's attack.

LOVELL'S LEADERSHIP

Lovell had never been the unanimous choice to tend to the defenses of New Orleans. After resigning from the army in 1854, he settled in New York City. This Northern connection, as well as his slowness in joining the Confederate cause, led many to view him with suspicion. For example, Braxton Bragg, who had coveted the New Orleans position for himself, wrote Governor Thomas Moore, "How do you get along with your new fledged Major General fresh from the lecture room of New York where he has been . . . instructing the very men he will have to oppose?" The fact that Lovell retreated from New Orleans without much of a fight seemed to support the claims that he had not been the right man for the job.

In spite of the low priority for resources assigned it by the Confederate government, Lovell did in fact expend great personal energy in improving New Orleans' military protection. He also identified the problems of unity of effort that plagued the city's defenses. However, Lovell must share some of the blame for not communicating these deficiencies to Richmond in a forceful enough way to result in meaningful change. Part of Lovell's problem in this area probably stemmed from his own failure to fully appreciate the threat posed to New Orleans from a southern approach. Like many others, Lovell did not heed the warnings associated with the Federal buildup after the capture of Ship Island. One of the principal advantages of the defender is the ability to prepare for the battle, and Lovell did not take advantage of this opportunity. While many of the problems in New Orleans were not of Lovell's making, he nonetheless failed to convince his superiors to make the decisions necessary to resolve them. Although a court of inquiry would vindicate him of any wrongdoing, Lovell's reputation still suffered greatly from the loss of New Orleans, both within the Confederate military and with the Confederate people.

in small groups, they all made it except for the *Varuna,* which was sunk, and three gunboats from the rear division that were forced to turn back. Farragut now sent word to Porter to demand the surrender of the forts, and to Butler to bring up the army transports from the Head of Passes. Farragut then pushed on toward New Orleans and anchored for the night fifteen miles below the city.

Farragut did not rest for long. Before dawn on April 25, he was up and moving toward New Orleans. By now the city was in panic and Lovell had torched the levee and retreated. As Farragut pulled alongside the city, he hammered it with broadsides and then dispatched his marines to take possession of the Federal mint, post office, and customhouse, and replace the Confederate flag with the Stars and Stripes on all public buildings. Captain Theodorus Bailey, commander of Farragut's Red Division, worked his way through an angry mob and demanded the city's surrender, but the mayor claimed to be under martial law and without authority. After Farragut threatened a bombardment, the mayor and the common council declared New Orleans an open city.

In the meantime, the forts had refused Porter's demand to surrender, so Porter resumed his bombardment. He made a second offer two days later, but still the forts refused. Finally, as word drifted downriver of New Orleans' fate, morale broke. At midnight on April 27, the troops mutinied, with half of them running off and the rest just sitting down. Brigadier General Johnson Duncan was left with no choice but to surrender. Commander Mitchell held out a little longer aboard the *Louisiana,* but ultimately blew her up and surrendered the remnants of the naval command.

On May 1, Butler and the army came up from their landing at Quarantine and began a controversial occupation of New Orleans. Butler gained such a terrible reputation in New Orleans that, for years after the war, the bottoms of chamber pots bore his likeness. Throughout the South he became known as "Beast Butler" for his oppressive occupation regime, or as "Spoons Butler" for his alleged pilfering of New Orleans' wealth. Most notorious was his general order that any Confederate woman who insulted or showed contempt for a Federal soldier would be treated as a "woman of the town plying her avocation."

UNREALIZED STRATEGIC SIGNIFICANCE

New Orleans was indeed a great victory for the Union, placing one of the South's premier cities and the mouth of the Mississippi under Federal control. Still, New Orleans was a limited victory in that the strategic momentum was lost. Like after so many other operations in the coastal campaign, the Federals lacked a detailed plan for what to do next.

One obvious target was the Confederate Mississippi River bastion at Vicksburg, about 400 miles above New Orleans, and Farragut made two attempts, one in May and another in June, to subdue the city. Both failed, with the latter effort clearly showing the need for a cooperating land force. Indeed, the Federals would not be able to wrest Vicksburg from Confederate control until some 43,000 men commanded by Major General Ulysses S. Grant, with the help of a powerful fleet commanded by Porter, did so on July 4, 1863, after a lengthy campaign of maneuver and siege.

In spite of this failure to rapidly follow up on the success, New Orleans was still a great Federal victory. It denied the Confederacy a key shipbuilding facility and the potential to build the ironclads that were so fearful to the Federal navy. It was a huge blow to Confederate morale and led Commander Porter to crow that the Southerners were now "broken backed." The Confederate diarist Mary Chesnut lamented, "New Orleans gone—and with it the Confederacy. Are we not cut in two?" Although a little premature, Chesnut's observation still captured the magnitude of the situation. The Federal victory at New Orleans was a huge step toward splitting the Confederacy in half and reopening the Mississippi River. It was the pivotal battle of the Gulf Campaign.

FARRAGUT'S LEADERSHIP

Secretary Welles had a difficult decision in appointing Farragut as the commander of the West Gulf Blockading Squadron. Not only did Farragut have substantial ties to the South (having been born in Tennessee and then marrying a woman from Virginia), he also had not previously commanded a large force. In spite of these considerations, Farragut proved to more than justify Welles's confidence in him. In Farragut, Welles found a man who "is a good officer in a great emergency, will more willingly take risks in order to obtain great results than any other officer in high position in either Navy or Army, and, unlike most of them, prefers that others should tell the story of his well-doing rather than relate it himself."

Farragut displayed two very sophisticated appreciations of the operational art at New Orleans. The first was an understanding that victory could be achieved by defeating either an enemy's force or the function of that force. Rather than attacking the significant force represented by Forts Jackson and St. Philip, Farragut instead negated the forts' function by pushing past them and threatening New Orleans itself. Once bypassed, the forts no longer served their intended function of protecting the city and became largely irrelevant. As soon as the defenders learned of the fate of New Orleans, morale broke, and the commander was forced to surrender.

Farragut also understood the need for joint operations between the army and the navy. While the navy could bypass the forts and threaten New Orleans, any long-term results would require a land force as well. Farragut needed Butler's soldiers to isolate the forts and occupy New Orleans. Without this asset, Farragut's navy may well have been able to conduct only a spectacular raid rather than achieve a decisive victory.

Farragut clearly enjoyed several advantages that were denied to Lovell. Farragut had a significant force and, Butler's self-serving personality notwithstanding, acceptable unity of effort. Nevertheless, it was Farragut who had to put these assets to use by detailed planning, levelheaded decision-making, and the exercise of appropriate risk. Farragut met these challenges and clearly outcommanded Lovell at New Orleans.

LEE VS. MCCLELLAN

ANTIETAM, 1862

Antietam was truly one of the pivotal battles of the Civil War. As General Robert E. Lee built on his victories in Virginia and launched an invasion into Maryland, the very existence of the United States stood in the balance. In desperation, President Lincoln had little choice but to turn to Major General George McClellan to meet the threat. The resulting battle was the bloodiest single day of the Civil War.

Although McClellan missed a spectacular opportunity to destroy Lee's army, the battle was enough of a victory to give Lincoln the chance he needed to issue the Emancipation Proclamation, a document that changed the nature of the

GEORGE B. MCCLELLAN

RANK: MAJOR GENERAL

BORN: 1826

EDUCATED: UNITED STATES MILITARY ACADEMY

MILITARY CAREER

VETERAN OF MEXICAN WAR

MEMBER OF DELAFIELD COMMISSION

RESIGNED FROM ARMY IN 1857

DEFEATED BY ROBERT E. LEE IN THE PENINSULA CAMPAIGN

DID NOT HOLD A FIELD COMMAND AFTER ANTIETAM

DIED: 1885

war and all but eliminated Confederate hopes of European intervention.

PRELIMINARIES

As a result of Lee's repulse of McClellan's Peninsula Campaign, McClellan received instructions on August 3, 1862, to return the army to a position south of Washington. In the meantime, a new command called the Army of Virginia had been activated in the middle of July under the leadership of Major General John Pope. Ultimately, most of the Army of the Potomac would fall under Pope's command.

Pope had a difficult threefold task. He was to protect Washington, ensure Federal control of the Shenandoah Valley, and draw Confederate strength away from Richmond, thereby relieving pressure on McClellan. This latter task would be accomplished by operating against the Confederate rail center at Gordonsville, Virginia. It was all a tall order, and Pope was clearly not up to the challenge. The dispersed Federal command, Pope's unfamiliarity with the eastern theater, and his generally abrasive personality all conspired against him.

Even more threatening to Pope were the aggressive designs of Lee. As soon as Lee was certain that McClellan was abandoning the peninsula, Lee went after Pope. McClellan had carried out his Peninsula Campaign with great deliberation and caution, and his withdrawal from the region would be equally unenergetic. Operating within

the enemy's decision cycle, Lee ordered the Army of Northern Virginia to move on the day of the Federal withdrawal. Before the first divisions of the Army of the Potomac had landed at Aquia Creek, Confederate forces had raced north to meet Pope just south of Manassas, and had him surrounded.

TURNING THE ENEMY

In the upcoming battle, Lee applied the lessons he had learned during the Seven Days' Battles about turning the enemy, and he built upon the remarkable partnership he had developed with Major General Thomas "Stonewall" Jackson during the campaign. On August 24, Lee ordered Jackson to cut Pope's line

ANTIETAM

Date	September 17, 1862
Location	Near Sharpsburg, Maryland
Result	Tactically inconclusive; Union strategic victory

Strength

Union: Army of the Potomac (87,000)	Confederate: Army of Northern Virginia (40,000)

Casualties and losses

12,401	10,316
2,108 killed	1,546 killed
9,540 wounded	7,752 wounded
753 captured/missing	1,018 captured/missing

ROBERT E. LEE

RANK: GENERAL

BORN: 1807

EDUCATED: UNITED STATES MILITARY ACADEMY

MILITARY CAREER

VETERAN OF MEXICAN WAR

SUPERINTENDENT OF THE UNITED STATES MILITARY ACADEMY

MILITARY ADVISER TO JEFFERSON DAVIS

LED ARMY OF NORTHERN VIRGINIA FROM 1862 UNTIL THE
  CONCLUSION OF THE WAR

DIED: 1870

of communication along the Orange and Alexandria Railroad, threatening Washington in the process. Marching fifty-seven miles in two days, Jackson descended upon the railroad, destroyed the Federal supply depot at Manassas Junction, and occupied a strong defensive position a few miles west of Manassas.

Pope mistakenly thought Jackson was weakened and, on August 29 and 30, the Federals attacked. In reality, Pope had fallen into a cunningly laid trap. As Jackson absorbed Pope's assault, Major General James Longstreet arrived on the scene and crashed into the Federal left with five divisions. Pope was sandwiched

between Jackson's anvil and Longstreet's hammer, and the Federal forces fled in panic. Pope withdrew his demoralized force northeast toward Washington, having suffered 14,500 casualties compared to 9,500 for Lee. The Battle of Second Manassas cleared northern Virginia of any major Federal presence and shifted the momentum in the eastern theater to the Confederates. With Pope defeated and McClellan's army withdrawn behind the defenses of Washington, Lee saw an opportunity to carry the war into Northern territory.

THE IMPORTANCE OF MARYLAND

Maryland was a slaveholding state with strong Confederate sympathies. If Maryland had seceded, the Federal capital of Washington would have been surrounded by Confederate territory, with Maryland on one side and Virginia on the other. After Fort Sumter, it seemed as if this disaster for the Union might come true. A secessionist mob had jeered and thrown objects as a group of soldiers from Massachusetts marched through Baltimore headed to Washington, and there were rumors that the Maryland legislature would soon vote for secession. Realizing the gravity of the situation and its potential catastrophic consequences for the Federal cause, Lincoln intervened and, suspending the writ of habeas corpus, imprisoned suspected Confederate activists and imposed military law. These extraconstitutional measures succeeded in keeping Maryland in the Union, but did not remove the Confederate sympathies from many of the state's citizens.

Thus, if Lee launched an offensive into Maryland, he would anticipate finding a fairly friendly population. The advance might even be enough to persuade Maryland to secede. Additionally, many observers thought a victory on Northern soil would result in the much-prized recognition of the Confederacy in Europe. The recent Southern victories, as well as frustration over the Federal blockade and its effect on European access to Confederate cotton, made many Europeans—especially the British—favor the South. Most importantly, the offensive

Opposite, top: Major General Ambrose Burnside (1824–81), seated in the center with his legs crossed, commanded the Union army's Ninth Corps. He is shown here with his staff. Photographs of commanders and their staffs taken either before or after a battle were very popular.

Below: Colorful Zouave uniforms included baggy pants, a vest, a short jacket, and leggings. The Ninth New York, known as the "Hawkins Zouaves," fought at Antietam.

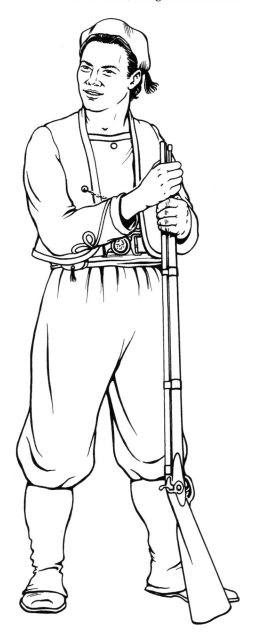

Left: The Confederate Fifth Texas Regiment charges the Federal Fifth New York Zouaves at the Battle of Second Manassas.

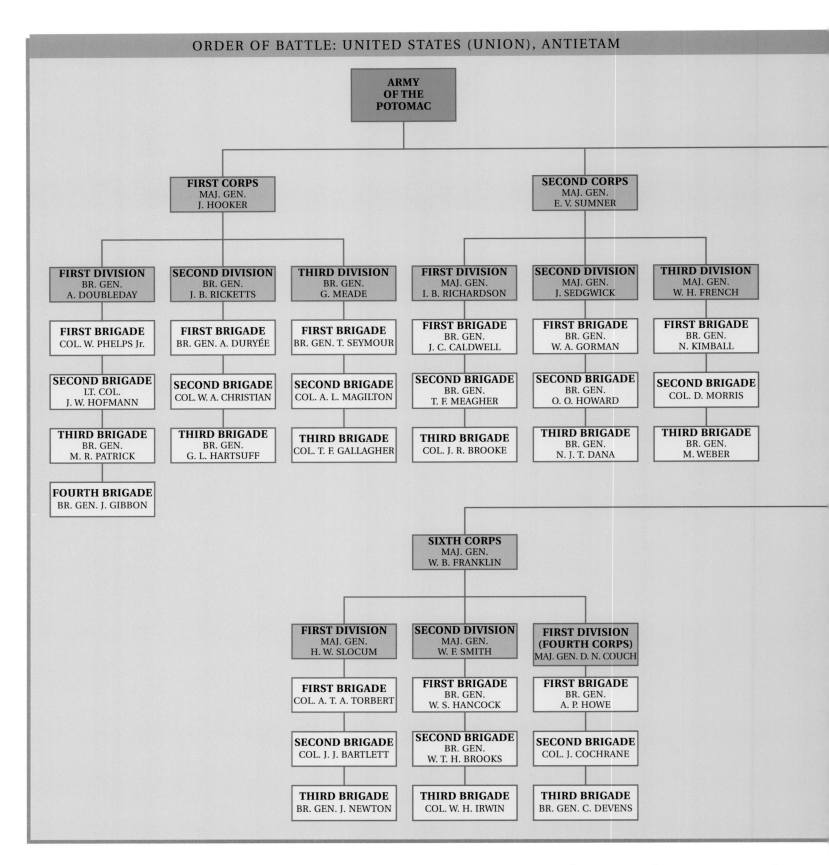

ORDER OF BATTLE: UNITED STATES (UNION), ANTIETAM

ARMY OF THE POTOMAC

FIRST CORPS
MAJ. GEN.
J. HOOKER

FIRST DIVISION
BR. GEN.
A. DOUBLEDAY

FIRST BRIGADE
COL. W. PHELPS Jr.

SECOND BRIGADE
LT. COL.
J. W. HOFMANN

THIRD BRIGADE
BR. GEN.
M. R. PATRICK

FOURTH BRIGADE
BR. GEN. J. GIBBON

SECOND DIVISION
BR. GEN.
J. B. RICKETTS

FIRST BRIGADE
BR. GEN. A. DURYÉE

SECOND BRIGADE
COL. W. A. CHRISTIAN

THIRD BRIGADE
BR. GEN.
G. L. HARTSUFF

THIRD DIVISION
BR. GEN.
G. MEADE

FIRST BRIGADE
BR. GEN. T. SEYMOUR

SECOND BRIGADE
COL. A. L. MAGILTON

THIRD BRIGADE
COL. T. F. GALLAGHER

SECOND CORPS
MAJ. GEN.
E. V. SUMNER

FIRST DIVISION
MAJ. GEN.
I. B. RICHARDSON

FIRST BRIGADE
BR. GEN.
J. C. CALDWELL

SECOND BRIGADE
BR. GEN.
T. F. MEAGHER

THIRD BRIGADE
COL. J. R. BROOKE

SECOND DIVISION
MAJ. GEN.
J. SEDGWICK

FIRST BRIGADE
BR. GEN.
W. A. GORMAN

SECOND BRIGADE
BR. GEN.
O. O. HOWARD

THIRD BRIGADE
BR. GEN.
N. J. T. DANA

THIRD DIVISION
MAJ. GEN.
W. H. FRENCH

FIRST BRIGADE
BR. GEN.
N. KIMBALL

SECOND BRIGADE
COL. D. MORRIS

THIRD BRIGADE
BR. GEN.
M. WEBER

SIXTH CORPS
MAJ. GEN.
W. B. FRANKLIN

FIRST DIVISION
MAJ. GEN.
H. W. SLOCUM

FIRST BRIGADE
COL. A. T. A. TORBERT

SECOND BRIGADE
COL. J. J. BARTLETT

THIRD BRIGADE
BR. GEN. J. NEWTON

SECOND DIVISION
MAJ. GEN.
W. F. SMITH

FIRST BRIGADE
BR. GEN.
W. S. HANCOCK

SECOND BRIGADE
BR. GEN.
W. T. H. BROOKS

THIRD BRIGADE
COL. W. H. IRWIN

**FIRST DIVISION
(FOURTH CORPS)**
MAJ. GEN. D. N. COUCH

FIRST BRIGADE
BR. GEN.
A. P. HOWE

SECOND BRIGADE
COL. J. COCHRANE

THIRD BRIGADE
BR. GEN. C. DEVENS

would remove the fighting from war-ravaged Virginia and give the state's farmers a chance to harvest their crops unmolested. In the meantime, Lee could feed his army from the abundant forage he would find in Maryland. There were many reasons to recommend an advance across the Potomac.

There were, however, an equal number of complications. Of greatest concern was the fact that offensive operations require a larger number of troops than defensive operations, and with just 45,000 soldiers in his command, Lee would be fighting the odds. Based on what he had seen on the peninsula

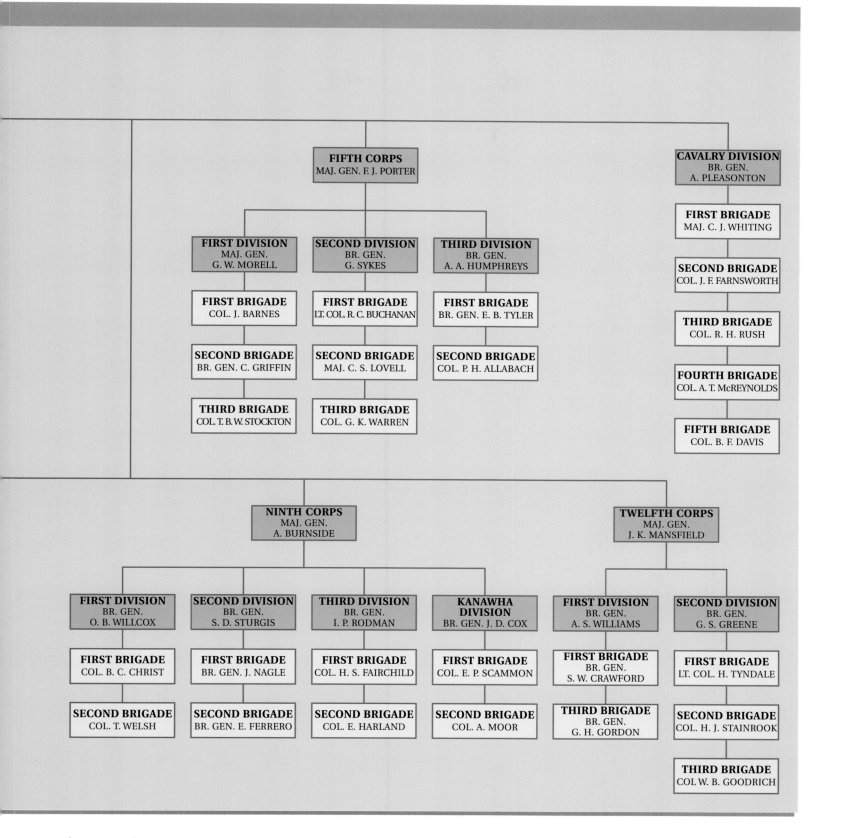

and at Second Manassas, however, Lee was confident in the superiority of the Confederate soldier. He had also had sufficient opportunity to size up McClellan, and Lee counted on his adversary's characteristic caution working in the Confederates' favor. Lee felt that the quality of his troops— and the corresponding deficiency he had seen thus far in the enemy—would offset his numerical disadvantage. On September 3, 1863, he wrote President Jefferson Davis, "The present seems to be the most propitious time since the commencement of the war for the Confederate Army to enter Maryland."

With this threat looming, President Lincoln was faced with a crisis. Pope's defeat at Second Manassas had clearly indicated that Pope was not the commander Lincoln needed, but the urgency of the current situation limited Lincoln's options for a replacement. Up to this point, Lincoln's experience with McClellan had been an exercise in frustration. It was only after great patience and prodding that McClellan had launched his highly anticipated Peninsula Campaign, only to have the offensive end in retreat. Rather than showing any humility in the wake of this failure, McClellan unashamedly wrote Lincoln the infamous "Harrison's Landing Letter," in which the defeated general offered his strategic advice for the larger war effort. Throughout the entire relationship, McClellan had shown nothing but disdain and contempt for Lincoln, but now Lincoln had little choice but to call on McClellan to see the army through the immediate crisis.

With this end in mind, Lincoln and Major General Henry Halleck went to McClellan's residence the morning of September 2 and found McClellan eating breakfast. Lincoln got right to the point, informing McClellan of the dire situation. Then, as McClellan reported it, Lincoln "asked me if I would, under the circumstances, as a favor to him, resume command and do the best that could be done." McClellan's inflated ego and pride in this time of crisis says as much about his character as Lincoln's humble submission for the good of the Union says about his.

THE CAMPAIGN BEGINS

Lee began crossing the Potomac River on September 4 and by September 7 had his army on the other side. The bands played "Maryland, My Maryland" as the weary Confederates marched through what must have appeared to be a cornucopia of agricultural bounty. Before long, however, unanticipated problems arose. As Lee marched into Maryland, he had expected the Federals to abandon their 13,000-man garrison at Harpers Ferry. This strategic location blocked the lower Shenandoah Valley, and with it Lee's communications to the South. Although the ground vastly favored the attackers—Jackson said he would rather "take the place forty times than undertake to defend it once"—the Federals stubbornly stayed in place. Colonel Dixon Miles was in command of the garrison. He was considered by most to be an alcoholic buffoon, but he had orders to defend Harpers Ferry to "the latest moment," and he took those orders literally. Lee was now compelled to deal with this threat to his rear.

Lee divided his army into four parts. Three of them under Jackson headed

Below: Harpers Ferry was strategically located on the railroad and at the northern end of the Shenandoah Valley. It also hosted a Federal arsenal.

toward Harpers Ferry to reduce the fort, and a fourth under Longstreet headed for Boonsboro to wait for Jackson to complete his mission. Lee divided his army still again in response to unfounded reports of Federal activity around Chambersburg, Pennsylvania. To meet this threat, Lee left a division commanded by Major General D. H. Hill in Boonsboro and shifted Longstreet northwest to Hagerstown, Maryland. To make matters worse for Lee, Jackson did not reach Harpers Ferry until September 13, a full day behind schedule. Upon arrival, Jackson encircled the Federal position, but Miles refused to surrender. "I am ordered to hold this place," he exclaimed, "and damn my soul to hell if I don't." Early on September 15, Jackson began shelling the Federal position, and Miles surrendered at 9:00 a.m. Miles's inept leadership compounded the natural disadvantages of the Federal position, but his stubbornness served to rob Lee of the quick operation he needed.

THE "LOST ORDER"

Lee had counted on the typically slow-moving McClellan to take three or four weeks to reorganize the Federal forces that had been defeated at Second Manassas. Instead, McClellan took fewer than seven days and headed after Lee. While Jackson was occupied at Harpers Ferry, McClellan advanced his army to Frederick, Maryland, within a day's striking distance of Lee's scattered command. In the process, McClellan fell upon an unbelievable piece of good fortune. On September 13, two Federal soldiers resting from the march at a farm just outside of Fredericksburg stumbled upon three cigars wrapped in a sheet of paper. Upon unwrapping the paper, the soldiers discovered it to be a copy of Special Orders 191, Lee's campaign plan. This priceless intelligence, famously known as the "Lost Order," was quickly forwarded to McClellan, who now had everything he needed to destroy Lee's dangerously scattered army.

But instead of acting decisively, McClellan, thinking that Lee's force was stronger that it was, moved slowly, taking six hours to issue orders. This meant it was not until the next day that Federal troops began marching to take advantage of the situation. In the meantime, intelligence had reached Lee that the Federals were strangely active. Fearing that McClellan would move to relieve Harpers Ferry, Lee ordered a full-scale defense of Turner's Gap, where the National Road from Frederick crossed South Mountain en route to Boonsboro. He told Major General Jeb Stuart, "The gap must be held at all hazards," and ordered Longstreet to march there from

> "A MAN LYING UPON THE GROUND ASKED FOR DRINK—I STOOPED TO GIVE IT, AND HAVING RAISED HIM WITH MY RIGHT HAND, WAS HOLDING THE CUP TO HIS LIPS . . . WHEN I FELT A SUDDEN TWITCH OF THE LOOSE SLEEVE OF MY DRESS—THE POOR FELLOW SPRANG FROM MY HANDS AND FELL BACK QUIVERING IN THE AGONIES OF DEATH—A BALL HAD PASSED BETWEEN MY BODY . . . CUTTING THROUGH THE SLEEVE, AND PASSING THROUGH HIS CHEST FROM SHOULDER TO SHOULDER."

CLARA BARTON, BATTLEFIELD NURSE AT ANTIETAM

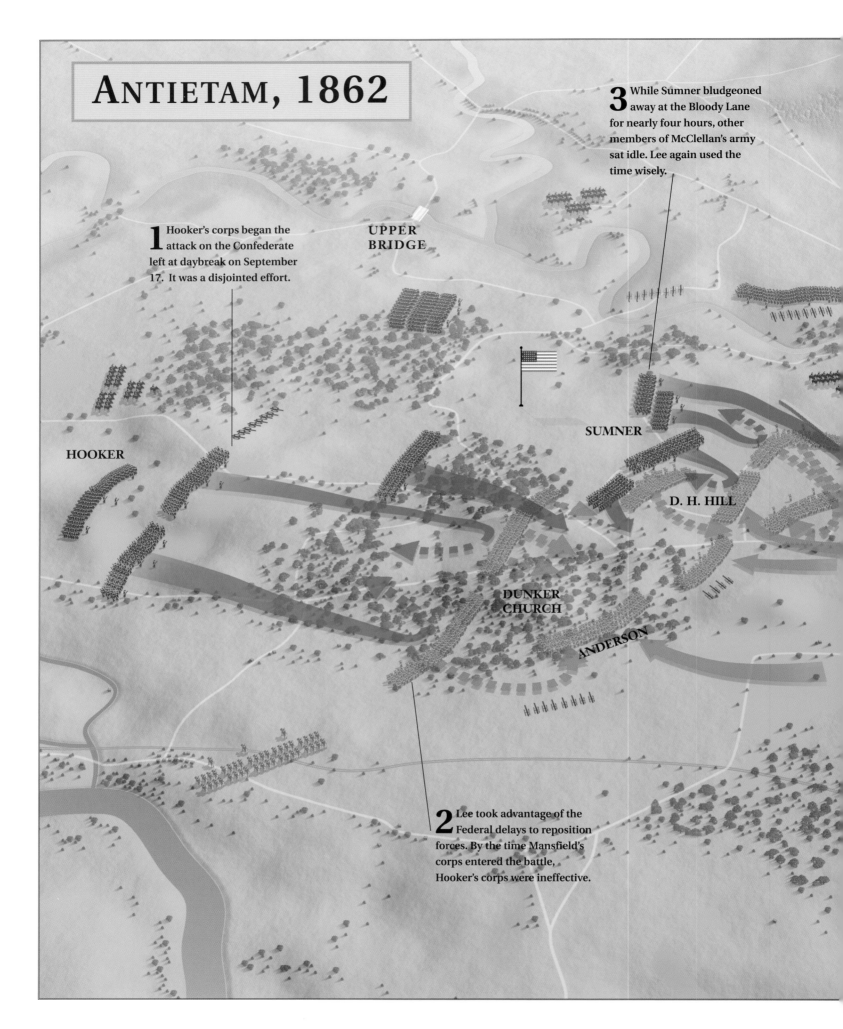

ANTIETAM, 1862

1 Hooker's corps began the attack on the Confederate left at daybreak on September 17. It was a disjointed effort.

UPPER BRIDGE

3 While Sumner bludgeoned away at the Bloody Lane for nearly four hours, other members of McClellan's army sat idle. Lee again used the time wisely.

SUMNER

HOOKER

D. H. HILL

DUNKER CHURCH

ANDERSON

2 Lee took advantage of the Federal delays to reposition forces. By the time Mansfield's corps entered the battle, Hooker's corps were ineffective.

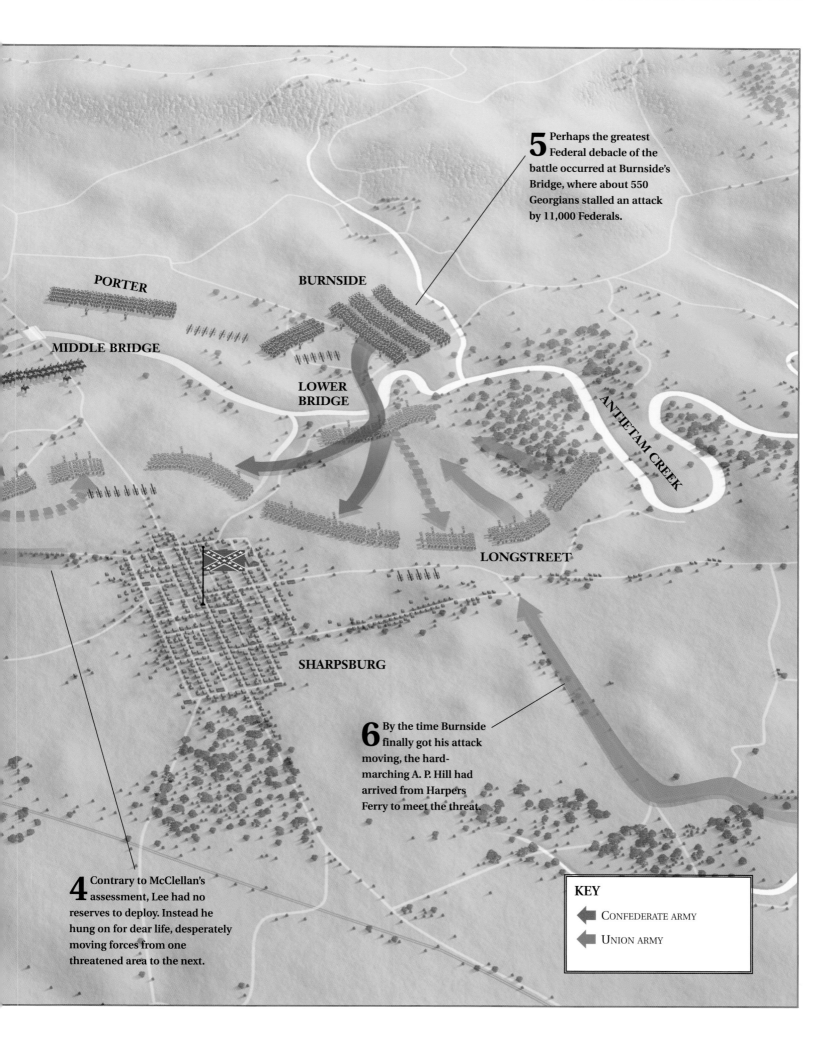

5 Perhaps the greatest Federal debacle of the battle occurred at Burnside's Bridge, where about 550 Georgians stalled an attack by 11,000 Federals.

PORTER

BURNSIDE

MIDDLE BRIDGE

LOWER BRIDGE

ANTIETAM CREEK

LONGSTREET

SHARPSBURG

6 By the time Burnside finally got his attack moving, the hard-marching A. P. Hill had arrived from Harpers Ferry to meet the threat.

4 Contrary to McClellan's assessment, Lee had no reserves to deploy. Instead he hung on for dear life, desperately moving forces from one threatened area to the next.

KEY

CONFEDERATE ARMY

UNION ARMY

Hagerstown with eight of his nine brigades to reinforce Hill's division. The Confederates also defended Crampton's Gap with three brigades belonging to Major General Lafayette McLaws and two regiments of dismounted cavalry.

McClellan's hesitancy had given Lee precious hours to react. As the Federals advanced on South Mountain early on September 14, they found strong Confederate positions waiting for them. Still, the Federals outnumbered the Confederates by more than two to one. In fierce fighting, the Federals worked their way through the gaps, but the delay was enough to allow Lee to concentrate at Sharpsburg and wait for Jackson to arrive at Harpers Ferry.

September 14 had been a close call for Lee, but things began looking up the next day when news arrived of the surrender of Harpers Ferry. Jackson had taken 11,000 prisoners and captured significant arms and equipment. More importantly, he would soon be able to reunite with Lee.

Until then, however, McClellan still had an opportunity to deal Lee a decisive blow. By the night of September 15, McClellan had four corps and part of a fifth within striking distance. Had he attacked early the next day, he would have outnumbered Lee by more than three to one. Instead, however, McClellan contented himself by exchanging

artillery fire with the Confederates throughout the day. After "a severe night's march," Jackson arrived at Sharpsburg with three divisions. Toward the evening, McClellan probed the Confederate left, a move that only served to telegraph his intentions for the next day. McClellan's hesitation had given Lee a chance to reassemble his dispersed forces, and now he had about 40,000 men available to oppose McClellan's 87,000.

THE BATTLE OF ANTIETAM

Although Lee had selected his position for an operational reason of concentrating his force rather than a tactical one, the ground still had several tactical advantages for the defender. Lee's line stretched across the angle formed by the junction of the Potomac River and Antietam Creek, the terrain feature that would give the battle its name. Limestone outcroppings and patches of woods gave Lee cover, while ravines and slight depressions gave him the opportunity to use interior lines to securely move reinforcements from one part of the battlefield to another. Interestingly, although Lee had two days to prepare his position, he did not build any breastworks. Later in the war, such improvements would have been undertaken as a matter of course.

McClellan's plan was to attack both Confederate flanks in a risky double

Below: The Rohrbach Bridge was the scene of some of the toughest fighting of the Battle of Antietam. Afterward, it became known as "Burnside's Bridge."

envelopment and then use his reserve to attack the center. Geography worked against such a scheme because the Antietam Creek would separate the wings of McClellan's attack, and the ground on the Confederate side aided the repositioning of reinforcements. McClellan envisioned the main attack occurring on the Confederate left, and Major General Joseph Hooker's First Corps began the battle there at daybreak on September 17. But instead of a Federal attack in force, the actual result was a piecemeal effort as individual divisions were thrown into the attack upon their arrival on the battlefield. Jackson thwarted each of Hooker's uncoordinated attacks, and Lee used the delays to send reinforcements to the threatened sector. By the time Major General Joseph Mansfield's Twelfth Corps entered the fighting, Hooker's command was ineffective for combat. McClellan had failed to mass his force in a way that would have allowed him to exploit his numerical advantage.

In the center of the Confederate line, Major General Edwin Sumner attacked with two divisions of his Second Corps. There the Confederates defended a 900-yard stretch of eroded road that formed a natural trench offering good protection. Rather than committing his reserves, McClellan held them back as a counter against any reserve force Lee might deploy. Such a precaution was entirely wasted because Lee had no reserves at all. Thus, while Major General William Franklin's Sixth Corps and Major General Fitz John Porter's Fifth Corps sat idle, Sumner bludgeoned away at the "Bloody Lane," finally gaining control of it after nearly four hours of fighting. It was another needless delay that gave Lee time to tend to urgent matters elsewhere.

While Hooker, Mansfield, and Sumner pounded away at the Confederate left and center, McClellan's plan called for Major General Ambrose Burnside's Ninth Corps to cross the Antietam using the Rohrbach Bridge and assault Lee's right. Instead, Burnside remained in position, allowing Lee additional freedom to reposition forces. By the time Burnside finally

attacked at 10:00 a.m., Lee had moved so many forces from in front of Burnside that Burnside now enjoyed an advantage of more than three to one. Still, Burnside's attack was so uninspired that the Confederates held on.

Brigadier General Robert Toombs commanded a brigade of 550 Georgians who opposed some 11,000 Federals. Taking advantage of the steep west bank of the Antietam and backed by artillery on the heights behind him, Toombs defended the bridge against one Federal attack after another. It was not until early afternoon that Burnside's men used a ford downstream to turn the Confederate position and force Toombs to relinquish his hold on the bridge. By then Burnside had suffered 500 casualties compared to just 160 for Toombs. More importantly, the already-delayed Federal attack on the Confederate right had been stalled for three full hours. The debacle resulted in the Rohrbach Bridge being rechristened "Burnside's Bridge."

It was now after 1:00 p.m., but in spite of the morning's fiascoes, the way finally seemed clear for McClellan to launch a full-scale assault. However, Burnside's men had exhausted both themselves and their ammunition in their fight to gain the bridge. Rather than continuing the Federal momentum, Burnside would have to call up Brigadier General

Above: During the Battle of Antietam, the Dunker Church was the focal point of a number of Federal attacks against the Confederate left flank. This painting shows Union troops advancing at the double. Although tactics of the time, such as Hardee's *Rifle and Light Infantry Tactics*, emphasized firepower, moving forward at the double in order to come to grips with cold steel was seen as a possible counter to the infantry firefight.

Orlando Willcox's reserve division, which was three-quarters of a mile behind Antietam Creek. It would take Willcox at least an hour to reach the bridge, and then his men would have to slowly funnel across. Apparently, no one thought of using the recently discovered ford as an additional means of crossing.

A HARD MARCH TO THE RESCUE

By the time Burnside got moving, help for the beleaguered Confederates was on the way. At 6:30 that morning, Lee had gotten a message through to Major General A. P. Hill at Harpers Ferry to rush his "Light Division" to Sharpsburg. One of Hill's men mused, "Why it was called the Light Division I did not learn; but I know that the name was applicable, for we often marched without coats, blankets, knapsacks, or any other burdens except our arms and haversacks, which were never heavy and sometimes empty." In this case, Hill's men lived up to their hard-marching reputation. Leaving one brigade behind to secure the captured supplies, Hill got the other five brigades on the road within an hour of receiving Lee's order. Marching along the same route Jackson had used a few days earlier, Hill drove his men nearly without a break. Having recently fortified themselves with the bounty captured at Harpers Ferry, the soldiers were up to the grueling task and covered fifteen miles in just six and a half hours.

It was now 2:00 p.m., and there were two miles left to march. Hill rode ahead to confer with Lee and reached him a half hour later. Lee, usually reserved by nature, was so relieved to see Hill that he hugged him. McClellan had been forced to threaten to relieve Burnside in order to get him moving, and it was not until 3:00 p.m., two hours after the capture of the Rohrbach Bridge, that Burnside finally got the entire Ninth Corps across to the west side of Antietam Creek. The inexcusably lethargic Federal attack had given Hill just enough time to come to the rescue of the handful of Confederates hanging on for dear life against the much larger enemy force. At 3:30 Lee could see Hill's 3,000 reinforcements arriving on the scene. They had marched seventeen miles in eight hours.

Hill divided his men, sending two brigades to guard his right flank and the other three to fill in on Toombs's right and prepare to attack. There Hill found a gap in the Federal line that left a perfect opening for the attack. At 3:40 he struck through a cornfield owned by John Otto. The attack broke the Federal far left and forced Burnside to retreat from the heights above the bridge. Outnumbered, Hill could not follow up on this advantage, but his timely arrival had saved the day for the Army of Northern Virginia.

Below: A part of the Roulettes' farm, at the Antietam battle site. Many farm families, including the Mummas and Roulettes, were caught in the middle of the Antietam battlefield.

By 5:30 the Battle of Antietam was all but over. After twelve hours of fighting, 12,400 Federals and 10,300 Confederates were casualties. It was the single bloodiest day in American military history. In spite of his losses, Lee did not immediately withdraw. It was not until around noon on September 18 that Jackson and Longstreet were able to convince the offensive-minded Lee that a counterattack was impossible. For his part, the ever-cautious McClellan felt that he had been too weakened to renew the fighting even though 24,000 of his troops had not been engaged in the first day's fighting and 12,000 fresh ones had arrived the morning of September 18. That night, Lee retired across the Potomac.

THE EMANCIPATION PROCLAMATION

While the Battle of Antietam itself was a tactical draw, the fact that Lee was forced to withdraw back to Virginia made it a strategic victory for the Union. This was enough to give President Lincoln the opportunity he had been waiting for to issue the Emancipation Proclamation. A few Federal generals, such as Ben Butler, John Frémont, and David Hunter, had already been pushing for such a move. Hunter, for example, had issued an order

after the capture of Fort Pulaski, Georgia, on April 11, 1862, that liberated all the slaves then in Federal hands. On May 9, Hunter issued another order freeing all the slaves in his Department of the South. Such a move was too much too fast for Lincoln, and he nullified the orders on May 19 on the grounds that Hunter had exceeded his authority.

While Hunter and others were pressing Lincoln to act more aggressively toward the Confederacy, there were also strong advocates of a more measured approach for conciliation. This policy assumed that it was only a minority of slaveholding aristocratic fire-eaters who had misguidedly led the South into secession and that popular support for the Confederacy was lukewarm at best. If the Federals treated the Southerners mildly, they would soon return to their senses and the Union would be restored. Adherents to the limited-war tradition modeled by Winfield Scott in the Mexican War, including McClellan, favored this approach.

At the outset of the war, Lincoln had been careful not to interfere with slavery, fearing it would alienate the border states, stoke Confederate resistance, and fracture support for the war in the North.

Above: This illustration shows the difficulty that faced the troops of Burnside's corps as they tried to push across the Rohrbach Bridge. Only one unit at a time could cross the bridge, so the Union troops were forced to launch piecemeal attacks rather than coordinated ones. Burnside seemed fixated on using the bridge as his crossing point, rather than a ford downstream.

Increasingly, however, Lincoln realized that the issue of slavery and the war were inseparable. Aside from any moral considerations, slave labor was sustaining the Confederate economy and was even being used to construct military fortifications. Gradually, Lincoln moved away from the policy of conciliation, and on July 22, 1862, he showed his cabinet a preliminary draft of the Emancipation Proclamation. Still, Lincoln needed a battlefield victory to give him an opportunity to make the proclamation public. Antietam provided that opportunity and on September 22, 1862, Lincoln announced, "That on the first day of January, in the year of our Lord one thousand eight hundred and sixty-three, all persons held as slaves within any State or designated part of a State, the people whereof shall then be in rebellion against the United States, shall be then, thenceforward, and forever free."

The Emancipation Proclamation changed the very nature of the war, giving it a completely new objective. Conciliation was no longer an option, and the war would take on an increasingly total nature. The move redefined and reinvigorated the Federal cause. The North was no longer merely fighting to restore a union it thought had never been legitimately separated. Now it was fighting for the freedom of a people. By the same token, the South was no longer fighting just for independence. It was fighting for the survival of its very way of life.

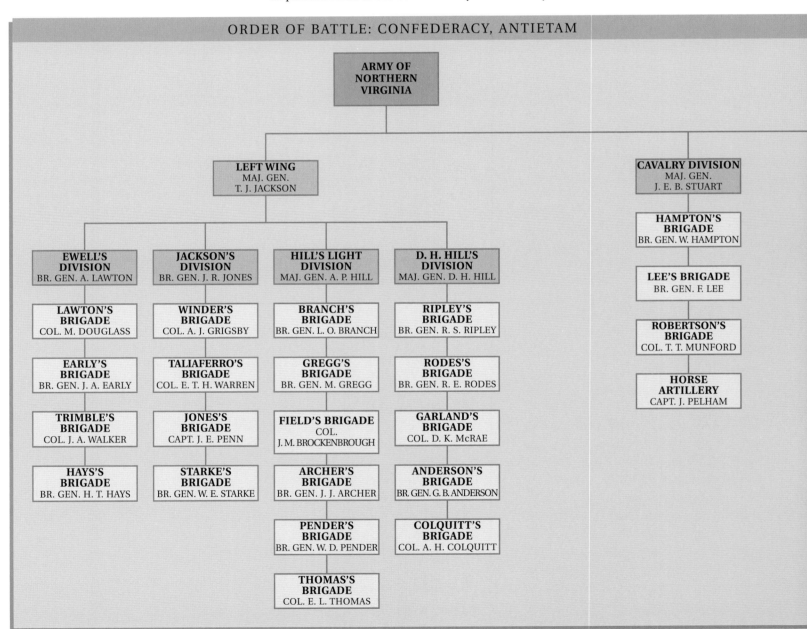

ORDER OF BATTLE: CONFEDERACY, ANTIETAM

ARMY OF NORTHERN VIRGINIA

LEFT WING
MAJ. GEN. T. J. JACKSON

CAVALRY DIVISION
MAJ. GEN. J. E. B. STUART

HAMPTON'S BRIGADE
BR. GEN. W. HAMPTON

LEE'S BRIGADE
BR. GEN. F. LEE

ROBERTSON'S BRIGADE
COL. T. T. MUNFORD

HORSE ARTILLERY
CAPT. J. PELHAM

EWELL'S DIVISION
BR. GEN. A. LAWTON

JACKSON'S DIVISION
BR. GEN. J. R. JONES

HILL'S LIGHT DIVISION
MAJ. GEN. A. P. HILL

D. H. HILL'S DIVISION
MAJ. GEN. D. H. HILL

LAWTON'S BRIGADE
COL. M. DOUGLASS

WINDER'S BRIGADE
COL. A. J. GRIGSBY

BRANCH'S BRIGADE
BR. GEN. L. O. BRANCH

RIPLEY'S BRIGADE
BR. GEN. R. S. RIPLEY

EARLY'S BRIGADE
BR. GEN. J. A. EARLY

TALIAFERRO'S BRIGADE
COL. E. T. H. WARREN

GREGG'S BRIGADE
BR. GEN. M. GREGG

RODES'S BRIGADE
BR. GEN. R. E. RODES

TRIMBLE'S BRIGADE
COL. J. A. WALKER

JONES'S BRIGADE
CAPT. J. E. PENN

FIELD'S BRIGADE
COL. J. M. BROCKENBROUGH

GARLAND'S BRIGADE
COL. D. K. McRAE

HAYS'S BRIGADE
BR. GEN. H. T. HAYS

STARKE'S BRIGADE
BR. GEN. W. E. STARKE

ARCHER'S BRIGADE
BR. GEN. J. J. ARCHER

ANDERSON'S BRIGADE
BR. GEN. G. B. ANDERSON

PENDER'S BRIGADE
BR. GEN. W. D. PENDER

COLQUITT'S BRIGADE
COL. A. H. COLQUITT

THOMAS'S BRIGADE
COL. E. L. THOMAS

Left: The major strategic outcome of the Battle of Antietam was that it provided President Lincoln an opportunity to issue the Emancipation Proclamation. Here, a contemporary magazine illustration shows the president writing the second proclamation on January 1, 1863. The first one, issued September 22, 1862, declared the freedom of all slaves in any of the Confederate states that did not return to Union control by January 1, 1863. The second order named the specific states where it applied.

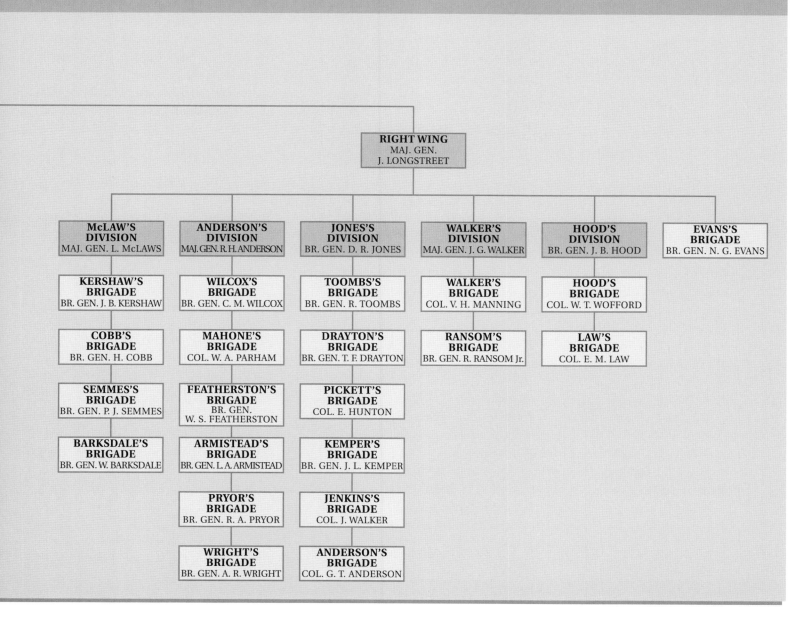

RIGHT WING
MAJ. GEN.
J. LONGSTREET

McLAW'S DIVISION MAJ. GEN. L. McLAWS	**ANDERSON'S DIVISION** MAJ. GEN. R. H. ANDERSON	**JONES'S DIVISION** BR. GEN. D. R. JONES	**WALKER'S DIVISION** MAJ. GEN. J. G. WALKER	**HOOD'S DIVISION** BR. GEN. J. B. HOOD	**EVANS'S BRIGADE** BR. GEN. N. G. EVANS
KERSHAW'S BRIGADE BR. GEN. J. B. KERSHAW	**WILCOX'S BRIGADE** BR. GEN. C. M. WILCOX	**TOOMBS'S BRIGADE** BR. GEN. R. TOOMBS	**WALKER'S BRIGADE** COL. V. H. MANNING	**HOOD'S BRIGADE** COL. W. T. WOFFORD	
COBB'S BRIGADE BR. GEN. H. COBB	**MAHONE'S BRIGADE** COL. W. A. PARHAM	**DRAYTON'S BRIGADE** BR. GEN. T. F. DRAYTON	**RANSOM'S BRIGADE** BR. GEN. R. RANSOM Jr.	**LAW'S BRIGADE** COL. E. M. LAW	
SEMMES'S BRIGADE BR. GEN. P. J. SEMMES	**FEATHERSTON'S BRIGADE** BR. GEN. W. S. FEATHERSTON	**PICKETT'S BRIGADE** COL. E. HUNTON			
BARKSDALE'S BRIGADE BR. GEN. W. BARKSDALE	**ARMISTEAD'S BRIGADE** BR. GEN. L. A. ARMISTEAD	**KEMPER'S BRIGADE** BR. GEN. J. L. KEMPER			
	PRYOR'S BRIGADE BR. GEN. R. A. PRYOR	**JENKINS'S BRIGADE** COL. J. WALKER			
	WRIGHT'S BRIGADE BR. GEN. A. R. WRIGHT	**ANDERSON'S BRIGADE** COL. G. T. ANDERSON			

MCCLELLAN'S LEADERSHIP

Military strategists characterize offensive operations as requiring surprise, tempo, concentration, and audacity. At Antietam, McClellan failed miserably in all four of these categories. Opportunities to destroy the enemy army were infrequent on the Civil War battlefield. At Antietam, McClellan's poor generalship cost the Federals one such opportunity.

Surprise is gained by attacking the enemy in a manner for which he is unprepared. The capture of the "Lost Order" gave McClellan one of military history's greatest opportunities to achieve surprise, but he failed to capitalize on it. Lee's army was dangerously scattered at the time McClellan received this intelligence boon, giving McClellan a remarkable opportunity to strike. Surprise, however, is a fleeting commodity. It must be exploited before the enemy realizes what is going on. McClellan failed to act before Lee could recover.

In addition, what frittered away his surprise was McClellan's failure to properly manage the tempo of the offense. As President Lincoln would later remark, everything McClellan did was plagued by "the slows." Rather than rapidly acting on the potential presented by the "Lost Order," McClellan took his time issuing his orders. In the process, he gave Lee a day to adjust to the situation. By then, the advantage McClellan had gained by knowing Lee's plan was greatly reduced.

Still, McClellan had an opportunity to use his vast numerical superiority to defeat Lee. However, mere total numbers often do not decide a battle. Those numbers must be employed at the decisive place and time to have the desired result. Concentration is the massing of overwhelming effects of combat power to achieve a single purpose. At Antietam, McClellan repeatedly failed to adhere to this characteristic of the offense. Instead, he broke up his attacks, allowing Lee to rush reinforcements from one spot to another to meet localized threats. Even then, the sheer weight of the Federal numbers had stretched the Confederates to the point of breaking. After the battle, Longstreet wrote, "We were so badly crushed that at the close of the day ten thousand fresh troops could have come in and taken Lee's army and everything in it." McClellan held the Fifth and Sixth corps in reserve—22,000 men remained largely idle and played no significant role in the battle.

But nearly all of McClellan's failures in the preceding three characteristics of the offense can be ascribed to his overall deficiency in the final characteristic of audacity. Offensive operations require boldness, violence of action, and willingness to take risks. These characteristics were simply not part of McClellan's personality. He was a brilliant administrator and builder of an army, but he lacked the killer instinct to use it. He was cautious to the point of paralysis, holding back his reserve for fear Lee would counterattack when in actuality Lee was doing all he could just to hold on. Even on September 18, McClellan still had a chance to deal Lee a decisive blow, this time with fresh troops who had begun to arrive as early as 7:00 a.m. Instead, McClellan let Lee slip away.

In addition to these changes generated on the American continent, the Emancipation Proclamation had a profound effect in Europe. The Confederacy had long hoped for European recognition and intervention, and Confederate sympathies in Britain were especially strong. Indeed, the hopes that a significant victory would seal European support had been one of the rationales for the advance into Maryland. Now, however, the Emancipation Proclamation made it virtually impossible for Europe to recognize the Confederacy. Britain had abolished slavery in 1833 and France had done likewise in 1848. They could hardly now pledge their support for a cause devoted to defending slavery. After the Emancipation Proclamation was issued, Confederate politician William Yancey lamented, "The feeling against slavery in England is so strong that no public man there dares extend a hand to help us . . . There is no government in Europe that dares help us in a struggle which can be suspected of having for its result, directly or indirectly, the fortification or perpetuation of slavery. Of that I am certain." The real significance of Antietam occurred not on the battlefield but in the social, political, and diplomatic developments it made possible through the Emancipation Proclamation.

LINCOLN FRUSTRATED

Few were as frustrated by McClellan's lack of audacity as President Lincoln. He implored McClellan to pursue Lee, but instead McClellan rested his army. After the battle, he had jubilantly telegraphed his wife that he had won a complete victory. The idea that a complete victory meant destroying Lee, not merely turning him back, seems to have been entirely lost on McClellan.

Major General Henry Halleck complained that McClellan "has lain still for twenty days since the Battle of Antietam, and I cannot persuade him to advance an inch. It puts me all out of patience." More than three weeks later, Halleck was still venting, "There is an immobility here that exceeds all that any man can conceive of. It requires the lever of Archimedes to move this inert mass." Lincoln was equally frustrated. He visited the Army of the Potomac at Sharpsburg and labeled it "McClellan's bodyguard." Finally, Lincoln could stand no more. On November 7, he replaced McClellan as commander of the Army of the Potomac with Ambrose Burnside, a man who had shown no great sense of audacity himself at Antietam.

LEE'S VICTORY

But these strategic and operational errors do not diminish the fact that Antietam was a tactical showcase for Lee and his lieutenants. In large part, this opportunity was made possible by a reorganization Lee had put into place after the Peninsula Campaign. Lee had experienced great difficulty in getting unity of effort among his nine divisions there, so he reorganized them into two "wings." At the time, Confederate law allowed no larger formation than a division, but these wings would serve as unofficial corps until the appropriate legislation was passed in November. Capably led by Longstreet and Jackson, and fresh from victory at Second Manassas, these new wings gave Lee the ability to operate effectively at a high level of command at Antietam. The result was a degree of cooperation and coordination that allowed Lee the tactical flexibility he needed to parry McClellan's disjointed attacks. In the final analysis, however, Lee's superior tactical generalship could only result in a stalemate at Antietam against the much larger Federal force. Thus, the victory on the diplomatic front that the Confederates had hoped for turned into a strategic defeat with the European reaction to the Emancipation Proclamation. In that sense, Antietam was an important turning point in the war. With European intervention no longer a real possibility and with the Federal abandonment of the policy of conciliation, after Antietam, Confederate war aims could be achieved only with a decisive victory on the battlefield.

LEE'S LEADERSHIP

Antietam was a battle that McClellan fought poorly, but it was also a battle that Lee probably should not have fought at all. Lee's army was in no condition to launch an invasion of Maryland. The men were exhausted after the fighting on the peninsula and at Second Manassas, and Lee lacked the numbers needed to wage an offensive. Lee simply expected too much from his soldiers, and his overconfidence nearly cost him his army. The decision to launch the campaign was a strategic error on Lee's part.

Operationally, Lee also made mistakes. Dividing his army in enemy territory was extremely risky and Lee's timetable for reducing Harpers Ferry proved to be overly ambitious. These operational realities then forced Lee into the tactical situation at Antietam. His taking a defensive position there was based solely on the need to wait for Jackson to join him. In fact, after the fighting on South Mountain, Lee had no viable offensive options. He had lost the element of surprise and stood in the face of a much larger enemy. Giving battle at Antietam offered Lee no military advantage.

An alternative would have been to cut his losses and retire across the Potomac. Lee's chief artilleryman, Brigadier General Edward Porter Alexander, pointed out that, with the capture of Harpers Ferry, the Confederates could have withdrawn and "left Maryland without a great battle, but we would nonetheless have come off with good prestige and a very fair lot of prisoners and guns, and lucky on the whole to do this, considering the accident of the 'lost order.' "

BUELL VS. BRAGG

PERRYVILLE, 1862

At about the same time General Robert E. Lee was conducting his Antietam Campaign, General Braxton Bragg and the Army of Mississippi were attempting another invasion of Northern territory. Bragg's plan was to join forces with units in eastern Tennessee commanded by Major General Edmund Kirby Smith and invade Kentucky.

At Perryville, Bragg fought a meeting engagement with Major General Don Carlos Buell and the Army of the Ohio.

Although Bragg bested Buell on the battlefield, the Confederates could not capitalize on the victory and Bragg was forced to withdraw from Kentucky.

PRELIMINARIES

On May 30, 1862, after a painfully slow march from Shiloh, Tennessee, Major General Henry Halleck took possession of the important railroad junction at Corinth, Mississippi. In the wake of Halleck's advance, General Pierre Gustave Toutant Beauregard had withdrawn to Tupelo and abandoned Corinth without a fight. Rather than pressing his advantage, Halleck, who always considered Corinth rather than Beauregard's army to be the true Federal objective, proceeded to scatter his force and dissipate its offensive power.

BRAXTON BRAGG

RANK: GENERAL

BORN: 1817

EDUCATED: UNITED STATES MILITARY ACADEMY

MILITARY CAREER

VETERAN OF MEXICAN WAR

RESIGNED FROM THE ARMY IN 1856

COMMANDED COAST BETWEEN PENSACOLA AND MOBILE

FINISHED WAR AS MILITARY ADVISER TO PRESIDENT DAVIS

DIED: 1876

Major General Don Carlos Buell commanded one part of Halleck's army. Buell had about 31,000 troops in this Army of the Ohio and was assigned the mission of moving east to Chattanooga, Tennessee, another important railroad center and the gateway to eastern Tennessee. Major General Ulysses S. Grant commanded the other part of the army, some 67,000 troops inefficiently spread throughout western Tennessee.

On July 11, 1862, President Lincoln ordered Halleck to Washington to serve as general-in-chief. Grant assumed Halleck's command more or less by default and chafed to go on the offensive, but he would need months to reconcentrate the forces Halleck had dispersed. Grant's immobility and the slow pace of Buell's advance gave General Braxton Bragg an opportunity to take the initiative. Rejecting the option of going after Grant, Bragg elected to move eastward toward Chattanooga, unite with Confederate forces in eastern Tennessee commanded by Major General Edmund Kirby Smith, and invade Kentucky. Bragg's aim was to turn Buell's flank and force him to retreat.

Such a move might even force Buell to abandon middle Tennessee. Moreover, like Lee in Maryland, Bragg anticipated finding a warm reception in Kentucky, a slaveholding state with strong Confederate sympathies. Success in Kentucky could possibly encourage the state to leave the Union. At a minimum, Bragg expected to draw thousands of Kentucky volunteers to his army. Leaving

a 16,000-man covering force under Major General Earl Van Dorn at Tupelo, Bragg set out on his operation in the middle of July.

The movement was a difficult one and required a circuitous route to avoid Buell's army. Beginning on July 23, Bragg moved the bulk of his 35,000-man force about 800 miles by rail from Tupelo to Montgomery, Alabama, south all the way to Mobile, then east to Atlanta, Georgia, and finally northwest to Chattanooga. Along the way, Bragg had to negotiate six different railroad gauges, a ferry across Mobile Bay, and a steamboat trip on the Alabama River. Commissary agents met the trains at various stations to conduct resupply operations. Transfer points were closely guarded to prevent desertions. In addition to this rail move, Bragg sent his cavalry, artillery, and wagon trains overland along a 430-mile

PERRYVILLE

Date	October 8, 1862
Location	Boyle County, Kentucky
Result	Confederate tactical victory; Union strategic victory

Strength	
Union: 16,000	Confederate: 22,000

Casualties and losses	
4,211	3,396
894 killed	532 killed
2,911 wounded	2,641 wounded
471 captured/missing	228 captured/missing

DON CARLOS BUELL

RANK: MAJOR GENERAL

BORN: 1818

EDUCATED: UNITED STATES MILITARY ACADEMY

MILITARY CAREER

VETERAN OF MEXICAN WAR

REINFORCED GRANT AT SHILOH

RESIGNED FROM THE ARMY ON JUNE 1, 1864

DIED: 1898

Above: This contemporary illustration shows the evacuation of Corinth by Beauregard's Confederate forces, May 30, 1862. Railroads were of critical importance to Civil War strategy because of their ability to provide interior lines.

route south to Tuscaloosa, Alabama, east to Rome, Georgia, and then north to Chattanooga. A meticulous stickler for detail, Bragg handled the complicated logistics of the operation very well.

In addition to Van Dorn, Major General Sterling Price commanded another Confederate force in Mississippi. Their armies threatened Grant's communications with Buell in Tennessee and represented possible reinforcements to Bragg. While Grant ultimately was able to hold these forces at bay during the Battle of Iuka on September 19 and the Second Battle of Corinth on October 3–4, at the time Bragg launched his campaign the Confederate armies in Mississippi were worrisome threats to the Federals.

On July 23, Grant telegraphed Halleck, "Since you have left here, the greatest vigilance has been kept up with cavalry to the front, but nothing absolutely certain of the movements of the enemy has been learned. It is certain, however, that a movement has taken place from Tupelo, in what direction or for what purpose is not so certain." It was an unsettling situation for the Federals.

By the end of July, Grant had determined that Bragg had shifted his headquarters to northern Georgia. The Federal War Department urged Buell to hurry his glacial movement to Chattanooga and get there before Bragg, but Buell continued to move agonizingly slowly. Bragg won the race, with the

Below: These guns are rifled Parrott thirty-pounders, capable of firing solid shot to destroy other guns or fortifications, or explosive fragmentation rounds for antipersonnel actions. They were extremely accurate to about one and a quarter miles, and capable of hitting a target about three times as far away, with some luck. Much of Braxton Bragg's Mexican War reputation stemmed from his employment of artillery at Buena Vista.

advance elements of his force reaching Chattanooga on July 27, and on July 31 Bragg met there with Major General Edmund Kirby Smith to develop a strategy.

CONFEDERATE DISUNITY

Smith had commanded the 18,000-man Department of East Tennessee since March and had set up his headquarters in Knoxville, a hundred miles northeast of Chattanooga. Beginning in the last week of June, Smith had sent out a series of alarming messages that outlined the

Below: Edmund Kirby Smith (1824–93) ended the war in the Trans-Mississippi Department, leading what for all practical purposes was a separate command.

danger to Chattanooga posed by Buell. Smith asked for reinforcements from various quarters, including Bragg, General Robert E. Lee, and the Confederate War Department.

Still, Smith's repeated concerns never seemed to match his own actions. He kept 9,000 men under his best commander, Brigadier General Carter Stevenson, north of Knoxville, where they faced Brigadier General George Morgan's 10,000 Federals in the Cumberland Gap. At Chattanooga, Smith posted just 9,000 men, mostly raw recruits commanded by the lackluster Major General John McCown, to oppose Buell's formidable 31,000 men. Bragg urged Smith to take personal command at Chattanooga, but Smith would not hear of it.

AMBITIONS IN KENTUCKY

Eventually, the reasons for Smith's reluctance to tie himself to Chattanooga became clear. He was secretly developing a plan to outflank Morgan and drive into Kentucky. Outwardly mild-mannered, Smith also had a deeply ambitious side. In letters to his wife, he compared himself to the conquistador Hernán Cortés and even Moses, and he predicted that his Kentucky Campaign would be hailed in the Confederate newspapers as "a stroke of inspiration and genius." Smith had no intention of conforming his grand plans to the designs of Bragg, and would prove very adept at manipulating both Bragg and the situation to his own advantage.

Bragg had a reputation as a severe disciplinarian and a martinet. One private wrote, "Breathe softly the name . . . Bragg, it has more terror than the [enemy] army" and "We . . . did not . . . so much love our country, as we feared Bragg." Still, for whatever reason, Bragg failed to exert his authority over Smith. Bragg was the senior of the two, but instead of taking command of their combined operations, Bragg treated Smith as an equal and independent commander. Perhaps Bragg considered himself a mere visitor in Smith's Department of East Tennessee and therefore felt the need to accord deference to his host. More likely, Smith's ambition and determination mastered the traditionally bureaucratic and indecisive Bragg. Regardless of the cause, the outcome was that instead of taking command, Bragg merely "arranged measures for mutual support and effective cooperation." In reality, Smith would never waver in his original plan to invade Kentucky, whether that supported and cooperated with Bragg's movements or not.

THE CAMPAIGN BEGINS

At the time of his July 31 meeting with Smith, Bragg's mounted units had not yet arrived, so it was decided that Bragg would wait for his entire force to close on Chattanooga while Smith would move immediately against Morgan in the Cumberland Gap. If, by the time Smith had driven off Morgan, Bragg's wagon trains had arrived, the two would then combine their forces and move into central Tennessee to cut off Buell.

A few days later, Smith was pleading with Bragg for reinforcements. Bragg obliged by sending his two best brigades, those of Brigadier General Patrick Cleburne and Colonel Preston Smith, to Major General Smith. Bragg now had just 27,000 men to oppose Buell's 31,000, while Major General Smith had more than 20,000 against Morgan's 10,000. Even that arrangement was not enough for the artful Smith. On August 9, he wrote Bragg a letter ostensibly outlining the plans reached in previous discussions, but in the midst of this seemingly routine communication, Smith proposed, "I understand General Morgan has at Cumberland Gap nearly a month's supply of provisions. If this be true then the reduction of the place would be a matter of more time than I presume you are willing I should take. As my move direct to Lexington, Kentucky, would effectually invest Morgan and would be attended with other most brilliant results in my judgment, I suggest I be allowed to take that course."

Rather than countermanding Smith, Bragg acquiesced, adding only the minor reservation that "it would be unadvisable, I think, for you to move far into Kentucky, leaving Morgan in your rear, until I am able to fully engage Buell and his forces on your left." That was all the encouragement Smith needed to launch his grand expedition. On August 13, he sent Colonel John Scott and his cavalry out as a screening force, and the next day Smith marched out of Knoxville with 6,000 men. Stevenson's division remained behind to check Morgan in the Cumberland Gap.

Smith's men had a difficult march as they bypassed Morgan. The region had recently experienced a drought, and forage was slim. The wagon trains lagged behind the infantry, making resupply inconsistent. Still Smith was proud, writing his wife, "Our men have marched night and day, and have carried their own subsistence in their haversacks for five days. Ragged, barefoot, they have climbed mountains, suffered starvation and thirst without a murmur."

MISPLACED CONFIDENCE

On August 18, Smith's exertions began to bear fruit. Arriving in Barboursville, Kentucky, Smith was well into Morgan's rear and astride his supply line to Lexington. Morgan soon realized he had

Above: Union troops in marching order. Civil War soldiers were forced to travel light, carrying their few possessions in a knapsack. Loops on top of the knapsack allowed the soldier to secure a blanket or greatcoat.

been flanked and withdrew his force out of the Cumberland Gap and into eastern Kentucky. Buoyed by these developments, Smith decided to press on to Lexington, where he would find supplies. He told Bragg such an operation would act as a diversion against Buell, and again Bragg passively accepted his junior's lead.

In reality, Smith's confidence was misplaced, and he was rapidly overextending himself. His men were short on rations, and Morgan still posed a threat to his rear. Ahead of him was more bad news. While advancing on Lexington, Scott's cavalry reported

clashing with Federal troops under the command of Colonel Leonidas Metcalfe. Scott chased the Federals toward Richmond, Kentucky, twenty miles southeast of Lexington, but along the way Scott learned heavy Federal reinforcements were due to arrive in Richmond on August 23.

Smith knew he was in trouble. He had not expected to meet enemy resistance so soon, but his supply situation compelled him to press on to Lexington. To remedy the problem, he again turned to Bragg, who Smith suggested should start moving across the Cumberland Mountains to draw the Federals away from Smith.

Smith also requested an additional 3,000 reinforcements from Brigadier General Humphrey Marshall's Department of Western Virginia. Remarkably, Bragg concurred with Smith's grandiose plan. On August 28, Bragg began moving his army north from Chattanooga toward Kentucky.

The next day, Smith set out for Lexington. Late in the afternoon, Scott's advance guard again ran into Metcalfe. In the first encounter, many of Metcalfe's men had turned and run away. This time the Federals fought better, holding the Confederates off until dark. Then Metcalfe broke off the engagement and withdrew toward Richmond. Smith made plans to launch an attack on the town early the next morning.

ON THE FEDERAL FRONT

The Federal commander at Richmond was Brigadier General Mahlon Manson. He had with him eight regiments of mainly raw recruits, and he was not certain of his chances against the advancing Confederates. During the night, Manson wrote his superior, Major General William "Bull" Nelson, to ask for advice. Nelson received Manson's message at 2:30 a.m. on August 29 and recommended retreat. In the meantime, he personally headed for Richmond to take charge of the situation.

Nelson's suggestion to retreat reached Manson too late to be of any value. As dawn broke on August 29, Cleburne had

Below: The wartime wedding of the dashing Confederate raider John Hunt Morgan (1825–64) and socialite Martha "Mattie" Ready was a great sensation.

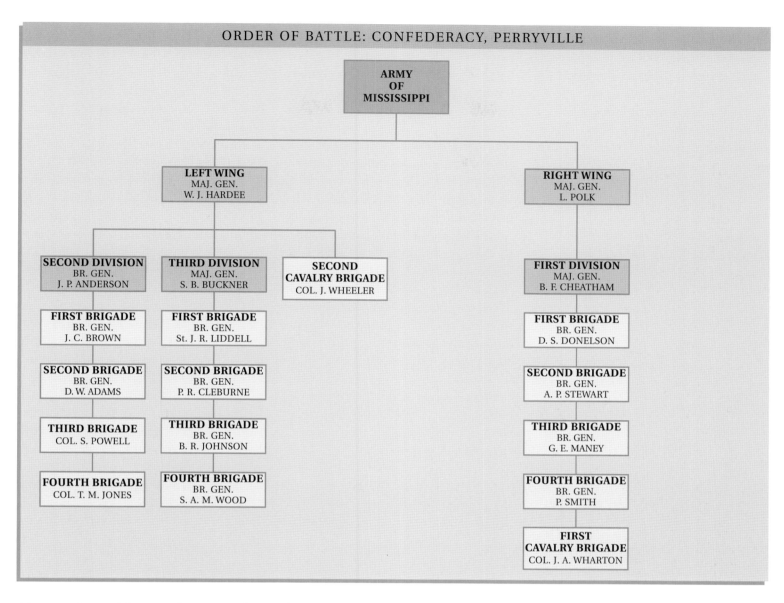

ORDER OF BATTLE: CONFEDERACY, PERRYVILLE

ARMY OF MISSISSIPPI

LEFT WING
MAJ. GEN.
W. J. HARDEE

SECOND DIVISION
BR. GEN.
J. P. ANDERSON

FIRST BRIGADE
BR. GEN.
J. C. BROWN

SECOND BRIGADE
BR. GEN.
D. W. ADAMS

THIRD BRIGADE
COL. S. POWELL

FOURTH BRIGADE
COL. T. M. JONES

THIRD DIVISION
MAJ. GEN.
S. B. BUCKNER

FIRST BRIGADE
BR. GEN.
St. J. R. LIDDELL

SECOND BRIGADE
BR. GEN.
P. R. CLEBURNE

THIRD BRIGADE
BR. GEN.
B. R. JOHNSON

FOURTH BRIGADE
BR. GEN.
S. A. M. WOOD

SECOND CAVALRY BRIGADE
COL. J. WHEELER

RIGHT WING
MAJ. GEN.
L. POLK

FIRST DIVISION
MAJ. GEN.
B. F. CHEATHAM

FIRST BRIGADE
BR. GEN.
D. S. DONELSON

SECOND BRIGADE
BR. GEN.
A. P. STEWART

THIRD BRIGADE
BR. GEN.
G. E. MANEY

FOURTH BRIGADE
BR. GEN.
P. SMITH

FIRST CAVALRY BRIGADE
COL. J. A. WHARTON

his men in position, ready to attack. Brigadier General Thomas Churchill's division was still on the move, so Cleburne harassed the Federals with artillery fire until the entire Confederate force was in position. The Federals were beginning to respond when Smith and Churchill arrived at about 7:30 a.m., and Smith ordered the attack to begin. The Federals were forced to fall back and re-form their lines. Then Colonel T. H. McCray's brigade crashed into the right flank and sent the Federals fleeing back to Richmond.

Right: This illustration shows Confederate infantry firing volleys into advancing Federal troops. Well-trained troops could fire, on average, three to four rounds per minute, causing devastation at ranges of up to 560 yards. Most engagements between infantry took place at less than 220 yards. Charging infantry were expected to cover 160 yards per minute, allowing the enemy to fire at least five rounds before engaging in hand-to-hand combat. Consequently, losses among charging troops could be staggering.

Opposite: This photograph taken after the battle shows a lane near Perryville flanked by lines of chevaux-de-frise and wooden palisades. These obstacles severely restricted the movement of enemy infantry—breaking up any charges—as well as ensuring that enemy cavalry did not carry out flanking maneuvers.

Nelson arrived on the scene at about 2:00 p.m. and managed to re-form a line on a ridge just south of the town. It was a formidable position anchored on a wall of stone in the Richmond cemetery, but when the Confederates renewed the attack at 5:00 p.m., the Federals were soon in full retreat. Nelson complained, "Our troops stood about three rounds, then struck by a panic, they fled in utter disorder."

The Federals withdrew along the road to Lexington, but Smith had earlier positioned a force to cut off such a move. He had sent Scott's cavalry on a wide sweep behind Richmond, and now Scott caught the fleeing Federals in a withering artillery fire. By the end of the day, Smith had captured 4,000 Federals, 10,000 stands of arms, nine guns, and a complete wagon train full of supplies. Additionally, the Federals suffered 206 killed and 844 wounded. Smith lost only 78 killed and 372 wounded.

SMITH HOLDS THE ADVANTAGE

It was an impressive Confederate victory that left Smith virtually unopposed in eastern Kentucky. He moved his headquarters to Lexington and sent a cavalry force to the state capital at Frankfort. Panic reached as far north as Cincinnati, Ohio, where Major General Lew Wallace drafted civilians into military service and threw together an emergency defense.

So far, Smith had been brash and aggressive, but now, when he seemingly held all the advantages, he turned passive. He went on the defense and waited to see what developed as a result of the move north that Bragg had initiated on August 28.

Up to that point, Buell had been indecisive and largely lethargic. In addition to the threats posed by Smith and Bragg, Brigadier General John Hunt Morgan, who spent July raiding into Kentucky from his base in Knoxville, also distracted Buell. In twenty-four days, Morgan, with fewer than 900 men, covered 1,000 miles, capturing and paroling 1,200 prisoners and picking up 300 new volunteers along the way before returning to Tennessee. On August 12, Morgan struck again, raiding the town of

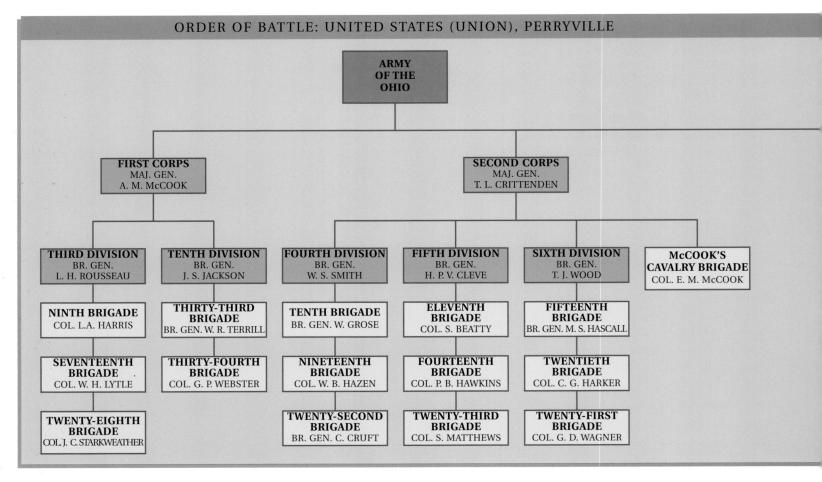

ORDER OF BATTLE: UNITED STATES (UNION), PERRYVILLE

ARMY OF THE OHIO

FIRST CORPS — MAJ. GEN. A. M. McCOOK

SECOND CORPS — MAJ. GEN. T. L. CRITTENDEN

THIRD DIVISION — BR. GEN. L. H. ROUSSEAU
TENTH DIVISION — BR. GEN. J. S. JACKSON
FOURTH DIVISION — BR. GEN. W. S. SMITH
FIFTH DIVISION — BR. GEN. H. P. V. CLEVE
SIXTH DIVISION — BR. GEN. T. J. WOOD
McCOOK'S CAVALRY BRIGADE — COL. E. M. McCOOK

NINTH BRIGADE — COL. L. A. HARRIS
THIRTY-THIRD BRIGADE — BR. GEN. W. R. TERRILL
TENTH BRIGADE — BR. GEN. W. GROSE
ELEVENTH BRIGADE — COL. S. BEATTY
FIFTEENTH BRIGADE — BR. GEN. M. S. HASCALL

SEVENTEENTH BRIGADE — COL. W. H. LYTLE
THIRTY-FOURTH BRIGADE — COL. G. P. WEBSTER
NINETEENTH BRIGADE — COL. W. B. HAZEN
FOURTEENTH BRIGADE — COL. P. B. HAWKINS
TWENTIETH BRIGADE — COL. C. G. HARKER

TWENTY-EIGHTH BRIGADE — COL. J. C. STARKWEATHER
TWENTY-SECOND BRIGADE — BR. GEN. C. CRUFT
TWENTY-THIRD BRIGADE — COL. S. MATTHEWS
TWENTY-FIRST BRIGADE — COL. G. D. WAGNER

Gallatin, Tennessee, and destroying the 800-foot railroad tunnel that had been cut through a mountain north of the town. Buell sent Brigadier General R. W. Johnson in pursuit of Morgan, but Morgan routed his would-be nemesis and captured Johnson and his staff. The raids did much to weaken Federal morale and discredit Buell.

In light of these developments, a frustrated Buell debated how to respond. He decided to concentrate his Army of the Ohio at McMinnville, Tennessee, a town on the Cumberland Plateau

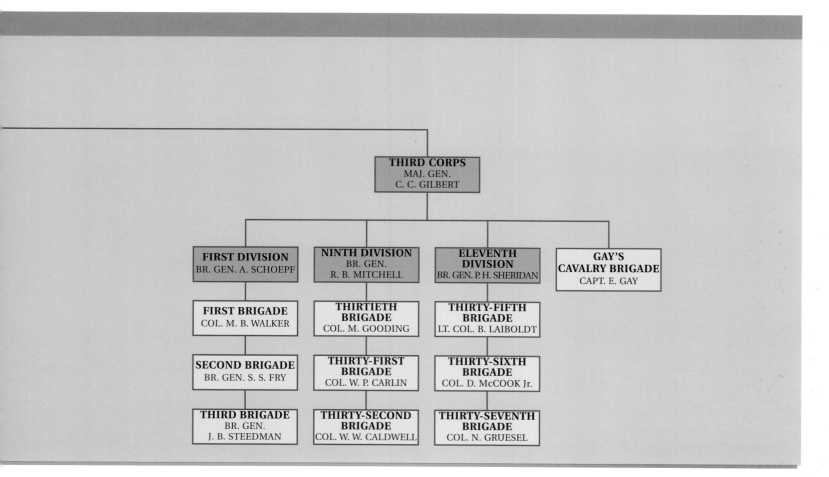

THIRD CORPS
MAJ. GEN.
C. C. GILBERT

FIRST DIVISION
BR. GEN. A. SCHOEPF

NINTH DIVISION
BR. GEN.
R. B. MITCHELL

ELEVENTH DIVISION
BR. GEN. P. H. SHERIDAN

GAY'S CAVALRY BRIGADE
CAPT. E. GAY

FIRST BRIGADE
COL. M. B. WALKER

THIRTIETH BRIGADE
COL. M. GOODING

THIRTY-FIFTH BRIGADE
LT. COL. B. LAIBOLDT

SECOND BRIGADE
BR. GEN. S. S. FRY

THIRTY-FIRST BRIGADE
COL. W. P. CARLIN

THIRTY-SIXTH BRIGADE
COL. D. McCOOK Jr.

THIRD BRIGADE
BR. GEN.
J. B. STEEDMAN

THIRTY-SECOND BRIGADE
COL. W. W. CALDWELL

THIRTY-SEVENTH BRIGADE
COL. N. GRUESEL

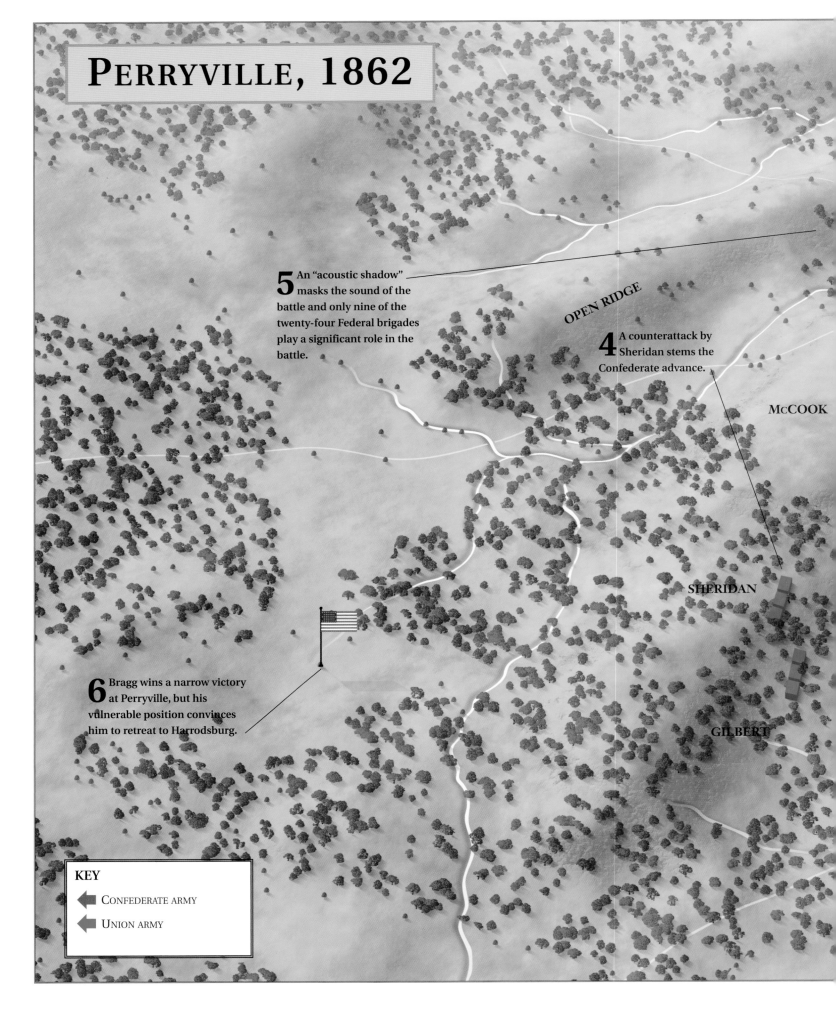

PERRYVILLE, 1862

5 An "acoustic shadow" masks the sound of the battle and only nine of the twenty-four Federal brigades play a significant role in the battle.

4 A counterattack by Sheridan stems the Confederate advance.

OPEN RIDGE

McCOOK

SHERIDAN

6 Bragg wins a narrow victory at Perryville, but his vulnerable position convinces him to retreat to Harrodsburg.

GILBERT

KEY

◄ CONFEDERATE ARMY

◄ UNION ARMY

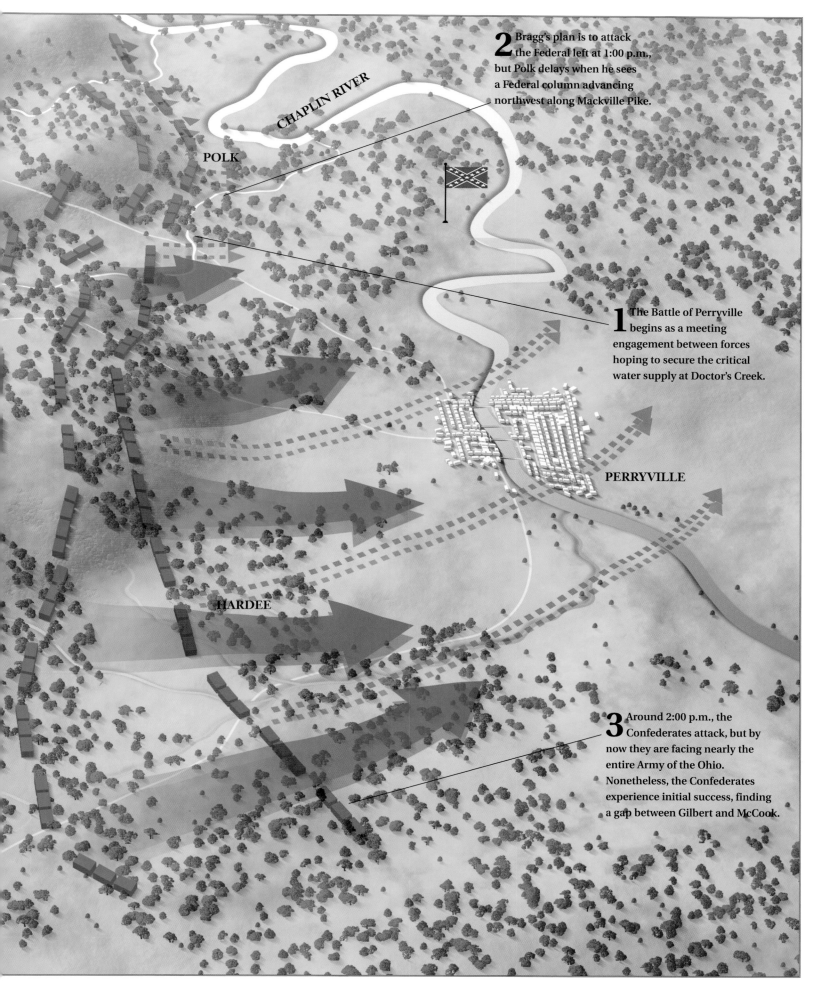

2 Bragg's plan is to attack the Federal left at 1:00 p.m., but Polk delays when he sees a Federal column advancing northwest along Mackville Pike.

CHAPLIN RIVER

POLK

1 The Battle of Perryville begins as a meeting engagement between forces hoping to secure the critical water supply at Doctor's Creek.

PERRYVILLE

HARDEE

3 Around 2:00 p.m., the Confederates attack, but by now they are facing nearly the entire Army of the Ohio. Nonetheless, the Confederates experience initial success, finding a gap between Gilbert and McCook.

Right: A Confederate cavalry officer charges with sword drawn. Cavalry soldiers fought from horseback armed with carbines, pistols, and especially sabers.

northwest of Chattanooga, where he could block any advance north by Bragg. It was a wise decision, but one on which Buell would fail to capitalize. By September 5, Bragg had established a headquarters in Sparta, just twenty miles northeast of McMinnville. Buell's army was well within striking distance, but the Federal general failed to attack. Instead he withdrew westward to Murfreesboro, thirty-five miles northeast of Nashville, in order to cover that city, which he feared was Bragg's objective.

However, Bragg was not headed for Nashville. Instead he marched his force north from Sparta, out of Tennessee to Glasgow, Kentucky, where he could seize the Louisville and Nashville Railroad. Bragg arrived in Glasgow on September 14 and made a two-day halt there to rest his tired troops. It was the first break they had taken since leaving Chattanooga seventeen days and 150 miles earlier. In spite of the vigorous marching, Confederate morale was high. While in Glasgow, Bragg issued a proclamation that began, "Kentuckians, I have entered your State with the Confederate Army of the West, and offer you an opportunity to free yourselves from the tyranny of a despotic ruler."

Bragg had good reason to be confident. By motivating Buell to recede toward Nashville, Bragg had already relieved north Alabama, Chattanooga, and much of middle Tennessee without firing a shot. Furthermore, Bragg found himself in a position between Smith and Buell. Bragg could use this advantage to either bring Smith to him or to move with Smith to capture Louisville or Cincinnati. Both of these key cities were closer to Bragg than they now were to Buell.

Bragg decided to combine with Smith against Louisville. Success there would severely disrupt Buell's deteriorating supply situation and might stimulate the flood of volunteers to the Confederate army that Bragg was counting on. By now Buell had slowly come to realize that his greatest threat was a union between Smith's and Bragg's forces, and he decided to move against Bragg on September 16.

BRAGG DRAWN INTO UNWANTED BATTLE

Before Buell could act on his newfound decisiveness, however, Bragg was moving, too. Instead of heading toward Buell, Bragg was headed north toward Munfordville. There a 4,000-man Federal garrison held a fort on the south bank of the Green River, guarding the Louisville and Nashville Railroad crossing point. Bragg had instructed Brigadier General James Chalmers to cut that rail line at Cave City, ten miles northwest of Glasgow. Accomplishing this task with ease, Chalmers then continued to, in what Bragg later described as an "unauthorized and injudicious" action, attack Munfordville. Chalmers was repulsed with heavy losses.

Bragg was now sucked into a battle he did not want, but he was "unwilling to allow the impression of a disaster to rest on the minds of my men." He committed four divisions to Munfordville and had the garrison surrounded by the middle of the afternoon on September 16. Bragg expected an almost immediate surrender, but instead the Federal commander at Munfordville, Colonel John Wilder, dragged out the proceedings until 6:00 a.m. the next day.

Bragg was now halfway across Kentucky. His victory at Munfordville and Smith's earlier one at Richmond were causes for much Confederate elation, but at this point Bragg seemed to lose his nerve. He told his men, "A powerful foe is assembling in our front and we must prepare to strike him a sudden and decisive blow," but instead of pressing his advantage, Bragg remained at Munfordville for several days, hoping Buell would advance from Bowling Green and attack him.

When Buell failed to attack, Bragg left Munfordville on September 21 and headed toward Bardstown in order to combine with Smith, who was still in Lexington. As soon as Bragg left Munfordville, Buell departed Bowling Green and headed for Louisville, where he arrived on September 25 and was immediately beset by problems. Upon arrival, Buell found himself in Major General Horatio Wright's Department of the Ohio, and it took some days to confirm that Buell was actually in charge. Then on September 29, in the culmination of a long-standing feud, Union Brigadier General Jefferson C. Davis shot and killed Bull Nelson. Nelson, the commander of the Army of Kentucky, had been the chief organizer of Louisville's defenses before Buell's arrival, and now Buell would be without this capable officer's assistance.

But the biggest crisis for Buell was that his irresolute action thus far in the campaign had finally so frustrated President Lincoln that he demanded Buell be relieved. On September 24, Major General Henry Halleck, Lincoln's general-in-chief, ordered Major General George Thomas to replace Buell. By this point, however, Buell had gained a local reputation as the man who had come to save Louisville and Cincinnati, and Halleck unsuccessfully attempted to retract the order. Thomas graciously resolved the situation by refusing command on the grounds that Buell had completed his plans for the defense and would be the best man to carry them out. Thomas would serve as Buell's second in command.

KENTUCKY FAILS TO PRODUCE HOPED-FOR VOLUNTEERS

These Federal difficulties were of little help to the Confederates. When Bragg

Below: Major General Henry Halleck became Lincoln's general-in-chief on July 11, 1862.

arrived at Bardstown, he found that Smith had neither sent supplies nor even left Lexington. In fact, Smith seemed completely uninterested in cooperating with Bragg and was apparently willing to let Bragg proceed to Louisville alone. Bragg, however, was in no position to make such a move. He had left Munfordville with only three days' worth of food and now had to scatter his men throughout the countryside to forage. In the meantime, Bragg and Smith appeared in Frankfort on September 30 and prepared to ceremoniously inaugurate a secessionist government. In spite of this gesture, Bragg had thus far failed to receive the influx of volunteers he had expected. On September 25, he wired Richmond,

"I regret to say we are sadly disappointed at the want of action by our friends in Kentucky. We have so far received no accession to this army. General Smith has secured about a brigade—not half our losses by casualties of different kinds. We have 15,000 stand to arms and no one to use them. Unless a change occurs soon, we must abandon the garden spot of Kentucky to its cupidity." To make matters worse, Grant's victories at Iuka and Corinth, Mississippi, eliminated the opportunity for Price and Van Dorn to provide Bragg with any reinforcements.

In the meantime, Buell seemed to have been infused with a new vigor after his brush with losing his command. By now he had a force of 60,000 troops, and he marched them out of Louisville to meet the advancing Confederates. On October 1, he formed his army into three corps, respectively commanded by Major Generals Alexander McCook, Thomas Crittenden, and Charles Gilbert, and dispatched them on three separate routes southeast to Bardstown. As Buell advanced, Bragg was still in the Kentucky capital of Frankfort, helping to install the newly proclaimed Confederate government. While he was thus occupied, his widely scattered force manned a fifty-mile front that extended from Bardstown northeast to Shelbyville.

MEETING ENGAGEMENT AT PERRYVILLE

Buell's plan was to launch a diversion on the Confederate right to conceal his main attack on the left. On October 2, this diversion struck Shelbyville, halfway between Lexington and Frankfort, and drove Cleburne's brigade back to Frankfort. Bragg fell for Buell's ruse by ordering Major General Leonidas Polk to march north from Bardstown and strike the Federal right flank as they advanced toward Frankfort. Bragg also told Smith to bring his 10,000-man force from Lexington. Amazingly, with his army under attack, Bragg remained in Frankfort to continue with the preparations for the inauguration scheduled for October 4.

Polk was less fooled by Buell's diversion than Bragg. Polk's cavalry had reported that

Below: Leonidas Polk (1806–64), the "Fighting Bishop," was much beloved by his men but possessed only mediocre military abilities.

Buell was moving south to Bardstown in force. Instead of following Bragg's order, Polk fell back to a supply depot at Bryantsville. As the inauguration ceremony in Frankfort was reaching its conclusion, gunfire could be heard to the west. Bragg belatedly realized his place was with his army, and he hurried to join Polk, leaving the newly appointed governor, Richard Hawes, to fend for himself.

Bragg now decided to concentrate his scattered army at Harrodsburg and, from there, turn north to meet Buell, who Bragg continued to think was headed for Frankfort. Bragg imagined a battle would be fought between Harrodsburg and Frankfort, in the vicinity of Versailles. He thus ordered Smith to halt his force north of the Kentucky River, near Versailles, to watch for the Federal advance.

Major General William Hardee had to cover twenty miles to march his corps to Bragg's appointed rendezvous at Harrodsburg. It was slow moving, water was scarce, and the advancing Federals continually harassed Hardee's march. On October 6, Polk ordered Hardee to halt in order to "force the enemy to reveal his strength." At the time of the order, Hardee's trailing division, 7,000 men commanded by Major General Simon Bolivar Buckner, was at Perryville. Polk

deployed another part of his force on a ridge to the north; the rest, commanded by Brigadier General St. John Liddell, were sent along a low range of hills to the west of the town. Colonel Joseph Wheeler's cavalry screened to the front.

STUMBLING INTO BATTLE

By this point, both armies were desperately looking for water. On the afternoon of October 7, Liddell sent two regiments still further west of his main line to secure Doctor's Creek and its precious water supply. On the Federal side, Brigadier General Phil Sheridan's brigade likewise had its eye on the valuable creek. The two enemies stumbled into each other at about 11:00 p.m. in what can best be described as a meeting engagement, and the Battle of Perryville was joined.

At first the Confederates repulsed the Federal attack, but renewed Federal efforts forced Liddell's men to abandon their position and withdraw east toward Perryville. During the night, Polk had arrived in Perryville with Major General Benjamin Cheatham's division and orders from Bragg to attack in the morning. At this point, neither side fully understood the complete situation, but what was developing significantly

Above: Many of the Union units at Perryville were composed entirely of raw recruits. Not yet used to army life, they were flung into desperate fighting against more experienced Confederate forces, and suffered accordingly.

favored the Federals. Buell's three-column advance and diversion on the Confederate right had fooled Bragg. As a result, Polk was preparing to attack 60,000 Federals with just 16,000 Confederates at Perryville. At the same time, Bragg was assembling 36,000 men at Versailles to meet a single Federal division of just 12,000 men.

"STRIKE WITH YOUR WHOLE STRENGTH"

Hardee was beginning to worry. He could not know that the main Federal attack was coming at Perryville, but he did know that, wherever the battle would be, Bragg was unprepared to meet it with his divided force. Pick either Perryville or Versailles, Hardee advised Bragg, and "strike with your whole strength."

Polk was also beginning to have his doubts, and he sensed the Federal army opposing him was much larger than he had anticipated. Upon learning that Sheridan had driven Liddell from Doctor's Creek, Polk decided to go on the defensive rather than attack. Growing impatient for Polk to proceed with the planned attack, Bragg rode to Perryville to assume command. He arrived at about 10:00 a.m. and was upset to find Polk on the defensive. Bragg immediately began preparing the troops to attack.

Bragg's plan was to focus his attack on the Federal left. He set the attack for 1:00 p.m., with Polk leading the charge. On the Federal side, Buell had intended to attack at 10:00 a.m, but confusion in getting his orders executed led him to postpone the attack until the next day. As Buell bided his time, the Confederates began to shell him with artillery fire at noon.

THE ODDS GROW STIFF

Bragg had expected a preliminary bombardment of an hour, followed by Polk's advance, but at 1:30 p.m. Polk had still not moved. Bragg then rode up to Polk to find out what was wrong, and Polk told him a Federal column was advancing northwest along the Mackville Pike. Polk feared that if he attacked, the unengaged Federals could descend upon

"MY STUDIES HAVE TAUGHT ME THAT BATTLES ARE ONLY TO BE FOUGHT FOR SOME IMPORTANT OBJECT . . . THAT IF THE RESULT IS REASONABLY UNCERTAIN, BATTLE IS ONLY TO BE SOUGHT WHEN VERY SERIOUS DISADVANTAGE MUST RESULT FROM A FAILURE TO FIGHT OR WHEN THE ADVANTAGES OF A POSSIBLE VICTORY FAR OUTWEIGH THE CONSEQUENCES OF PROBABLE DEFEAT. THESE RULES SUPPOSE THAT WAR HAS A HIGHER OBJECT THAN THAT OF MERE BLOODSHED."

FROM BUELL'S TESTIMONY FOR THE MILITARY COURT OF INQUIRY

Left: Confederate cavalry ride at a reenactment of the Battle of Perryville. Civil War reenacting is a popular pastime. These reenactors are carrying the first national flag of the Confederacy, commonly called the "Stars and Bars."

115

BRAGG'S LEADERSHIP

Conceptually, Braxton Bragg's Kentucky Campaign showed much promise, but its ultimate failure rests with Bragg's inability to adhere to the principles of war of unity of effort, objective, and security. Bragg's conduct as a whole shows he had profound skill as a strategist and administrator, but little aptitude as a commander or leader. The logistical planning that made Bragg's movement from Tupelo to Chattanooga possible is impressive and clearly demonstrates his organizational skills. However, as Bragg closed with the enemy, he seemed to make up the campaign as he went along. The Kentucky Campaign clearly showed that Bragg was operating beyond his capabilities at the level of army commander.

Bragg's usual problem in obtaining unity of effort was an irascible personality that tended to alienate many who served under him. However, in a display seemingly contrary to this characteristic, he was entirely too deferential to Smith. In the process, Bragg allowed himself to be manipulated by Smith for Smith's own ambitious designs. Bragg completely failed to exert his will over his junior commander, and the two acted largely as competing rather than cooperating forces. The biggest threat to Buell's army was if Bragg and Smith combined forces. By allowing Smith to act independently, Bragg failed to achieve the unity of effort necessary to bring this threat to fruition.

Bragg also failed to adhere to the principle of objective, choosing to pursue political goals rather than Buell's army. Even Smith saw the problem. When Bragg complained that the expected rush of Confederate volunteers had not materialized, Smith coyly suggested that if Bragg defeated Buell, perhaps the volunteers would follow. Bragg's obsession with the inauguration ceremonies in Frankfort, even while his army was under attack, also clearly shows where Bragg felt his attention needed to be. By focusing on the political aspects of the campaign, Bragg missed the true objective of Buell's army.

Finally, Bragg failed in the area of security in that he never understood the true disposition of Buell's force. He was completely bamboozled by Buell's demonstration, in part probably because of the importance Bragg himself attached to Frankfort. He also kept his force widely dispersed and therefore poorly prepared to concentrate once the battle developed.

his flank, so he was waiting until the enemy took their positions in the Federal defense. Under these circumstances, Bragg agreed to the delay.

What Bragg did not know was that the approaching Federals were part of McCook's corps and their arrival meant that now nearly the entire Army of the Ohio was on the field. When the Confederates finally attacked at around 2:00 p.m., they were facing very stiff odds.

Nonetheless, the Confederate forces experienced initial success, finding a gap between the corps of Gilbert and McCook, and driving the Federals back until the Twenty-eighth Brigade, under Brigadier General John Starkweather, stopped the penetration. Remarkably, Buell did not know until 4:00 p.m. that a fierce battle was on. Atmospheric conditions masked the sounds of the battle, and he arrived on the scene too late to have a real impact. Other commanders also suffered from this "acoustic shadow," and Gilbert and Crittenden were also slow to react. The end result was that only nine Federal brigades were heavily engaged while fifteen others that were within close supporting distance played little part.

In the meantime, however, the aggressive Sheridan was able to counterattack, claiming he "had driven the enemy before him, and whipped them like hell." In the process, though, Sheridan advanced too far in front of the rest of the Federal line, and he was forced to halt his advance and consolidate his position just west of Perryville. By nightfall, the Confederates still held advanced positions, but the lines were so disjointed they could not be used to any advantage. Skirmishing continued after dark, but in essence the battle was over.

FEDERAL BLUNDERS SAVE THE CONFEDERATES

The Federals lost 4,211 in the fighting, compared to 3,396 on the Confederate side. Bragg had won a victory, but he was still facing the entire Army of the Ohio. He was in a dangerous situation that he had survived thus far thanks only to Federal blunders. He wisely decided to withdraw to Harrodsburg, where he could gather his forces and prepare to counter any Federal move. The ever-cautious Buell, who was convinced he faced Bragg's entire army, did not pursue until the morning. By then Bragg was gone.

Smith joined Bragg in Harrodsburg on October 10. Wheeler's cavalry fought an effective rearguard action against Buell's tepid pursuit as Bragg withdrew from Kentucky to Morristown, Tennessee. Buell broke off his pursuit on October 12 and withdrew to Glasgow and Bowling Green. Buell had repelled Bragg's invasion, but he had also missed a golden opportunity to gain a great victory. Bragg's poor performance in the Kentucky Campaign severely hampered his reputation in the Confederacy. His problems continued when, after the Battle of Chickamauga, several high-ranking officers signed a petition requesting that Bragg be removed from command. Nonetheless, President Davis continued to support Bragg until, finally, after the loss of Chattanooga, Bragg asked to be relieved. Bragg was a fairly sound strategist, but the Kentucky Campaign illustrated his fatal flaw of being unable to bring to fruition his conceptual thoughts in the face of a freethinking enemy.

REFLECTED FAILURE

Then, in another failure shared with McClellan, Buell allowed Bragg to withdraw unmolested. Like many of the Federal generals, Buell lacked the killer instinct. He considered a battle to be a victory merely by not losing. President Lincoln expected much more, and Buell's failure to severely damage Bragg was the last straw. On October 25, Lincoln replaced Buell as commander of the Army of the Ohio with Major General William Rosecrans. Still, Lincoln owed Buell at least some debt of gratitude. Earlier the president had said, "I hope to have God on my side, but I must have Kentucky. I think to lose Kentucky is nearly the same as to lose the whole game." If nothing else, Buell secured Kentucky for Lincoln at Perryville.

BUELL'S LEADERSHIP

Buell's reputation also suffered from the Kentucky Campaign. Buell is sometimes called "the McClellan of the West," and while this moniker is not completely accurate, the comparison is in some ways apt. At almost the same time that Buell was resisting Bragg's invasion of Kentucky, Major General George McClellan was battling General Robert E. Lee's invasion of Maryland. While both Buell and McClellan turned back the Confederates, both commanders missed opportunities to severely damage their foes. Both men showed excessive caution and both failed to get their entire armies into the battle.

Like McClellan, Buell was highly criticized for his slow movements. His plodding advance on Chattanooga is a good example. Buell seemed to fail to understand the urgency of the situation and instead devoted much energy to securing railroads and building up supply depots. He spent a full two weeks on an extremely inefficient operation to build a pontoon bridge across the Tennessee River at Bridgeport. While these logistical challenges must be acknowledged, Buell's slow advance stands in stark contrast to the achievement of Bragg's much more energetic move of 800 miles from Tupelo.

Buell displayed the same methodical caution when he failed to attack Bragg at Sparta, instead withdrawing to Murfreesboro. Buell's concern for Nashville led him to surrender much of middle Tennessee without even opposing Bragg. In the process, he allowed Bragg to gain the advantageous position of being able to either bring Smith to him or move with Smith to capture Louisville or Cincinnati. It was only when Louisville—and his job—was in peril that Buell found the energy to act.

Buell's battle plan at Perryville was sound, and his diversion worked exactly as he intended it to. However, after that, Buell lost control of the situation both by failing to get his attack started when he wanted it to and then by being out of position to command the battle effectively. His failure to bring his entire force to bear is another strong similarity with McClellan's actions at Antietam. In the end, it was the aggressiveness of subordinates like Sheridan that saved Buell at Perryville.

LEE VS. HOOKER

CHANCELLORSVILLE, 1863

In the Battle of Chancellorsville, General Robert E. Lee defeated Major General Joseph Hooker in what many consider Lee's greatest victory of the Civil War. It is also a sterling example of the difference a general can make.

While Hooker possessed the initial advantage, Lee simply outgeneraled his opponent. Sending Lieutenant General Stonewall Jackson on a bold flank march, Lee shattered the Federal defense and created widespread panic. In the process, however, Jackson became a casualty, a loss Lee could ill afford.

PRELIMINARIES

Major General Ambrose Burnside had been reluctant to accept command of the Army of the Potomac after the Battle of Antietam, and his poor performance at Fredericksburg on December 13, 1862, proved his concerns were well founded. There the Federals lost more than 12,500 men in six futile frontal assaults against the strong Confederate defense put in place by Lee. Observing the wreckage, Lee commented, "It is well war is so terrible—otherwise we would grow too fond of it."

Burnside tried to redeem himself in January 1863 with a renewed offensive northwest of Fredericksburg. Torrential rains conspired against the hapless Burnside and the operation ended up

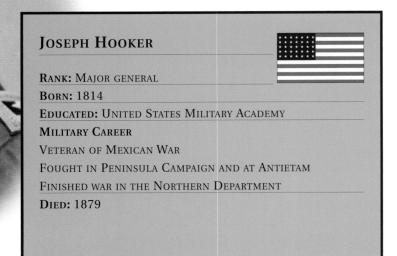

JOSEPH HOOKER

RANK: MAJOR GENERAL
BORN: 1814
EDUCATED: UNITED STATES MILITARY ACADEMY
MILITARY CAREER
VETERAN OF MEXICAN WAR
FOUGHT IN PENINSULA CAMPAIGN AND AT ANTIETAM
FINISHED WAR IN THE NORTHERN DEPARTMENT
DIED: 1879

being nothing more than the infamous "Mud March." By now the army had lost confidence in Burnside, and several of his subordinate commanders were clamoring for him to be relieved. Leading the chorus was Brigadier General Joe Hooker, who had commanded the "Center Grand Division," consisting of the Second and Third corps, at Fredericksburg in December. Hooker accused Burnside of "blundering sacrifice," "madness," and "follies," and when Burnside complained to President Lincoln of Hooker's insubordination, the president, by now himself exhausted by Burnside, relieved him and placed Hooker in command of the Army of the Potomac.

AS A FATHER MIGHT WRITE HIS SON

While justified in his frustration with Burnside, Hooker was still a volatile and bellicose critic with a loose mouth. He allegedly complained that "both the army and government needed a dictator," and word of this statement had reached Lincoln. Thus, when Lincoln placed Hooker in command, the president advised Hooker, "I have placed you at the head of the Army of the Potomac. Of course I have done this upon what appear to be sufficient reasons. And yet I think it best for you to know that there are some things I regard to which I am not satisfied with you. I believe you to be a brave and skillful soldier, which, of course, I like. You have confidence in yourself, which is a valuable, if not indispensable, quality.

You are ambitious, which, within reasonable bounds, does good rather than harm; but I think that during General Burnside's command of the Army you have taken counsel of your ambition, and thwarted him as much as you could, in which you did a great wrong to the country . . . I have heard, in such way as to believe it, of your recently saying that both the Army and the Government needed a Dictator. Of course it was not for this, but in spite of it, that I have given you the command. Only those generals who gain success can set up dictators. What I ask of you is military success, and I will risk the dictatorship." A humbled Hooker noted, "That is just such a letter as a father might write to his son." He then put the army into winter quarters at Falmouth, Virginia, and began preparing for the spring campaign.

CHANCELLORSVILLE

Date	April 30–May 6, 1863
Location	Spotsylvania County, Virginia
Result	Confederate victory

Strength	
Union: Army of the Potomac (133,868)	Confederate: Army of Northern Virginia (59,500)

Casualties and losses	
17,287	12,764
1,606 killed	1,665 killed
9,762 wounded	9,081 wounded
5,919 missing	2,018 missing

ROBERT E. LEE

RANK: GENERAL

BORN: 1807

EDUCATED: UNITED STATES MILITARY ACADEMY

MILITARY CAREER

VETERAN OF MEXICAN WAR

SUPERINTENDENT OF THE UNITED STATES MILITARY ACADEMY

MILITARY ADVISOR TO JEFFERSON DAVIS

LED ARMY OF NORTHERN VIRGINIA FROM 1862 UNTIL THE
   CONCLUSION OF THE WAR

DIED: 1870

HOOKER'S INITIATIVES

Hooker's first order of business was to restore the flagging morale of the post-Burnside army. Building on the considerable experience with staff and organizational administration he had gained during the Mexican War, Hooker initiated a series of reforms that breathed new life into the Army of the Potomac. Among his most important decisions was to appoint Major General Daniel Butterfield as his chief of staff. Having been a chief of staff himself in Mexico, Hooker knew what the job required and what he wanted. Butterfield proved to be a skilled administrator who would provide invaluable assistance to Hooker in implementing his reforms.

With Butterfield's help, Hooker's administrative initiatives were far-reaching. He abolished the army's four unwieldy "grand divisions" of two army corps each and replaced them with a more streamlined structure of seven infantry and one cavalry corps. This consolidation of the army's cavalry under one commander greatly improved what had previously been a scattered and dysfunctional asset.

Hooker addressed the problem of desertions by both tightening travel restrictions and offering amnesty to any soldier who returned to the army by April 1. The results were impressive. In January, deserters had accounted for 30 percent of the army's absentees, but by March 31 Hooker had reduced that number to less than 4 percent.

Hooker also made several changes to improve morale, such as instituting an enlightened furlough policy, instilling unit pride by implementing a system of distinctive unit badges, and improving rations. Hooker announced, "My men shall be fed before I am fed, and before any of my officers are fed." He began sponsoring sporting events such as ball games, sack races, steeplechases, and greased pole competitions. Hooker's reforms even extended to the press, insisting on stricter accountability, and thereby reducing security leaks, by

Below: General Ambrose Burnside (standing in center, with sideburns and mustache) with his staff. Burnside had left the Army of the Potomac dispirited and demoralized, and Hooker set out to rebuild it.

requiring bylines. To oversee all these reforms, Hooker increased the powers of his inspectors general.

CULTIVATING RELIABLE MILITARY INTELLIGENCE

Perhaps the most important of Hooker's reorganizing efforts was the work he did in the area of military intelligence. Hooker appointed Colonel George Sharpe as the head of his Bureau of Military Information and gave him the far-reaching task of developing a reliable intelligence-gathering system virtually from scratch.

The problem was that, prior to Sharpe, intelligence officers had simply collected raw information and passed it on to the commander in bulky reports with no effort to evaluate or analyze it. A vast network of spies with impressive access to the Confederacy fed much of the previous intelligence system, but few other sources were available to corroborate their findings. The result was a haphazard and inefficient system that was of little value to the commander. Sharpe reversed these deficiencies by coordinating the information acquired from prisoners, deserters, refugees, contrabands, infantry and cavalry reports, balloon observations, and signal stations into an ordered and evaluated form. As a result, unlike his predecessors, Hooker had a reliable picture of the Confederate army and could make decisions based on accurate intelligence.

Hooker's administrative reforms were perhaps the greatest contribution he made to the army. Indeed, Francis Walker, assistant adjutant general of the Second Corps, felt that during the period of Hooker's reforms, "the Army of the Potomac never spent three months to better advantage." One of Hooker's corps commanders pronounced the difference Hooker had made as being "magical."

As Hooker considered how to use his reinvigorated army, he was strongly influenced by the advice of Brigadier General Montgomery Meigs, the Federal army's quartermaster general. Meigs wrote Hooker, "What is needed is a great and overwhelming defeat and

destruction of [Lee's] army." Meigs suggested a bold, rapid turning movement around the Confederate left flank to threaten the enemy rear—"such a move as Napoleon made at Jena, as Lee made in his campaign against Pope."

Meigs was pressing for a decisive Napoleonic victory. "Throw your whole army upon [Lee's] communications," Meigs counseled. "Interpose between him and Richmond . . . and he fights, if you are successful, he has no retreat." To seal the victory, Meigs proposed unleashing Hooker's newly reorganized cavalry against Lee's lines of communications.

MEIGS'S ADVICE IN ACTION

Hooker soon began working on a plan along the lines of Meigs's suggestion. Resources certainly were not a problem. Hooker had 134,000 troops available, more than enough to do the job. He decided to commit only a third to Meigs's suggested turning movement and use another third to attack across the Rappahannock River to fix Lee at Fredericksburg. With Lee thus distracted, the turning force could gain Lee's flank and then the Confederates would be crushed between the two parts of the Federal army. For added flexibility, Hooker still had the final third of his force held as a reserve that could reinforce either wing.

Above: This Civil War period illustration shows General George Stoneman's (1822–94) 7,500 Union cavalry raiding through Virginia during the Chancellorsville Campaign. Stoneman's forces struck deep into the Confederate rear areas, destroying crucial supply depots and cutting Lee's lines of communication and supply.

Above: A sergeant from the First Virginia Cavalry. As a rule, the Confederate cavalry was better than its Union counterpart, as they were recruited from country-bred men who could already ride and shoot.

Hooker also ordered his newly created cavalry corps, commanded by Major General George Stoneman, to precede the main turning movement by two weeks and raid Lee's lines of communication. Only a small cavalry brigade commanded by Brigadier General Alfred Pleasonton would remain with Hooker's main body.

On April 13, Stoneman left Falmouth with a force of 10,000 men. However, a severe storm prevented the fording of the Rappahannock for two weeks and Stoneman ended up not crossing until April 29, the same day as the infantry. The raid caused alarm in Richmond, but turned out to be of no practical use to Hooker's overall operation. In fact, by dispatching Stoneman on this mission,

Hooker denied himself a reconnaissance asset that would have been of much greater use to him. Instead, it was the Confederate cavalry that would play a key role in the upcoming Battle of Chancellorsville.

When Hooker initiated his great turning movement on April 28 and Major General John Sedgwick launched his fixing attack with his Sixth Corps across the Rappahannock the next day, Lee was at as great a disadvantage as any he experienced during the war. With just 59,500 troops, Lee faced an army more than twice his size. Soon reports from Major General Jeb Stuart's cavalry were coming in that the Federals had crossed the Rappahannock not just to Lee's front, but also twenty-five miles to the

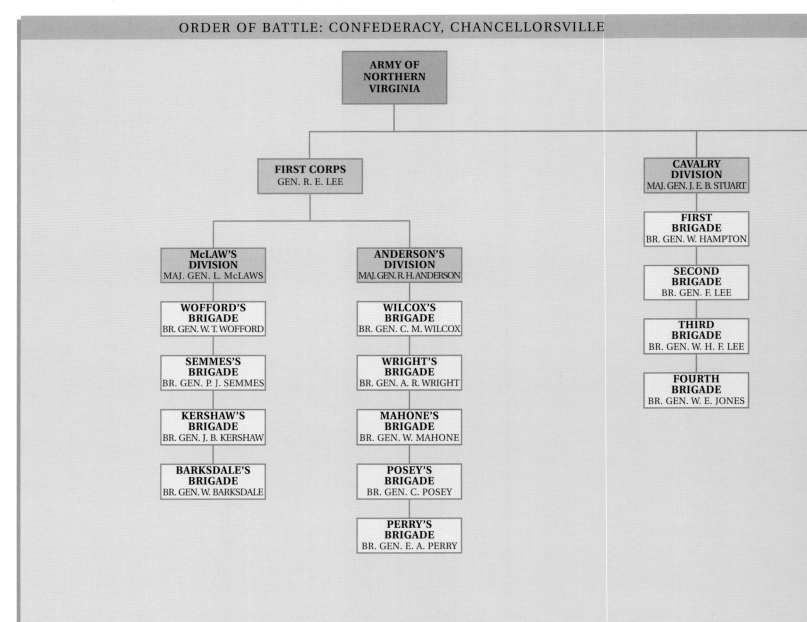

ORDER OF BATTLE: CONFEDERACY, CHANCELLORSVILLE

ARMY OF NORTHERN VIRGINIA

FIRST CORPS
GEN. R. E. LEE

CAVALRY DIVISION
MAJ. GEN. J. E. B. STUART

McLAW'S DIVISION
MAJ. GEN. L. McLAWS

ANDERSON'S DIVISION
MAJ. GEN. R. H. ANDERSON

FIRST BRIGADE
BR. GEN. W. HAMPTON

WOFFORD'S BRIGADE
BR. GEN. W. T. WOFFORD

WILCOX'S BRIGADE
BR. GEN. C. M. WILCOX

SECOND BRIGADE
BR. GEN. F. LEE

SEMMES'S BRIGADE
BR. GEN. P. J. SEMMES

WRIGHT'S BRIGADE
BR. GEN. A. R. WRIGHT

THIRD BRIGADE
BR. GEN. W. H. F. LEE

KERSHAW'S BRIGADE
BR. GEN. J. B. KERSHAW

MAHONE'S BRIGADE
BR. GEN. W. MAHONE

FOURTH BRIGADE
BR. GEN. W. E. JONES

BARKSDALE'S BRIGADE
BR. GEN. W. BARKSDALE

POSEY'S BRIGADE
BR. GEN. C. POSEY

PERRY'S BRIGADE
BR. GEN. E. A. PERRY

northwest at Kelly's Ford. Lee found himself in the middle of a giant set of jaws that Hooker was about to snap shut. Conventional wisdom would have dictated that Lee should withdraw, but the audacious Lee had something else in mind. Sensing that Sedgwick's attack was a diversion, Lee saw an opportunity to strike Hooker's divided army a serious blow. To do so, however, Lee would have to take the dangerous step of dividing his own small army.

INTO THE WILDERNESS

Leaving just 10,000 men commanded by Major General Jubal Early to watch Sedgwick, Lee rushed the rest of his army west of Fredericksburg to the tiny country crossroads of Chancellorsville

in the middle of a part of Virginia ominously called the Wilderness. Chancellorsville boasted just one building, a two-and-a-half-story brick farmhouse that stood along the intersection of the Orange Turnpike with the Orange Plank Road, Ely's Ford Road, and River Road. The preponderance of the Wilderness region's terrain consisted of twisted undergrowth that would impede large troop movements and greatly favor an outnumbered army fighting on the defense.

Hooker had taken his force across the Rappahannock with great stealth, going to such lengths as covering his pontoons with pine boughs to muffle the sound of men and equipment crossing over them. Once on the other side of the river, he

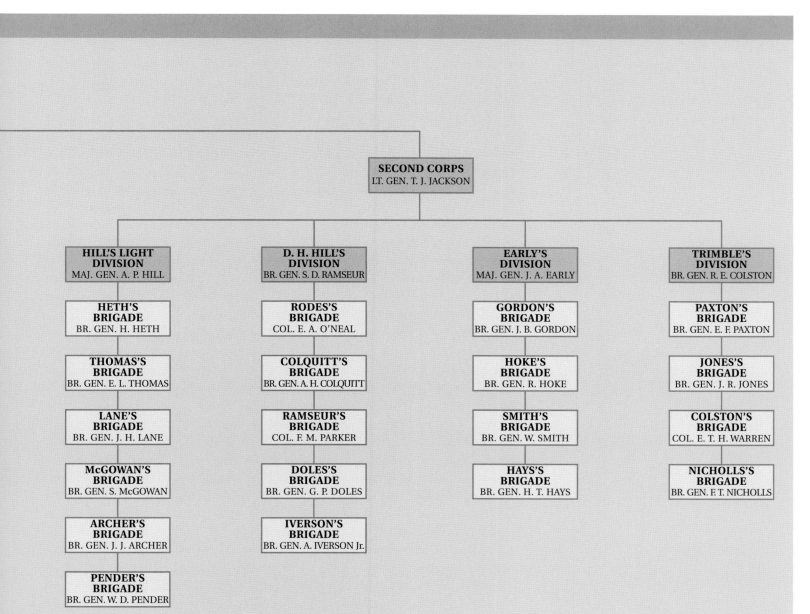

Above: Cavalryman J. E. B. ("Jeb") Stuart (1833–64) was a brilliant source of intelligence for Robert E. Lee and a critical part of the Confederate success at the Battle of Chancellorsville.

cleverly used hills to screen his movement from Stuart's cavalry. The result was that Hooker had a day's head start on Lee, and by midafternoon on April 30, the Federals had reached the key road junction at Chancellorsville. Hooker had encountered virtually no opposition up to this point and had negated Lee's advantage of holding a river line. Hooker's plan seemed to be working to perfection.

Filled with confidence in the campaign's progress thus far, the usually reserved Major General George Meade, commander of Hooker's Fifth Corps, exuded, "This is splendid. Hurrah for Old Joe. We are on Lee's flank and he doesn't know it." Equally proud, Hooker crowed to a newspaper reporter, "The Rebel army . . . is now the legitimate property of the Army of the Potomac."

All was indeed well for the Army of the Potomac up to this point, but then Hooker made a crucial mistake. What Hooker should have done next was to press eastward and break clear of the Wilderness. He could then cross Banks' Ford downstream and significantly shorten the distance between the two wings of his army. Instead, he decided to halt at Chancellorsville and await the arrival of additional troops. Other Federal officers on the scene lamented this loss of momentum. Meade, whose earlier exuberance was now tempered, wrote his wife, "We are across the river and have out-maneuvered the enemy, but are not yet out of the woods."

ARRIVAL AT ZOAN CHURCH
The delay would prove costly for the Federals because, while Hooker remained stationary, Lieutenant General Stonewall Jackson was marching fast. Jackson had left the Fredericksburg lines at 3:00 a.m. on May 1 and arrived at Zoan Church five hours later. The small Baptist meetinghouse stood on a commanding ridge that was the highest ground for miles. It also represented the edge of the tangled Wilderness.

When Jackson arrived, Major General Richard Anderson and Major General Lafayette McLaws were already at Zoan Church with their divisions and had begun to prepare defensive positions. Although his own corps had not yet closed, Jackson ordered Anderson and McLaws to stop digging and advance forward, ready to attack. Jackson's decisive action was critical in shaping the Battle of Chancellorsville, because when Hooker finally got moving again later that morning, he collided with the small but aggressive Confederate force. The unexpected stiff resistance caught the Federals off guard, and the initial reports seem to have created an unwarranted panic on Hooker's part. He quickly ordered his generals to fall back to the Wilderness and assume a defensive posture. The decision was the turning point of the battle, and it was not well received by Hooker's lieutenants.

ANGER AND DISBELIEF
When Twelfth Corps commander Major General Henry Slocum received the order, he told Hooker's messenger, Washington Augustus Roebling—later the builder of the Brooklyn Bridge—"You are a damned liar! Nobody but a crazy man would give such an order when we have victory in sight! I shall go and see General Hooker myself, and if I find out that you have spoken falsely, you shall be shot on my return." An angry Meade supposedly complained, "If we can't hold the top of a hill, we certainly can't hold the bottom of it." In spite of the protests, the order stood.

Major General Darius N. Couch was Hooker's senior corps commander, and he was also deeply unhappy with this change in plan. When Couch took his concerns to Hooker, however, Hooker reassured him by saying, "It is all right, Couch. I have got Lee just where I want him; he must fight me on my own ground." Couch was incensed and knew exactly what had been lost. "To hear from his own lip that the advantages gained by the successful marches of his lieutenants were to culminate in fighting a defensive battle in that nest of thickets was too much," Couch recalled, "and I retired from his presence with the belief that my commanding general was a whipped man."

Hooker earlier had gained the nickname "Fighting Joe Hooker" from the tagline of a series of newspaper reports during the Peninsula Campaign. The copyist headed them "Fighting-Joe Hooker," and newspapers across the country removed the hyphen and used "Fighting Joe Hooker" as a subheading. Hooker supposedly was not fond of the nickname, but it did fit his reputation as an aggressive combatant. Now, with Hooker's characteristic boldness and confidence fading, the chances of Federal success were also sinking fast.

Left: The two-and-a-half-story brick farmhouse at the key road junction was the distinguishing feature of Chancellorsville.

Below: Robert E. Lee embodied the Confederate cause and came closer than any other general to bringing the South victory. The loss of his trusted lieutenant Stonewall Jackson at Chancellorsville cost him dearly.

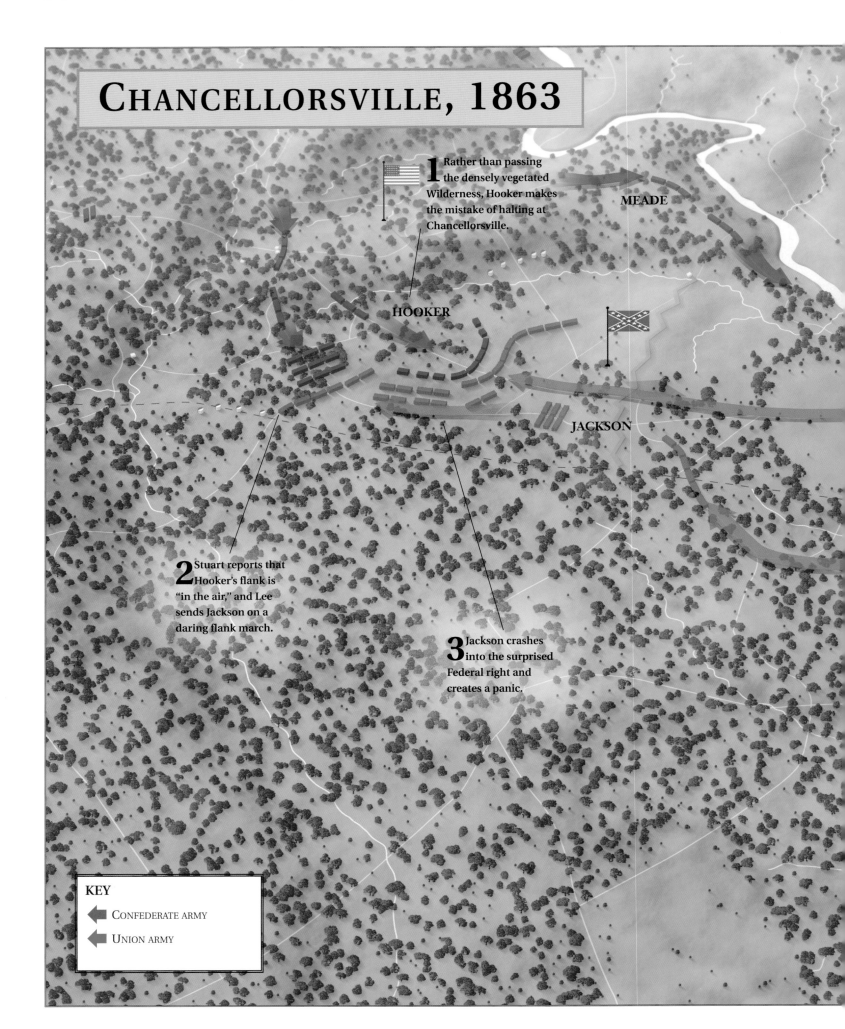

CHANCELLORSVILLE, 1863

1 Rather than passing the densely vegetated Wilderness, Hooker makes the mistake of halting at Chancellorsville.

MEADE

HOOKER

JACKSON

2 Stuart reports that Hooker's flank is "in the air," and Lee sends Jackson on a daring flank march.

3 Jackson crashes into the surprised Federal right and creates a panic.

KEY

◄ CONFEDERATE ARMY

◄ UNION ARMY

5 The Federals withdraw across the Rappahannock, much to Lee's frustration.

FALMOUTH

FREDERICKSBURG

EARLY

SEDGWICK

A. P. HILL

4 Over the next few days, Lee stubbornly presses the attack, but is unable to destroy Hooker.

ORDER OF BATTLE: UNITED STATES (UNION), CHANCELLORSVILLE

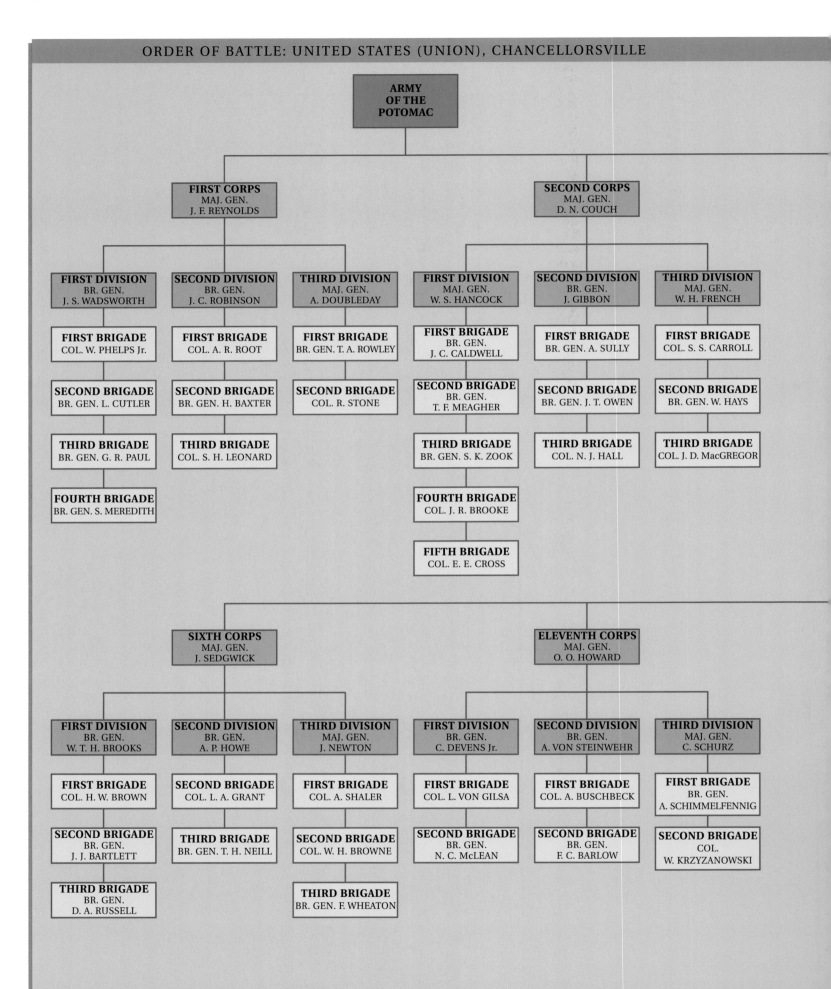

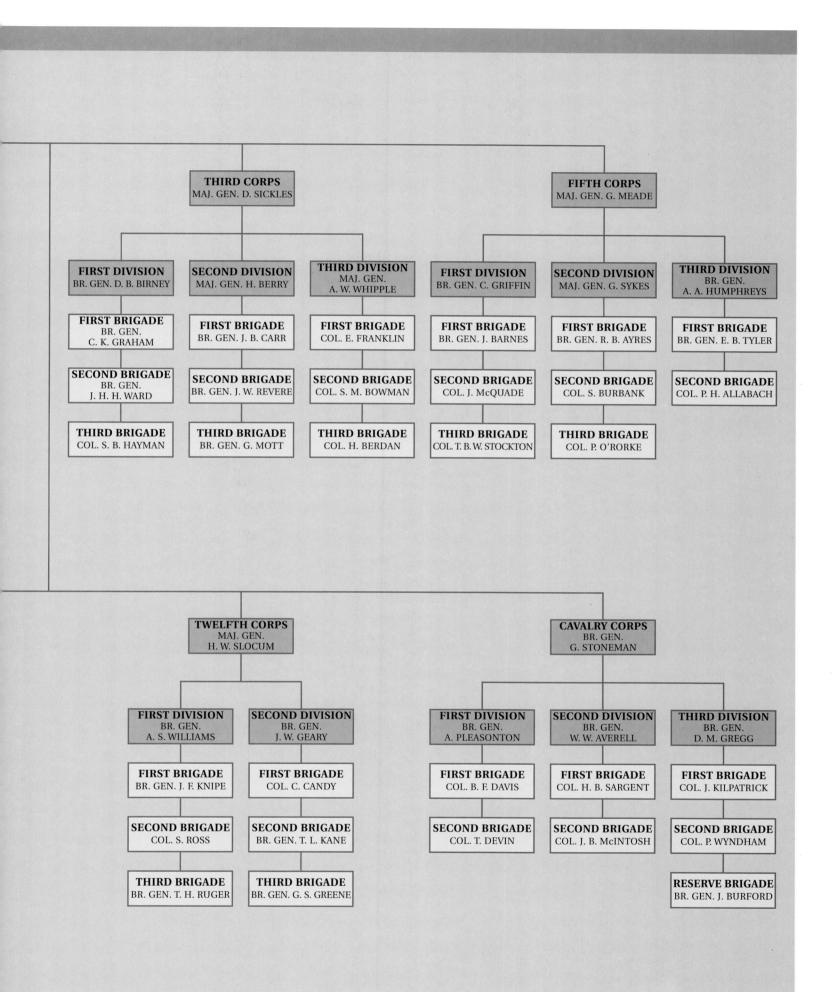

Above: The Union army's First Sharpshooters was a regiment composed entirely of men with excellent shooting skills. The sharpshooters fought with distinction at Chancellorsville, Gettysburg, the Wilderness, and many other major actions. With their fast-firing rifles, they were constantly pushed to the front of the line and consequently suffered heavy casualties—of 2,570 men who served with the regiment, about 1,300 were killed or wounded in the course of the war.

Right: Sabers drawn, the Federal Eighth Pennsylvania Cavalry engages with Confederate infantry at Chancellorsville. Cavalry rarely used sabers in the Civil War; revolvers and carbines proved to be more effective skirmishing weapons. The few roads of the Wilderness region were critical to movement and provided opportunities for both counterattack and ambush.

Such a cautious move on Hooker's part suited the offensive-minded Lee just fine. On the evening of May 1, he met with Jackson at the intersection of the Orange Plank Road and the Furnace Road to discuss the options. Using discarded Federal cracker boxes as stools, the great Confederate command team studied the situation. Lee could ill afford a costly frontal attack against the strong Federal defense, and he knew it. Then at around midnight, Stuart rode up with information that Hooker's right flank was "in the air." By that Stuart meant there was no obstacle to protect this vulnerable point of attack. Lee and Jackson immediately turned their energies to determining a way to take advantage of this situation.

LEE AND JACKSON IN COMMAND

Closely studying the map, Lee asked Jackson, "How can we get at those people?" and then traced a general direction of advance that would put Jackson beyond the right flank in Hooker's rear. With this concept in mind, Jackson dispatched his topographical engineer, Major Jedediah Hotchkiss, and his chaplain, Tucker Lacy, to locate a route that could accomplish Lee's intent. With the help of Colonel Charles Wellford, a local resident, they determined such a road did exist, which could support Jackson's maneuver.

Before dawn, Lee and Jackson decided to undertake one of the biggest gambles in American military history. "What do you propose to do?" Lee asked Jackson.

"Go around here," Jackson answered, tracing a route on the crude map.

"What do you propose to make this movement with?" asked Lee.

"With my whole corps," answered Jackson.

Lee then asked, "What will you leave me?" to which Jackson replied, "The divisions of Anderson and McLaws."

"Well," Lee said calmly, "go on."

This quaint exchange represented the Lee-Jackson command team at its best. Lee would develop the broad conceptual guidance, and Jackson, without need for detailed instructions, would use his own

Above: The accidental shooting of Stonewall Jackson by his own men made the Confederate victory at Chancellorsville extremely costly.

"**CAPTAIN SMITH SPRANG TO HIS SIDE, AND . . . A BEAM OF MOONLIGHT . . . RESTED UPON THE PALE FACE OF THE SUFFERER. THE CAPTAIN WAS STARTLED . . . AND CRIED OUT: 'OH! GENERAL, ARE YOU SERIOUSLY HURT?' 'NO,' HE ANSWERED, 'DON'T TROUBLE YOURSELF, MY FRIEND, ABOUT ME.'"**

DR. HUNTER MCGUIRE, MEDICAL DIRECTOR OF GENERAL STONEWALL JACKSON'S CORPS

initiative and understanding of Lee's intent to elaborate on it and execute it flawlessly.

Lee and Jackson had thus decided that Jackson's corps of about 30,000 troops would follow a series of country roads and paths through the woods to reach the Federal right flank while Lee, with the remaining 14,000 infantry, would occupy a position more than three miles long and divert Hooker's attention away from Jackson.

Once in position, Jackson would assail the Federal weak point while Lee continued to hold on. It was an extremely risky plan. Counting the contingent Lee had left with Jubal Early at Fredericksburg, the Army of Northern Virginia would now be divided into three pieces against a Federal army more than twice its size. Success depended on Jackson's ability to get to the Federal flank before Hooker realized Lee's predicament and attacked.

Jackson's route began at Catherine Furnace and followed Furnace Road south and southwest to Brock Road. Instead of turning north and passing dangerously close to the enemy, the route moved south about 600 yards and then turned sharply right along a lesser road branching out of the Brock Road

and running parallel to it but on the western side. In this way, Jackson would be concealed from the enemy. The lesser road would eventually loop back onto the Brock Road just about a mile below the Orange Plank Road. Jackson's men would have to march about ten and a half miles.

"PRESS ON, PRESS FORWARD"

Jackson's men began moving at about 8:00 a.m. In spite of the concealed route, as the Confederates traversed a small clearing about a mile into the march, Federal scouts perched in treetops at Hazel Grove spotted them. The Federals lobbed artillery shells at Jackson's men and notified Hooker of the enemy movement. Hooker correctly ascertained that the Confederates were heading toward his right flank, and he warned Major General Oliver Howard, whose Eleventh Corps defended that sector, to be on the lookout.

As the morning progressed, however, Hooker grew to believe that Lee was actually withdrawing, and Hooker became increasingly less concerned about his right flank. He ordered Couch's Third Corps to harass the tail end of Lee's "retreating" army. Couch succeeded in overwhelming Jackson's rear guard and captured an entire regiment. However, the action actually backfired on Hooker, because it drew 20,000 Federal troops toward Catherine Furnace and away from Howard's corps, thus further isolating the Federal flank.

Jackson's men continued to march. Although they were hungry and thirsty and suffered from early afternoon temperatures of about 80°F, Jackson's urgings for them to "press on, press forward" kept them going. By around 4:00 p.m., they had completed the ten-and-a-half-mile route. At the end of their march, they encountered a tangle of undergrowth and thickets that made it difficult to deploy into attack formation, but before 6:00 p.m. Jackson was in position with six of his fifteen brigades astride the Orange Turnpike, west of Chancellorsville, facing east toward the exposed Federal flank.

Jackson then gave the order to Major Eugene Blackford, commander of the skirmishers, "You can go forward then," and unleashed the attack. As many of the Federal soldiers were preparing their meals, rabbits, deer, and other animals began bounding out of the woods. The surprised soldiers did not have to wait long to learn the cause of the stampede. With bloodcurdling rebel yells, the Confederates poured out of nowhere into Hooker's flank. The Eleventh Corps was overwhelmed. A few units rallied and attempted to make a stand, but the overall situation was hopeless. As new units arrived, Jackson fed them into the battle, and within three hours, the Confederates had surged forward two miles. Hooker's line was folded into a U, centered on the large house at the Chancellorsville crossroads. There Federal resistance stiffened, and the Confederate onslaught slowed.

VICTIMS OF FRIENDLY FIRE

With darkness falling, Jackson was desperate to press his victory. By now, however, the rapid advance had left him uncertain of the exact disposition of his troops. With a group of staff officers accompanying him, Jackson rode forward to reconnoiter the situation, and in the darkness and confusion some North Carolina troops mistook the party for the enemy and opened fire. Jackson was hit in the left arm. Major General A. P. Hill, Jackson's senior division commander, was also struck.

It was not until midnight that Stuart arrived and assumed command of Jackson's troops. With no real idea of Jackson's plans, Stuart mounted several weak attacks against Hooker's main body throughout May 3, but without great success. Hooker continued to try to hang on until Sedgwick, according to the original plan, could advance the twelve miles from Fredericksburg and descend upon Lee's rear. It was a seemingly irrational decision to count on Sedgwick's one corps when Hooker had six of his own, but by this point Hooker had long ceased to think offensively. For example, Hooker had Major General

George Meade's Fifth Corps in an excellent position north along the Ely's Ford Road. As the Confederate advance moved eastward across his front, Meade stood in the ideal position to deal a devastating flank attack. He awaited the order to strike with growing impatience, but Hooker remained mute.

HOOKER IS RENDERED INSENSIBLE

Hooker had established his headquarters at the Chancellorsville house, and Confederate artillery had already hit the building several times. At about 9:00 a.m., as Hooker observed the battle from the porch near the front entrance of the house, another round struck solidly against the pillar near where Hooker stood. The cannonball split the heavy column in two, and half of it crashed into Hooker. He fell to the floor and lay insensible for half an hour or more. At

Below: Dead soldiers of William Barksdale's Mississippi Brigade line the Sunken Road of the Second Battle of Fredericksburg. The photograph was taken by Union officer Captain Andrew J. Russell.

HOOKER'S LEADERSHIP

There is perhaps no better example in the Civil War of one general totally dominating another than what Lee did to Hooker at Chancellorsville. Hooker had a brilliant strategic plan to gain Lee's flank, and the plan's initial execution was flawless. Hooker's only planning error was in keeping his cavalry out of touch with his headquarters. While Stoneman's raid caused some excitement in Richmond, it had virtually no effect on Lee and left Hooker without his main intelligence-gathering asset.

After achieving the initial surprise, however, Hooker proceeded to make one mistake after another. Instead of fighting at Chancellorsville to win, he fought so as not to lose. He became tentative and cautious and forfeited his initial advantage. His decision to halt at Chancellorsville on April 30 rather than pushing on to Banks' Ford and connecting the wings of his army created a vulnerability that Lee could exploit. The next day, Hooker pulled back in the face of Jackson's smaller but more aggressive force and completely surrendered the initiative in the campaign.

While Howard and his division commanders must also share some of the blame for the Federal flank's lack of security, Hooker, as the commander, did nothing to fulfill this critical responsibility during the preparation of the defense. Had Stoneman's cavalry been available to screen the flank, the problem would likely have been abated.

Even after Jackson's stunning but incomplete success on the flank, Hooker still had a chance to recover. The Confederates were disorganized and outnumbered. A more resolute Hooker could have counterattacked and turned the Confederate position, but instead he withdrew. Even to this point, the damage the Army of the Potomac and its commander had suffered was much more psychological than physical, and it is therein that lies Hooker's undoing. Hooker's failure at Chancellorsville was a failure of the nerve.

Contemporary observers and modern-day historians have long debated what exactly happened to Hooker. How could the self-assured Hooker, who once bragged, "May God have mercy on General Lee, for I will have none," be reduced to such a state? Theories range from being shell-shocked to being a coward, from being drunk to being not drunk, from suffering a nervous breakdown to simply being outgeneraled, and from being unintelligent to being afraid of Lee. For his part, Hooker dismissed all these possible explanations. "For once I lost confidence in Hooker," he told Major General Abner Doubleday, "and that is all there was to it."

this point the Confederates were winning the battle, but its final outcome was not yet decided. Hooker still had numerous reserves available to throw against the exposed Confederate left flank and turn defeat into victory. Instead, Hooker took no action as he recovered from his injury and refused to relinquish full control to Couch, his second in command. Rather than counterattacking, Hooker withdrew north of Chancellorsville around noon.

In the meantime, Sedgwick's attack at Fredericksburg had defeated Early's small force, and his troops were now moving west, threatening Lee's success at Chancellorsville. A hodgepodge Confederate force, built largely around Brigadier General Cadmus Wilcox's brigade, found good defensive terrain at Salem Church to resist the Federal advance. By 4:00 p.m., Wilcox had been driven inside the church itself and was using the building as a fort. Learning of Sedgwick's success, Lee had earlier sent four brigades under McLaws's command to aid Wilcox, and these reinforcements arrived just in time to strengthen the Confederate line. About an hour later, Sedgwick launched a series of attacks that lasted until dark, but was unable to break through the defense.

With Hooker still inactive, Lee was able to send additional strength to battle Sedgwick shortly after daylight on May 4. Leaving only Jackson's old corps, now commanded by Stuart, to contain the Federals around Chancellorsville, Lee sent Anderson to assail Sedgwick. That meant only 25,000 Confederates were keeping watch on Hooker's 75,000, but by now Lee had clearly taken the measure of Hooker and considered the risk small. It was almost dark before all the Confederate forces were in position to attack, but they then kept nearly continuous pressure on Sedgwick throughout the night. Against this new threat, Sedgwick decided to withdraw northwest across the Rappahannock near Banks' Ford. Hooker knew Sedgwick was in trouble, but had done nothing to help him.

The campaign wound down over the next few days. Lee was frustrated by his inability to destroy Hooker and was upset when he learned the Federals had withdrawn across the Rappahannock. When Brigadier General Dorsey Pender brought Lee the disappointing news, Lee vented, "Why, General Pender, that is what you young men always do. You allow those people to get away. I tell you what to do, but you don't do it. Go after them and damage them all you can!" By then, however, Hooker was safely out of harm's way.

In actuality, Lee would have been ill advised to attack Hooker on May 6. Hooker's withdrawal in effect spared Lee the costly mistake of attacking a strong defensive position and suffering unacceptable losses. Many observers point to Lee's stubborn desire to press the attack at Chancellorsville as an indication that his offensive strategic approach was simply out of touch with the limited Confederate resources available to him.

Lee inflicted 17,000 casualties on Hooker at Chancellorsville, suffering 13,000 himself. Still, Lee's losses represented one-fifth of his force. Even great victories such as Chancellorsville sapped the Army of Northern Virginia of manpower it could ill afford to lose. But of all Lee's losses, the one most critical to the Confederate cause was Stonewall Jackson. Jackson's left arm had been amputated as a result of his wound, and at first it appeared that he would recover. Complications soon developed, however, and Jackson died. When Lee first learned of the amputation, he said that Jackson "has lost his left arm, but I have lost my right." Now with Jackson gone, Lee would be without his most capable general.

The victory at Chancellorsville gave Lee the momentum he needed to launch a second invasion into Northern territory, but at the ensuing Battle of Gettysburg, Lee would sorely miss Jackson, the one subordinate who could make Lee's audacious strategies work. The Army of Northern Virginia would never again have the vigor it possessed before Jackson's death. Chancellorsville was an amazing victory for Lee, but a costly one as well.

LEE'S LEADERSHIP

Lee's Chancellorsville victory was among the most lopsided in the Civil War, but some observers attribute the outcome more to Hooker's failure than to Lee's brilliance. In fact, they argue, had Hooker shown stronger leadership, the results would have been disastrous for Lee. By dividing his army, Lee did take an exceptional risk, but such audacity is what makes the great commanders great. What mitigated Lee's risk-taking was his uncanny ability to read his opponents. Whether against Major General George McClellan on the Virginia peninsula or against Lieutenant General Ulysses S. Grant at Spotsylvania, Lee was somehow able to anticipate the actions of his opponents. Once Lee saw Hooker pull back in the face of Jackson at Zoan Church, Lee knew that he was in control. From then on he forced his will on Hooker, and Hooker submitted.

In addition to understanding his opponent, another characteristic of Lee's generalship that served him well at Chancellorsville was his use of intelligence. As an engineer serving with Winfield Scott in Mexico, Lee had performed numerous daring reconnaissance missions such as at Cerro Gordo, where he found a concealed route to turn the Mexican army. In Mexico, Lee learned the importance of reconnaissance and how to act upon intelligence of the enemy and the terrain. Indeed, his entire strategic approach came to be based on such knowledge.

Lee greatly benefited from the talents of Jeb Stuart. The cavalry was the premier intelligence-gathering source in the Civil War, and certainly at this stage of the war the Confederates enjoyed a great advantage in this department. The Federals simply had nothing to match Stuart and, at Chancellorsville, what cavalry Hooker had, he frittered away on Stoneman's raid. Stuart, on the other hand, had a great knack for interpreting what he saw on his rides and providing Lee with a perceptive intelligence summation. Stuart's discovery that Hooker's flank was "in the air" was the information that made Jackson's turning movement conceptually possible. Lee then used the skilled mapmaker Jedediah Hotchkiss and local residents to find the exact route that would make this concept practical. At Chancellorsville, Lee's understanding of the enemy and the terrain was critical to his success.

GRANT VS. PEMBERTON

VICKSBURG, 1863

During the Vicksburg Campaign, Major General Ulysses S. Grant and his Federal Army of the Tennessee struggled against Lieutenant General John Pemberton, commander of the Confederate Department of Mississippi and East Louisiana, for control of the Mississippi River.

While the campaign ended with the siege of Vicksburg, the true brilliance of Grant's generalship lay in his use of maneuver to trap Pemberton's force inside the city. The Battle of Champion Hill was decisive in the campaign because it was after that defeat that Pemberton withdrew to Vicksburg and was subjected to Grant's siege. The only way a besieged force can survive is either by breaking out itself or by being relieved by the attack of an outside force. Neither of these two possibilities was going to happen at Vicksburg, and the Federals won control of the strategic Mississippi

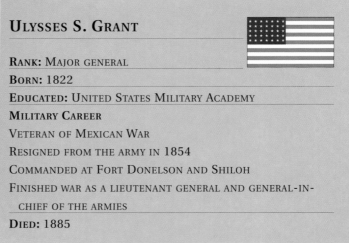

ULYSSES S. GRANT

RANK: MAJOR GENERAL

BORN: 1822

EDUCATED: UNITED STATES MILITARY ACADEMY

MILITARY CAREER

VETERAN OF MEXICAN WAR

RESIGNED FROM THE ARMY IN 1854

COMMANDED AT FORT DONELSON AND SHILOH

FINISHED WAR AS A LIEUTENANT GENERAL AND GENERAL-IN-
   CHIEF OF THE ARMIES

DIED: 1885

River. The campaign clearly showed both Grant's genius as a modern general and Pemberton's limitations. In both men, these results were shaped by experiences they had had earlier in their careers.

PRELIMINARIES

The Mississippi River dominated the western theater of the Civil War. It was the main north–south artery in the interior of the United States, and farmers in places like Illinois and Wisconsin had long relied on it to get their goods to the market. In fact, at the time of the Civil War, the Mississippi River was the single most important economic feature of the continent. With the outbreak of hostilities, Confederate forces closed the Mississippi to navigation, which threatened to strangle Northern commercial interests. For the Confederacy, the agricultural produce of the relatively peaceful trans-Mississippi Confederacy was making a substantial contribution to the Confederate armies in Virginia and Tennessee. If the Federals could gain control of the Mississippi River, they would not only secure the free flow of their internal commerce, they would cut the Confederacy in two in a way that challenged its very identity as a nation.

Lieutenant General Winfield Scott had recognized this importance of the Mississippi in the opening stages of the war. His original Anaconda Plan had envisioned an amphibious attack on New Orleans from the Gulf of Mexico that would serve as a springboard for securing the Mississippi and splitting the South in two. Although Scott's plan had been rejected, various Federal operations at places like Columbus, Kentucky, and Island No. 10 near the Kentucky-Tennessee border had in fact gobbled up control of much of the river. On May 1, 1862, Admiral David Farragut had captured New Orleans and began working upstream. By November, the Confederates controlled only the stretch of river between Vicksburg, Mississippi, and Port Hudson, Louisiana. Still, that was enough to block Federal commerce and maintain a tenuous rail connection with the trans-Mississippi Confederacy. President Lincoln had understood the situation and put it in perspective. "See what a lot of land these fellows hold, of which Vicksburg is the key! The war can never be brought to a close until that key is in our pocket," he told his civil and military leaders.

VICKSBURG

Date	May 18–July 4, 1863
Location	Warren County, Mississippi
Result	Union victory

Strength

| Union: Army of the Tennessee (77,000) | Confederate: Army of the Mississippi (33,000) |

Casualties and losses

10,142	9,091
1,581 killed	1,413 killed
7,554 wounded	3,878 wounded
1,007 missing	3,800 missing
	29,000 surrendered

JOHN C. PEMBERTON

RANK: LIEUTENANT GENERAL

BORN: 1814

EDUCATED: UNITED STATES MILITARY ACADEMY

MILITARY CAREER

VETERAN OF MEXICAN WAR

COMMANDED DEPARTMENT OF SOUTH CAROLINA, GEORGIA, AND FLORIDA

RESIGNED MAY 18, 1864, AND FINISHED THE WAR AS A LIEUTENANT COLONEL OF ARTILLERY

DIED: 1881

"We can take all the northern ports of the Confederacy, and they can defy us from Vicksburg."

TERRAIN

What made Vicksburg so formidable was the terrain. About 300 miles downstream from Memphis, Tennessee, Vicksburg stood at a hairpin turn in the Mississippi and dominated the river from a high bluff. The river channel there narrowed to a quarter of a mile and ran 100 feet deep. The current velocity was about six knots, making navigation treacherous. Under such geographic conditions, the Confederate guns at Vicksburg could block any river transportation.

Foreboding terrain protected the city from the land approaches as well. To the north of Vicksburg was the Yazoo River

Below: Building, repairing, guarding, and attacking railroads consumed much of the Civil War activity. Railroads represented the key strategic means of moving troops and supplies for both sides.

Delta, which sprawled along the eastern bank of the Mississippi for about 140 miles. In some places, it was forty miles wide. The delta was a patchwork of swamps and waterways that would bar the way of any large army attempting to move overland. What roads that did exist were made of dirt that quickly turned to mud in the heavy rains.

On the western side of the Mississippi in Louisiana, the land was just as flat and swampy, if not more so. Roads there would have to be corduroyed with logs to support military traffic.

FEDERAL FORCES

Major General Ulysses S. Grant was in command of the Federal Army of the Tennessee. Ostensibly Grant controlled four corps, but most of his Sixteenth Corps, led by Major General Stephen Hurlbut, remained in Memphis during the Vicksburg Campaign performing rear area missions. This left Grant with three corps, consisting of 44,000 effectives, to form his maneuvering force during the campaign.

Two of Grant's corps commanders were capable and highly trusted. Major General William Sherman commanded the Fifteenth Corps and Major General James McPherson led the Seventeenth Corps. Sherman was the more senior of the two and had greater experience, but McPherson was competent and already showed great promise. Grant's other corps commander, Major General John McClernand, was more of a problem. A prewar Democratic Party congressman, McClernand had used his political connections to persuade President Lincoln to allow him to raise the Eighteenth Corps for what McClernand envisioned as an independent expedition to open the Mississippi. McClernand was ambitious and self-serving, and would prove to be a continual source of irritation to Grant.

Where the Federals had a dramatic advantage over the Confederates was with their naval forces. Flag Officer David D. Porter commanded the Mississippi River Squadron, which consisted of sixty combat vessels. About twenty of these

Above: Mexican War hero Winfield Scott (1786–1866) profoundly influenced many Civil War generals, including Grant.

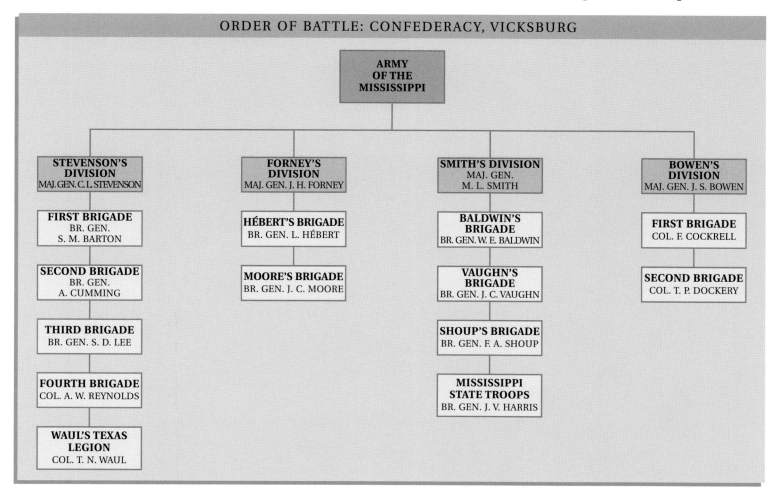

ORDER OF BATTLE: CONFEDERACY, VICKSBURG

- **ARMY OF THE MISSISSIPPI**
  - **STEVENSON'S DIVISION** MAJ. GEN. C. L. STEVENSON
    - **FIRST BRIGADE** BR. GEN. S. M. BARTON
    - **SECOND BRIGADE** BR. GEN. A. CUMMING
    - **THIRD BRIGADE** BR. GEN. S. D. LEE
    - **FOURTH BRIGADE** COL. A. W. REYNOLDS
    - **WAUL'S TEXAS LEGION** COL. T. N. WAUL
  - **FORNEY'S DIVISION** MAJ. GEN. J. H. FORNEY
    - **HÉBERT'S BRIGADE** BR. GEN. L. HÉBERT
    - **MOORE'S BRIGADE** BR. GEN. J. C. MOORE
  - **SMITH'S DIVISION** MAJ. GEN. M. L. SMITH
    - **BALDWIN'S BRIGADE** BR. GEN. W. E. BALDWIN
    - **VAUGHN'S BRIGADE** BR. GEN. J. C. VAUGHN
    - **SHOUP'S BRIGADE** BR. GEN. F. A. SHOUP
    - **MISSISSIPPI STATE TROOPS** BR. GEN. J. V. HARRIS
  - **BOWEN'S DIVISION** MAJ. GEN. J. S. BOWEN
    - **FIRST BRIGADE** COL. F. COCKRELL
    - **SECOND BRIGADE** COL. T. P. DOCKERY

were available at any one time for use in the Vicksburg Campaign. Of those that ultimately participated, thirteen were ironclads. But while the Mississippi River Squadron represented a powerful contribution to Grant's effort, Porter reported to the Navy Department in Washington rather than to Grant. Neither Grant nor Porter had the authority to act as a joint commander and direct the combined efforts of the army and the navy. Instead, Grant and Porter would have to cooperate with each other in order to achieve unity of effort.

CONFEDERATE FORCES

Commanding the far-flung Confederate Department of Mississippi and East

Below: Stephen Hurlbut's (1815–82) Civil War service was marred by corruption and drunkenness. He remained in Memphis for most of the Vicksburg Campaign.

Louisiana was Lieutenant General John Pemberton. Pemberton was responsible for not just the river defenses at Vicksburg and Port Hudson but also the field forces confronting Grant in northern Mississippi. To handle these wide threats, Pemberton had more than 43,000 effectives organized into five infantry divisions with no intermediate corps headquarters. The commanders of the divisions in Pemberton's charge were a mixed bag. Brigadier General John Bowen was Pemberton's most tactically proficient subordinate, but Pemberton also had to deal with the likes of Brigadier General William Loring, who was antagonistic and showed little loyalty to or respect for his commander.

Pemberton also suffered from a paucity of naval support. By the time of Vicksburg, the River Defense Fleet had been reduced to possessing no ironclads and only a handful of gunboats. The Confederates did succeed in capturing two Federal ironclads in February 1863, but this brief triumph scarcely elevated the Confederate naval prowess.

The final reality that conspired against Pemberton was the Confederate departmental system, a convoluted command structure based on geography and not operational need. Pemberton's department ended at the Mississippi River, and he had no control over Confederate forces on the other side.

THE FIRST ATTEMPT

So with the disadvantage of terrain, a rough parity in troop strength, and a huge naval advantage, Grant opened his first attempt to wrest control of the Mississippi River in November 1862. Grant's plan involved advances on two axes, which were to converge in the Vicksburg-Jackson region. Grant personally led 45,000 troops southward from near La Grange in western Tennessee while Sherman conducted a river-borne expedition from Memphis to the Yazoo River just above Vicksburg. Grant's column advanced methodically, rebuilding the Mississippi Central Railroad as it went. Pemberton seemed reluctant to give battle, but on December

20 he received a stroke of good fortune when Confederate cavalry under Brigadier General Nathan B. Forrest and Major General Earl Van Dorn raided Grant's extended line of communications in several places. Forrest wrecked a good portion of the railroad from which Grant received his supplies, and Van Dorn destroyed the major Federal advanced depot at Holly Springs. These losses compelled Grant to call off the overland campaign and return to Tennessee. In the process, however, Grant made conclusions about his ability to live off the countryside that would be very influential later in the campaign.

Sherman's effort fared even worse than Grant's. Sherman had sailed down the Mississippi to Chickasaw Bluffs, just north of Vicksburg. There, Sherman was supposed to seize Vicksburg while Grant distracted Pemberton. Grant's retreat after Holly Springs, however, allowed Pemberton to bolster his lines at Chickasaw Bluffs, terrain that already favored the defender and provided little room for offensive maneuver. On December 29, Sherman suffered a stiff repulse and, like Grant, had to withdraw.

While Sherman was in the process of returning north, McClernand reclaimed the troops he considered Sherman had "borrowed" from him and proceeded to lead an expedition up the Arkansas River that ultimately captured the Confederate fort at Arkansas Post on January 10, 1863. As McClernand planned more operations in the interior of Arkansas, Grant ordered him to return with his force to the Vicksburg area. McClernand, who disputed Grant's authority over him, reluctantly complied, and subsequent orders from Major General Henry Halleck compelled McClernand to bring his force under Grant's command. Tensions continued to exist between Grant and McClernand, however, and Grant would eventually find an opportunity to relieve his troublesome subordinate on June 18. For the time being, though, Grant decided that his newly united force would operate against Vicksburg by way of the river, not overland. On January 30, Grant established a headquarters at Young's Point, Louisiana, on the west bank of the Mississippi River, just ten miles above Vicksburg, and got to work.

FAILED SCHEMES

Before the Army Corps of Engineers tamed it in the twentieth century, the Mississippi would periodically flood,

Below: The Federal naval advantage was especially pronounced by the presence of thirteen ironclads in Porter's fleet.

more or less inundating the entire floodplain. During these floods, only the tops of the levees remained above water, and many of the tributaries and abandoned channels that surrounded the river were rendered temporarily navigable. Such was the case in early 1863 when unusually heavy rains filled the floodplain and kept the river well above flood stage from mid-January until early April. Grant endeavored to use this situation to his advantage.

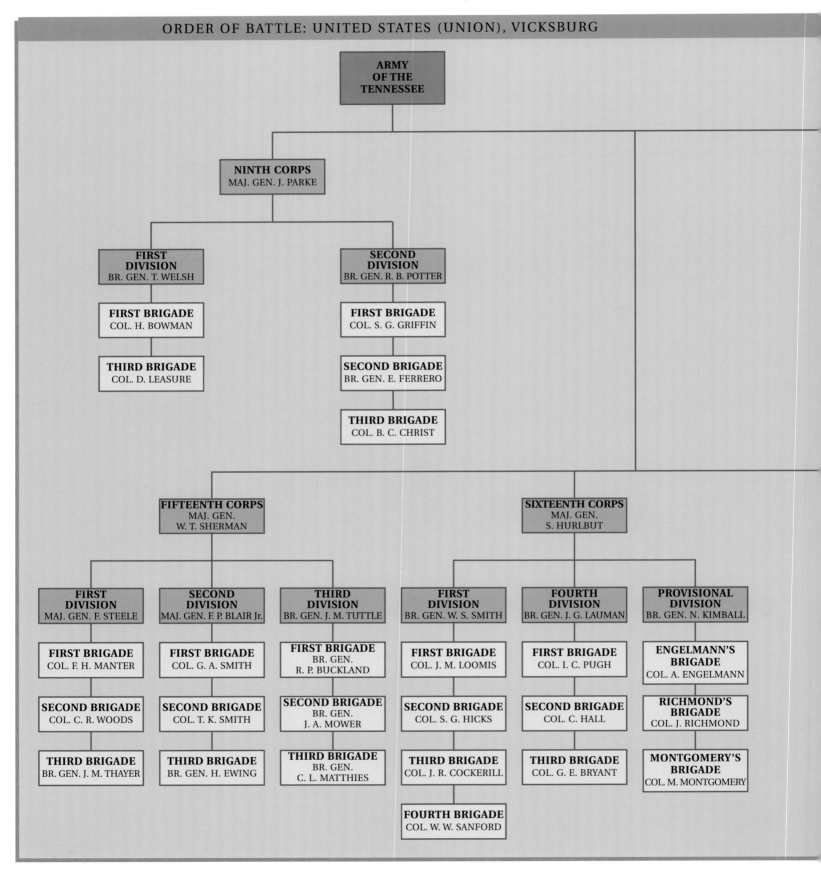

ORDER OF BATTLE: UNITED STATES (UNION), VICKSBURG

- **ARMY OF THE TENNESSEE**
  - **NINTH CORPS**
    MAJ. GEN. J. PARKE
    - **FIRST DIVISION**
      BR. GEN. T. WELSH
      - **FIRST BRIGADE**
        COL. H. BOWMAN
      - **THIRD BRIGADE**
        COL. D. LEASURE
    - **SECOND DIVISION**
      BR. GEN. R. B. POTTER
      - **FIRST BRIGADE**
        COL. S. G. GRIFFIN
      - **SECOND BRIGADE**
        BR. GEN. E. FERRERO
      - **THIRD BRIGADE**
        COL. B. C. CHRIST
  - **FIFTEENTH CORPS**
    MAJ. GEN. W. T. SHERMAN
    - **FIRST DIVISION**
      MAJ. GEN. F. STEELE
      - **FIRST BRIGADE**
        COL. F. H. MANTER
      - **SECOND BRIGADE**
        COL. C. R. WOODS
      - **THIRD BRIGADE**
        BR. GEN. J. M. THAYER
    - **SECOND DIVISION**
      MAJ. GEN. F. P. BLAIR Jr.
      - **FIRST BRIGADE**
        COL. G. A. SMITH
      - **SECOND BRIGADE**
        COL. T. K. SMITH
      - **THIRD BRIGADE**
        BR. GEN. H. EWING
    - **THIRD DIVISION**
      BR. GEN. J. M. TUTTLE
      - **FIRST BRIGADE**
        BR. GEN. R. P. BUCKLAND
      - **SECOND BRIGADE**
        BR. GEN. J. A. MOWER
      - **THIRD BRIGADE**
        BR. GEN. C. L. MATTHIES
  - **SIXTEENTH CORPS**
    MAJ. GEN. S. HURLBUT
    - **FIRST DIVISION**
      BR. GEN. W. S. SMITH
      - **FIRST BRIGADE**
        COL. J. M. LOOMIS
      - **SECOND BRIGADE**
        COL. S. G. HICKS
      - **THIRD BRIGADE**
        COL. J. R. COCKERILL
      - **FOURTH BRIGADE**
        COL. W. W. SANFORD
    - **FOURTH DIVISION**
      BR. GEN. J. G. LAUMAN
      - **FIRST BRIGADE**
        COL. I. C. PUGH
      - **SECOND BRIGADE**
        COL. C. HALL
      - **THIRD BRIGADE**
        COL. G. E. BRYANT
    - **PROVISIONAL DIVISION**
      BR. GEN. N. KIMBALL
      - **ENGELMANN'S BRIGADE**
        COL. A. ENGELMANN
      - **RICHMOND'S BRIGADE**
        COL. J. RICHMOND
      - **MONTGOMERY'S BRIGADE**
        COL. M. MONTGOMERY

Although he was just a few miles north of Vicksburg, Grant still faced the problem of getting into a position from which he could assault what had become "the Gibraltar of the West." Grant had to get his army out of the floodplain and onto high ground on the Vicksburg side of the river. The heavy rains and high river levels effectively eliminated any sort of direct approach across the lowlands. Instead, Grant explored ways to bypass the Vicksburg fortifications by

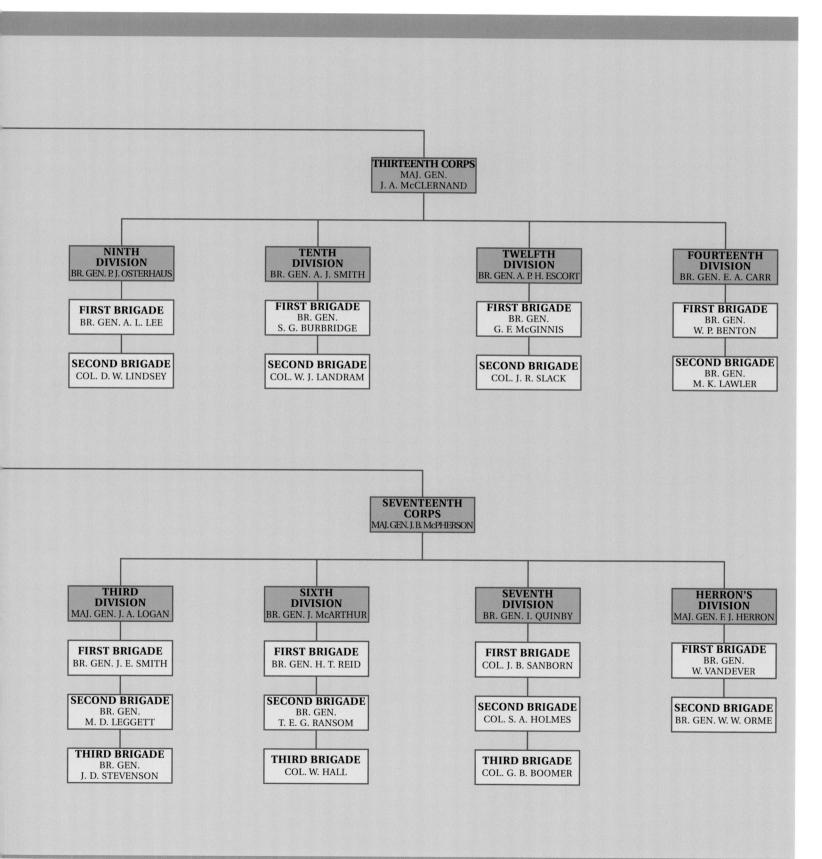

Right: Confederate defenses along the high bluffs around Vicksburg made "running the gauntlet" particularly hazardous, but Porter accomplished the daring mission. Pictured are seven gunboats, a tug, a captured Confederate ram, three transport ships, and coal barges that ran the gauntlet of thirty-seven guns on the night of April 16, 1863.

water so as to approach the city from the less-protected land side.

Thus, from January through March 1863, Grant tried four separate plans to break through to Vicksburg. First was the Lake Providence scheme in which his engineers tried to connect a series of creeks, old river channels, swamps, and bayous into a waterway capable of carrying vessels around Vicksburg to the south. Once that was accomplished, Grant intended to march his army down to the vessels, which would then ferry the soldiers across the river to the dry ground on the eastern shore. After weeks of arduous labor, the plan was abandoned. Next came the canal bypass scheme in which Grant tried to dig a canal across the peninsula formed by the great bend in the river directly opposite Vicksburg. Grant hoped this action would change the course of the Mississippi so that its main channel would bypass Vicksburg. This effort also failed and gave way to the Steele's Bayou expedition. Similar to the Lake Providence scheme, this plan hoped to create a waterway through the Yazoo Delta. But Confederate sharpshooters eventually convinced the Federal gunboats to turn back from the narrow passageway. Finally, Grant tried to create a waterway running from the Yazoo Pass at the northern end of the delta. Like its predecessors, this scheme failed.

In spite of these abortive efforts, Grant never lost his optimism. He later claimed that he never expected the schemes to work, but only undertook them to keep his men busy and to create the illusion of activity necessary to silence his critics. Fortuitously for Grant, the failures also created a certain amount of bewilderment in his opponent Pemberton. The seemingly haphazard endeavors gave the Confederate general the impression Grant was operating everywhere and left Pemberton in a state of confusion when Grant finally attacked in earnest after the water levels began to drop in late March. In April, Grant set aside his "bayou expeditions" and decided to outflank Vicksburg on foot.

APRIL CAMPAIGN

Grant's new strategy was to avoid a frontal assault on the Confederate defenses by marching his army down the west side of the Mississippi to a point below Vicksburg. There the troops would meet vessels that would ferry the men across the river. To accomplish this, the transports would have to run the gauntlet past the Vicksburg batteries. It was a daring move, but other vessels had made the run and Grant was willing to take the chance.

On March 31, Grant began his overland march with McClernand in the lead, followed by McPherson. Sherman's corps stayed behind to protect the base of operations above Vicksburg. To create a diversion, Grant sent a detachment commanded by Major General Frederick Steele to Greenville, Mississippi, where the Federals then moved inland and operated along Deer Creek. The idea was to convince Pemberton that Grant had abandoned his campaign against Vicksburg in favor of operations upriver. In addition to this ruse, several Federal steamers returning north toward Memphis further strengthened, albeit unintentionally, Pemberton's perception that Grant was withdrawing.

The biggest diversion, however, was Colonel Benjamin Grierson's cavalry raid. On April 17, Grant sent Grierson and 17,000 men from La Grange through Mississippi on a generally diagonal route from northeast to southwest. Along the way, Grierson sent out small detachments in various directions. The haphazard pattern of the Federal appearances convinced Pemberton that the Federals were everywhere and left him in a quandary as to how to respond.

With these movements and diversions in motion, it was time to get the Federal river transports below Vicksburg. On the night of April 16–17, Porter ran the batteries at Vicksburg with eight of his gunboats and three transports. More steamers made the dash five days later. With Porter's vessels south of Vicksburg, Grant now had the means to cross to the east bank of the Mississippi without facing the stiffest Confederate defenses. By the time Pemberton figured out what Grant was up to, it was too late.

GRAND GULF AND PORT GIBSON

As Grierson eluded Pemberton's feeble attempts to run him down, Grant launched another diversion. This time, Sherman conducted a demonstration at Snyder's Bluff north of Vicksburg to distract Pemberton from Grant's main effort at Grand Gulf. Grand Gulf lay about thirty miles south of Vicksburg and it was the first place below the city where the river met the bluffs. There the Confederates had built two forts and

established a formidable defense. Grant's plan was for Porter's ships to shell the Confederates into submission and then ferry McClernand's men across the river.

On April 28, eight Federal gunboats began a fierce bombardment that lasted five hours but could not defeat the staunch defense of Brigadier General John Bowen's Confederates. Porter assessed Grand Gulf to be "the strongest place on the Mississippi," but the setback was only a momentary one for the Federals. Grant received intelligence from a runaway slave that, just twelve miles south of Grand Gulf, there was an undefended crossing at Bruinsburg. Grant moved his men there and began crossing the Mississippi on April 30. By the end of the day, Grant had 22,000 Federal troops on the Mississippi side of the river.

Poor intelligence combined with Grant's diversions had left Pemberton confused and unprepared for the Federal attack. The Confederates had just 8,000 troops in the Grand Gulf area, and Bowen rushed these to Port Gibson to meet McClernand's advance inland. The outmanned Bowen fought tenaciously, but McClernand, eventually reinforced by McPherson, forced the Confederates to withdraw. Pemberton had missed his opportunity to defeat Grant before the Federals were safely ensconced on high, dry ground on the Mississippi side of the river. The Confederates evacuated the outflanked fortress at Grand Gulf, and Porter promptly occupied it and began turning it into a logistical base.

His foothold in Mississippi secure, Grant paused from May 3–9 to evaluate his options, bring his supply trains forward, and allow Sherman's corps to join the main body. The addition of Sherman's two divisions gave Grant 42,000 men, with more reinforcements and supplies arriving regularly.

LOGISTICS

Grant's location afforded him plenty of options. He was squarely between Vicksburg and Port Hudson, Louisiana, and about forty miles west of Jackson. In addition to being the capital of

Above: Major General John A. McClernand's Thirteenth Corps led the way through the Louisiana wetlands, provided the vanguard across the Mississippi, fought the Battles of Port Gibson and Champion Hill, and penetrated the defenses of Vicksburg.

Below: This Confederate cavalryman carries a guidon, or pennant-shaped flag. The two chevrons on this soldier's sleeve indicate he is a corporal.

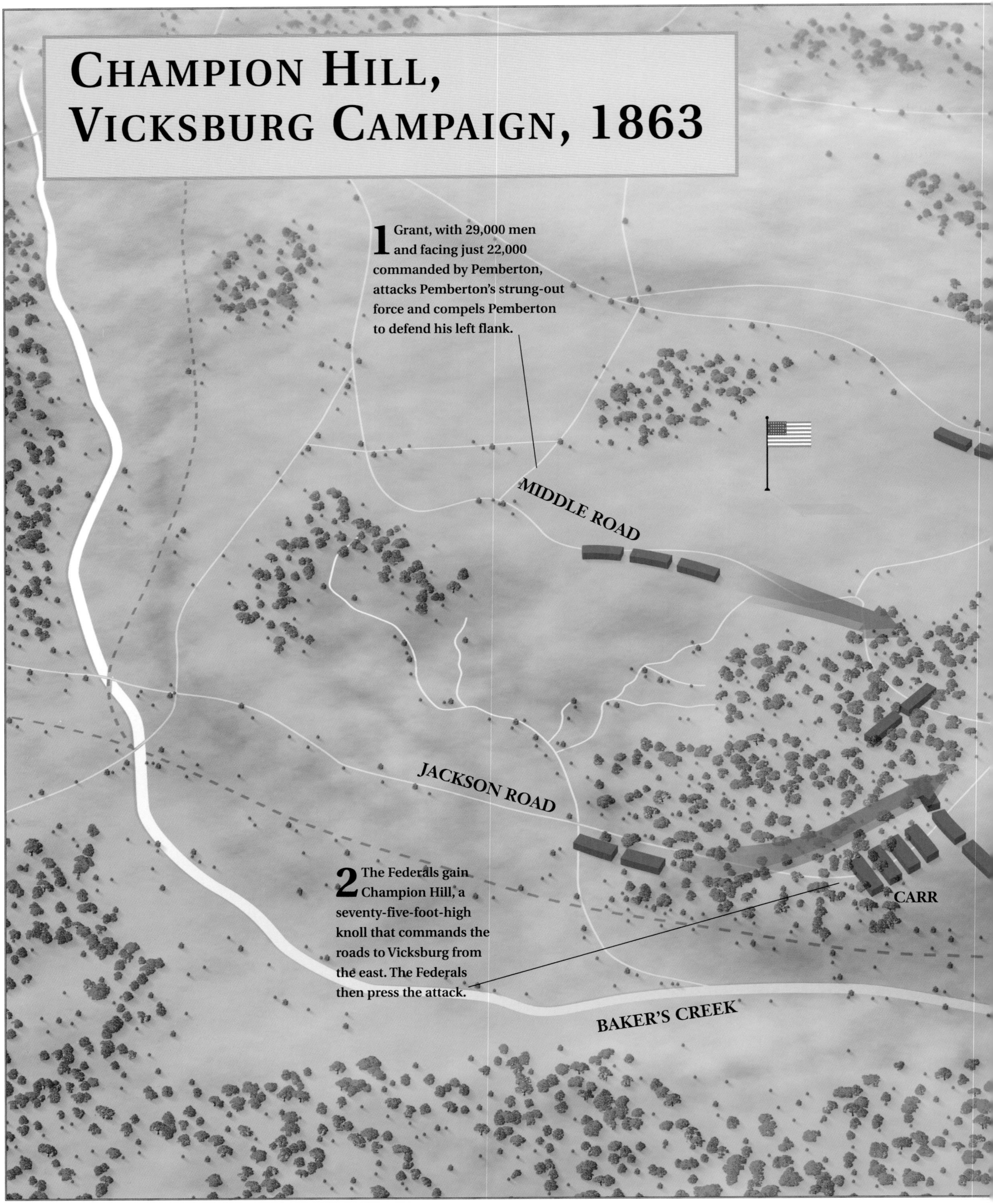

CHAMPION HILL, VICKSBURG CAMPAIGN, 1863

1 Grant, with 29,000 men and facing just 22,000 commanded by Pemberton, attacks Pemberton's strung-out force and compels Pemberton to defend his left flank.

MIDDLE ROAD

JACKSON ROAD

2 The Federals gain Champion Hill, a seventy-five-foot-high knoll that commands the roads to Vicksburg from the east. The Federals then press the attack.

CARR

BAKER'S CREEK

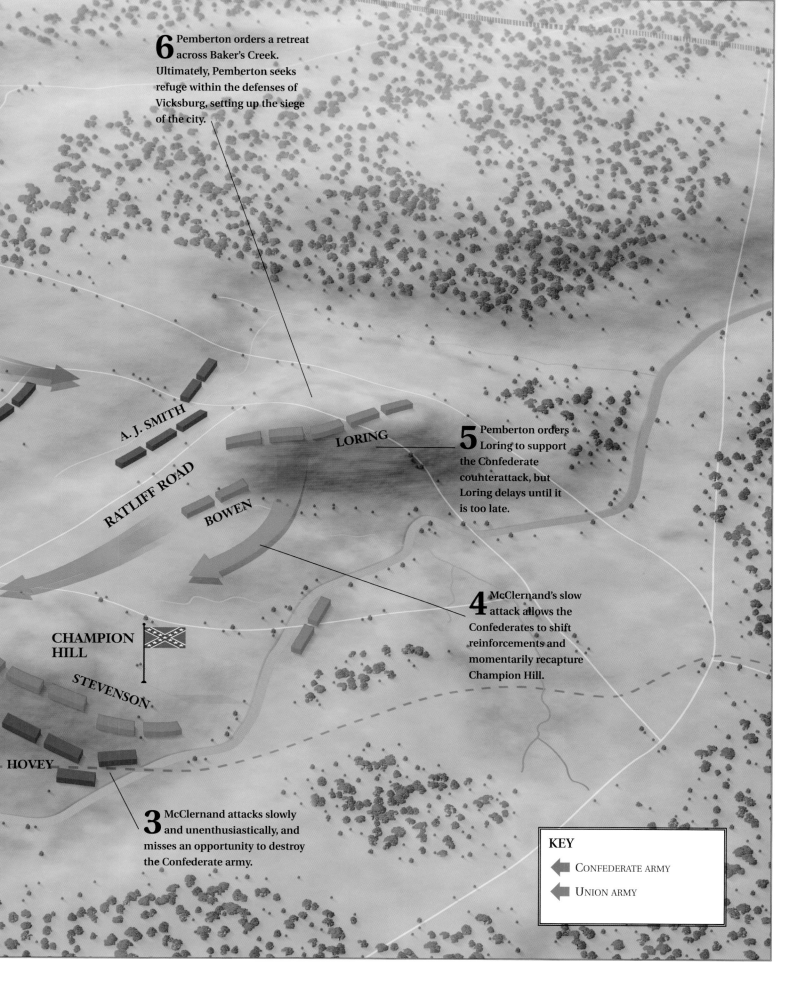

6 Pemberton orders a retreat across Baker's Creek. Ultimately, Pemberton seeks refuge within the defenses of Vicksburg, setting up the siege of the city.

A. J. SMITH

LORING

RATLIFF ROAD

BOWEN

5 Pemberton orders Loring to support the Confederate counterattack, but Loring delays until it is too late.

CHAMPION HILL

STEVENSON

4 McClernand's slow attack allows the Confederates to shift reinforcements and momentarily recapture Champion Hill.

HOVEY

3 McClernand attacks slowly and unenthusiastically, and misses an opportunity to destroy the Confederate army.

KEY

Confederate army

Union army

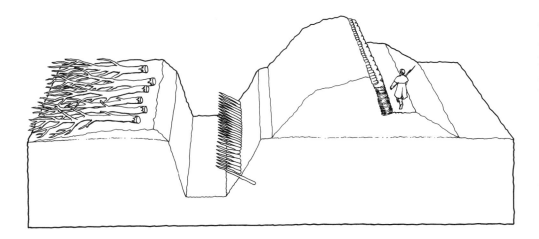

Above: Abatis, formed by felled trees, sharpened and pointed toward the enemy, were common obstacles employed in the Civil War. These defenses were designed to break up the impetus and formations of enemy attacks while providing superb protection from rifle and cannon fire.

Mississippi, Jackson was the site of the convergence of four railroads. One of these, the Southern Railroad, was Vicksburg's main line of supply. If Grant could cut that railroad, he would make Vicksburg much more vulnerable to attack. However, if Grant marched toward Jackson, he would be exposing his own line of supply, and the earlier raids of Forrest and Van Dorn had made Grant well aware of the consequences of such a risk.

While Grant considered these circumstances, he received word that Major General Nathaniel Banks had begun operating on the Red River and would not be able to join Grant for an attack on Port Hudson for several days. With this new development, Grant "determined to move independently of Banks, cut loose from my base, destroy the rebel force in rear of Vicksburg or invest or capture the city." Grant proposed to live off the land.

GRANT REDUCES HIS DEPENDENCE

Grant exaggerated when he said he "cut loose" from his line of supply. In fact, he would also benefit from his newly established base at Grand Gulf and a steady stream of wagons to keep him supplied. But while Grant still received supplies by wagons, he was also drawing from the Confederate countryside. Even scavenger teams brought in supplies. The result was "an abundant array of farm vehicles, ranging from long-tongued wagons designed for hauling cotton bales, to elegant plantation carriages, upholstered phaetons, and surreys. The vehicles were drawn by an equally odd assortment of horses, mules, and oxen—probably the most unmilitary military train ever assembled." The system worked. One of Grant's privates bragged, "We live fat." In deciding to reduce his logistics, Grant was able to facilitate maneuvers.

With this option now open, Grant set off in a northeastward direction, up the watershed between the Big Black and Bayou Pierre, with an objective of cutting the railroad link between Vicksburg and Jackson. The Federals advanced on a wide front, with McClernand's corps on the left, Sherman's coming up in the center, and McPherson's on the right. The multiple axes both facilitated foraging and kept Pemberton guessing.

RAYMOND AND JACKSON

As Grant cut a swath toward central Mississippi, Pemberton offered little resistance. Divided by instructions from President Davis to "hold both Vicksburg and Port Hudson" and from General Joe Johnston to strike Grant, Pemberton played it safe and consolidated his forces west of the Big Black to protect Vicksburg. Pemberton thus kept two of his five divisions near the Vicksburg fortifications and used the other three to fortify and guard the Big Black River near Edwards. In the meantime, Davis sent reinforcements to Jackson and told Johnston to take command in Mississippi.

For the time being, however, the forces in Jackson consisted only of a small brigade that Brigadier General John Gregg had recently brought there from Port Hudson. Thinking he faced only a small detachment, Gregg marched out of Jackson and encountered an entire division of McPherson's corps at Raymond on May 12. Gregg fought valiantly but was simply outnumbered. After an engagement that was characterized by uncoordinated attacks and counterattacks, Gregg pulled back to Jackson.

Gregg's tenacious resistance, as well as reports that Johnston was assembling an army in Jackson, convinced Grant to modify his plans. Rather than risk being caught in between Pemberton and

Johnston, Grant decided to shift his objective from the railroad and first deal with Johnston before then turning his attention to Pemberton. On May 13, Grant sent Sherman and McPherson on two separate axes toward Jackson, while McClernand waited in reserve to prevent any advance by Pemberton. That same day, Johnston arrived in Jackson and, betraying his predetermined pessimism for the entire affair, declared, "I am too late." Behind a small screen from Gregg, Johnston withdrew to the north. On May 14, the Federals began their assault on Jackson.

Jackson could offer little in the way of resistance to Grant, and he took the city with fewer than 300 casualties. He then proceeded to neutralize anything of military value, which led residents to nickname Jackson "Chimneyville" in allusion to the only structures left standing in the city. With Johnston out of the picture and Jackson under his control, Grant had Vicksburg isolated. He could now turn west and deal with Pemberton.

CHAMPION HILL

While Sherman remained in Jackson to finish the destruction of industrial and transportation assets, Grant sent McClernand and McPherson west. By this point Pemberton was in an advanced state of bewilderment and shattered confidence. In a council of war on May 14, his subordinates convinced him to abandon his own inclination to fight Grant from prepared positions on the Big Black and instead launch an offensive southward against Grant's line of communication. Having barely begun this movement on May 15, Pemberton received orders from Johnston to march eastward and unite forces with him near Clinton. Pursuant to this new order, Pemberton had just started to countermarch on May 16 when Grant's forces surprised the

Below: In this highly dramatized 1887 chromolithograph, Major General John Logan (1826–86), seen left of center with hat in hand, leads his Third Division of the Seventeenth Corps at Champion Hill to attack the Confederate left flank on May 16, 1863. The railroad connecting Vicksburg to Jackson is in the background. As Logan's division crashed into two brigades from Alabama and Georgia, General Grant, at the nearby Champion House, instructed a staff officer to "go down to Logan and tell him he is making history today."

"WE WERE BLOCKADED ON EVERY SIDE, COULD GET NOTHING FROM WITHOUT, SO HAD TO MAKE EVERYTHING AT HOME; AND HAVING BEEN HERETOFORE ONLY AN AGRICULTURAL PEOPLE, IT BECAME NECESSARY FOR EVERY HOME TO BE SUPPLIED WITH SPINNING WHEELS AND THE OLD-FASHIONED LOOM, IN ORDER TO MANUFACTURE CLOTHING FOR THE MEMBERS OF THE FAMILY. MY DUTIES . . . WERE NUMEROUS AND OFTEN LABORIOUS . . . AND THIS WAS THE CASE WITH THE TYPICAL SOUTHERN WOMAN."

VICTORIA V. CLAYTON, WIFE OF CONFEDERATE GENERAL HENRY D. CLAYTON OF ALABAMA, WRITING OF THE CHANGES SOUTHERN WOMEN WERE FACING AS THE WAR CLOSED IN ON THEM, IN *WHITE AND BLACK UNDER THE OLD REGIME*, 1899

Confederates in the vicinity of Champion Hill, east of Vicksburg.

The Battle of Champion Hill proved to be the decisive engagement of the campaign. Grant's preparations prior to the battle had allowed him to converge from three directions with a force ratio advantage of three to two over the Confederates. Outgeneraled, Pemberton was forced to order a broad retreat, leaving behind Brigadier General Lloyd Tilghman to act as rear guard.

Pemberton withdrew the rest of his army to the east side of the Big Black

River, where he waited for the rear guard to join him. While Pemberton lingered, McClernand struck the dejected Confederates on May 17. Pemberton escaped, thanks to some well-placed infantry and artillery on the west bank of the Big Black and the burning of the railroad bridge across the river. The Confederates had now escaped into their considerable defenses at Vicksburg and, with Grant close on his heels, Pemberton prepared to meet the Federal attack. He was safe for the time being, but his defeat at Champion Hill had cost him the

ability to maneuver and had given Grant the advantage of time.

In spite of this victory, Grant was frustrated that he had not been able to finish off Pemberton. Impetuously, Grant hurled two assaults against the Vicksburg fortifications, one on May 19 and a second on May 22, but both failed. Grant then decided to lay siege to Vicksburg, concluding that the trapped Confederates "could not last always." Grant also used McClernand's conduct during and after the May 22 assault to finally relieve his troublesome subordinate.

THE SIEGE

The siege phase of the campaign lasted six weeks, and the results were largely inevitable. Grant's force became stronger every day thanks to his solid logistical base, which provided reinforcements and supplies. Pemberton, on the other hand, became steadily weaker as both his army and the civilian population of Vicksburg consumed the finite provisions in the city. The only way for the Confederates to break the siege was either for Pemberton's force to attack outward to escape or for an external

Above: Grant's siege was of the deliberate, formalized European style that slowly but surely defeated Confederate resistance.

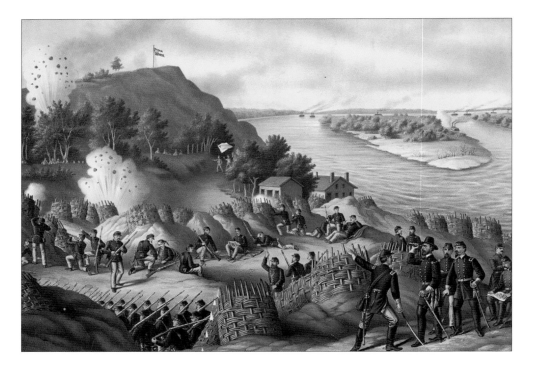

Above: On May 18, 1863, General Sherman's Fifteenth Corps drove Confederate sharpshooters from Martha Edwards's farmhouse (center). The encircled Vicksburg garrison eventually surrendered on July 4, 1863. Throughout the siege of Vicksburg, the Federals attempted to disrupt the defense by exploding mines beneath Confederate positions.

force to come to their relief. Pemberton lacked the audacity and initiative necessary to attempt the former, and Johnston certainly lacked the offensive spirit to come to Pemberton's aid.

Even in such a desperate situation, support from the trans-Mississippi was grudging. Lieutenant General Dick Taylor complained, "To go two hundred miles and more away from the proper theater of action in search of an indefinite something is hard, but orders are orders." By the time a token effort was mounted to relieve some pressure on Pemberton with an attack on Milliken's Bend on June 7, it was too late. The vagaries of the Confederate departmental system served to thwart unity of effort in the defense of Vicksburg. Surrounded within the confines of the beleaguered city, Pemberton was on his own.

Using formalized European siege tactics, Grant dug fortifications facing the Confederate works and battered the Confederate strong points with siege batteries. Porter's vessels contributed to the siege both with fire from the river and by delivering supplies. Within the siege lines, the Federal troops dug approaches and exploded mines on June 25 and July 1, but undertook no general assaults after the failed effort on May 22. As the siege dragged on, Confederate morale within the city deteriorated. Pemberton

even received a letter signed "Many soldiers" that suggested surrendering so that the men would not desert. When Pemberton polled his generals to see if they thought a breakout from Vicksburg was possible, they unanimously said no. On July 3, Pemberton began negotiations with Grant.

The Federal commander initially demanded unconditional surrender, but later agreed to terms that allowed the Confederates to give up their weapons and then be paroled. On July 4, the Federals took control of Vicksburg, just one day after the failure of Pickett's Charge sealed the Federal victory at Gettysburg. Within a week, Banks captured the Confederate stronghold at Port Hudson, thus opening the length of the Mississippi River to Federal traffic. Summarizing the development, President Lincoln declared that the mighty Mississippi once again flowed "unvexed to the sea."

Often overshadowed by the twin Federal victory at Gettysburg, Vicksburg is arguably the more decisive of the two battles. With the parole of Pemberton's army, the Confederacy lost critical manpower. The Federals could now concentrate on the only remaining Confederate army in the west—the Army of Tennessee. In addition to facilitating their own commerce, by controlling the Mississippi River the Federals also bisected the Confederacy, leaving it with logistical and strategic problems as well as damaging the Confederacy's sense of national unity.

REASONS FOR DEFEAT: PEMBERTON'S INEXPERIENCE

The Confederate victory at First Manassas had dispelled most people's hopes of a short war, and both the Federal and Confederate sides began building large armies that consisted of volunteer as well as conscripted soldiers. The result was armies of a size that had never before been seen in the United States, and providing senior leadership for such large numbers of men would stress both the Confederate and Federal armies. As casualties took their toll,

junior officers were often promoted before they were ready, many gaining levels of responsibility that they simply could not handle. Sadly for the Confederate cause, Pemberton fell into that category.

Pemberton was just a captain in the U.S. Army before he tendered his letter of resignation on April 24, 1861. A Pennsylvanian, Pemberton's decision to join the Confederacy is usually attributed to the fact that his wife was a Virginian. Upon reporting to Richmond, Pemberton was nominated by Virginia governor John Letcher to be a lieutenant colonel of volunteer state troops.

On June 15, Pemberton was designated a major in the Confederate army. Just two days later, he bypassed the ranks of lieutenant colonel and colonel and was promoted to brigadier general.

His meteoric rise in rank is hard to explain, and certainly did him no service in developing him as a commander.

Pemberton was posted in the Norfolk area until November, when President Davis reorganized the coasts of South Carolina, Georgia, and northern Florida into a single department and named General Robert E. Lee as its commander. Responding to South Carolina governor Francis Pickens's complaint that Lee lacked brigadier generals, Davis dispatched Pemberton to Charleston on November 29. On January 14, 1862, Pemberton was promoted to major general, and in March he was given command of the Department of South Carolina and Georgia. His principal mission in this capacity was to ensure the defense of Charleston. It would be a formative experience for Pemberton.

Above: This late nineteenth-century line illustration shows Grant (left) and Pemberton meeting to agree on surrender terms. Initially, Grant offered Pemberton only unconditional surrender, but later agreed to terms.

PEMBERTON'S LEADERSHIP

John Pemberton was a loyal, sincere, dedicated man who failed at Vicksburg simply because he found himself in a situation that grossly exceeded his capabilities. Pemberton is a classic example of the "Peter Principle," Dr. Laurence J. Peter's theory that individuals in an organization ultimately rise to their "highest level of incompetence."

At Vicksburg, Pemberton approached his duties in a detached and bureaucratic fashion as if he were still Worth's aide. He made little contribution as a battlefield leader, acting more as an administrator than combat general. As Grant began presenting Pemberton with multiple threats and diversions, Pemberton became confused and paralyzed. For example, Grierson's cavalry raid completely stymied Pemberton and drew his attention away from the real threat posed by Grant. Pemberton's ability was limited to dealing with the known. He lacked the flexibility necessary to deal with an ambiguous situation, such as the one developing around him at Vicksburg.

As Grant closed in, Pemberton was left with a choice—defend from Vicksburg or strike Grant. Pemberton's commander, Joe Johnston, ordered him to unite his forces and attack Grant, even if that meant abandoning Vicksburg. Conversely, President Davis instructed Pemberton to "hold both Vicksburg and Port Hudson." Pemberton lacked the flexibility to deal with such a confused and complicated situation.

By April 30, the Federal navy had successfully passed the Confederate positions both at Vicksburg and Grand Gulf, and Grant's army had crossed the Mississippi River unopposed at Bruinsburg. Pemberton seems to have understood intellectually the significance of these developments, writing President Davis on May 1 that the "enemy's success in passing our batteries has completely changed the character of defense." However, Pemberton seems to have lacked the mental flexibility to adjust to the new situation. After Grant crossed the river, Pemberton should have realized his primary concern was defeating Grant's army rather than holding Vicksburg. Instead, Pemberton chose to defend Vicksburg, applying the lesson he had learned from his experience in Charleston. In so doing, Pemberton surrendered the initiative—and the advantages of maneuver and the offensive—to Grant.

A successful defense requires flexibility. Commanders must focus their planning on preparations in depth, use of reserves, and the ability to shift the main effort. Pemberton failed to display this flexibility. He did not anticipate Grant crossing the Mississippi south of Vicksburg. In fact, he believed Grant had abandoned the effort and withdrawn toward Memphis. Pemberton also inefficiently diverted units from his strategic reserve to chase after Grierson's diversion. Finally, he failed to shift his main effort from defending Vicksburg to defeating Grant when the situation required.

Vicksburg was a fluid and changing situation, and Pemberton lost control of it. In the absence of certainty and afraid to make a critical error, Pemberton remained passive. He no doubt did his best, but at Vicksburg, against the likes of Grant, Pemberton's best was simply not good enough.

As Pemberton surveyed the situation, he became increasingly concerned about his ability to defend the city. Governor Pickens, however, stressed to Pemberton that "the defense is to be desperate, and if they can be repulsed, even with the city in ruins, we should unanimously prefer it." Lee added that Pemberton must be willing to fight "street by street and house by house as long as we have a foot of ground to stand upon." Pemberton's stay in Charleston was marked by conflict with Pickens, and on August 28 he was informed that he was being replaced as commander. However, Pemberton took with him from his Charleston experience the lesson that he should focus on terrain rather than the enemy. He had spent his energies on preparing to defend a fixed location rather than maneuver a force in the field. These experiences would negatively shape Pemberton's conduct during the Vicksburg Campaign.

Pemberton had also had a formative experience during the Mexican War that served him poorly at Vicksburg. In Mexico, Pemberton was assigned as an aide to Brigadier General William Jenkins Worth, an abrupt, unimaginative, and unsophisticated leader who set a poor example for Pemberton regarding broad, responsive, flexible, and anticipatory thought. Pemberton's biographer concluded, "Pemberton might have been better served for the future if he had been influenced by a different role model. Worth had an inflexible, sometimes abrupt nature. Colleagues would someday describe Confederate General John Pemberton as having the same characteristic."

CONCENTRATED FORCES

At Vicksburg, Grant showed his skill as a general in being able to acheive unity of effort. He realized immediately that Porter's naval component gave the Federals a huge advantage and would be critical to Federal success. Grant involved Porter early in the planning, explaining, "I had had in contemplation the whole winter the movement by land to a point below Vicksburg from which to operate—my recollection was that

Admiral Porter was the first one to whom I mentioned it. The cooperation of the Navy was absolutely essential to the success (even to the contemplation) of such an enterprise." In the absence of formal command authority, Grant worked by means of communication, personality, and shared purpose to achieve unity of effort with Porter. As a result, Grant benefited from Porter's transportation, shelling, and logistical support. The Vicksburg Campaign was truly a joint affair, and Grant's leadership made that happen.

LINCOLN ACKNOWLEDGES THE GENIUS OF GRANT

President Lincoln was among the many who recognized Grant's military genius in the Vicksburg Campaign. In a letter after the fall of Vicksburg, Lincoln wrote, "My Dear General: I write this now as a grateful acknowledgement for the almost inestimable service you have done the country. I wish to say a word further. When you first reached the vicinity of Vicksburg, I thought you should do, what you finally did—march the troops back across the neck, run the batteries with the transports, and thus go below; and I never had any faith, except a general hope that you knew better than I, that the Yazoo Pass expedition and the like, could succeed. When you got below, and took Port Gibson, Grand Gulf and vicinity, I thought you should go down the river and join Gen. Banks; and when you turned northward East of the Big Black, I feared it was a mistake. I now wish to make the personal acknowledgement that you were right, and I was wrong." Lincoln now fully appreciated what he had in Grant. After suffering through a series of commanding generals who did not meet his expectations, Lincoln finally found the right man for the job. In fact, perhaps the most important legacy of Vicksburg is that the victory propelled Grant to his promotion to lieutenant general and appointment as general-in-chief in March 1864. In this capacity, Grant brought a new approach to the war effort that would result in total victory.

GRANT'S LEADERSHIP

At Vicksburg, Grant literally ran circles around Pemberton. Grant's performance during the campaign modeled the persistence, understanding of maneuver and logistics, and ability to achieve unity of effort that were the hallmarks of his generalship. If there had been any doubt before, the Vicksburg Campaign marked Grant for greatness.

After the failure of the Chickasaw Bayou expedition, Grant faced a difficult situation. He could have withdrawn his army to the drier ground upriver at Memphis and waited for spring. Instead, he launched his series of expeditions designed to turn the strong Confederate defenses. All the attempts failed, but they showed Grant's persistence. A man of lesser determination might have succumbed to defeatism and quit. Instead, Grant pressed on and demonstrated the perseverance required of a good leader. His efforts later bore fruit by compounding Pemberton's confusion amid the flurry of Federal activity.

Another outstanding aspect of Grant's generalship at Vicksburg was his mastery of maneuver, the movement of forces in relation to the enemy to gain positional advantage. By marching down the west side of the Mississippi River and then crossing at Bruinsburg, Grant turned Pemberton's defense. By marching inland to Jackson, Grant then isolated Pemberton from possible reinforcements. Finally, at Champion Hill, Grant achieved success at the decisive point, the location where a commander gains a marked advantage over his opponent. Champion Hill was the decisive point in the campaign because Grant's victory there compelled Pemberton to withdraw to Vicksburg. Once subjected to a siege, Pemberton had little chance of success. The Vicksburg Campaign is most associated with the climactic siege of the city, but the greatness of Grant's leadership was not in the siege itself but in the maneuver that made it possible.

One thing that allowed Grant to perform this maneuver was his logistical acumen. While Pemberton had developed negative traits in Mexico observing the inflexible and unimaginative Worth, Grant had learned logistical risk as a quartermaster under Winfield Scott. In moving from Vera Cruz to Mexico City, Scott found he was sapping his force by garrisoning various supply depots along the way to defend against guerrilla attacks. Instead, he resolved to cut loose from his supply line and live off the land.

In a situation similar to Scott's, Forrest and Van Dorn's raids in December 1862 had shown Grant how vulnerable his supply line was. After crossing the Mississippi, Grant decided to follow Scott's example and cut loose from his supply line in order to give him the freedom needed to execute the maneuver he sought. Grant did not cut loose completely. He continued to receive supplies brought forward by wagons, but he did not occupy and garrison his supply route, and this is where, like Scott, Grant assumed risk. It was Grant's mastery of logistics and his willingness to take logistical risks that made his brilliant maneuver possible.

LEE VS. MEADE

GETTYSBURG, 1863

Perhaps the most famous battle of the Civil War, the Battle of Gettysburg was fought between General Robert E. Lee's Army of Northern Virginia and Major General George Meade's Army of the Potomac.

Gettysburg was Lee's second invasion of the North and another effort to gain the decisive victory that would perhaps lead to European intervention or a negotiated peace. Instead, Meade defeated Lee in a three-day battle that forced Lee back into Virginia and eliminated the Army of Northern Virginia as a future offensive threat.

PRELIMINARIES

Chancellorsville had been a great victory for the Confederates, but the loss of Lieutenant General Stonewall Jackson was costly. Lee had previously had two corps commanders, with Jackson leading one corps and Lieutenant General James Longstreet leading the other. Each corps had about 30,000 men, and Lee felt that with Jackson gone there was no one commander who could replace him and handle a unit that large. Instead, Lee reorganized the Army of Northern Virginia into three corps. Longstreet would take command of one, Lieutenant General Dick Ewell would lead Jackson's

ROBERT E. LEE

RANK: GENERAL

BORN: 1807

EDUCATED: UNITED STATES MILITARY ACADEMY

MILITARY CAREER

VETERAN OF MEXICAN WAR

SUPERINTENDENT OF THE UNITED STATES MILITARY ACADEMY

MILITARY ADVISER TO JEFFERSON DAVIS

LED ARMY OF NORTHERN VIRGINIA FROM 1862 UNTIL THE
   CONCLUSION OF THE WAR

DIED: 1870

old Second Corps, and Lieutenant General A. P. Hill would command the new Third Corps. Ewell and Hill had both served ably as division commanders, but it remained to be seen if they were up to the challenge of a corps command.

Building on the momentum of his victory at Chancellorsville, Lee proposed a second invasion of Northern territory. Lee's loyalties had always been first and foremost to Virginia. Shortly after resigning from the U.S. Army, he said, "I devote myself to the service of my native state, in whose behalf alone, will I ever again draw my sword." This loyalty had a profound influence on Lee's strategic thinking, and now an invasion into Northern territory would relieve some of the ravages Virginia had suffered as the principal battleground of the war.

However, there were others who looked to the west as being the more important theater. This "western bloc" included such influential Confederate figures as Secretary of War James Seddon, Senator Louis Wigfall of Texas, Generals Joe Johnston and Pierre Gustave Toutant Beauregard, and even Lee's "old war horse," Longstreet. Even President Jefferson Davis, a native Mississippian, had leanings toward the west. With Lieutenant General John Pemberton's army reeling under pressure from Major General Ulysses S. Grant's Vicksburg Campaign, there was considerable support for sending reinforcements from Virginia west instead of mounting an offensive in the eastern theater.

Lee countered these arguments, saying that an invasion of the North would cause such alarm that the Federals would be forced to divert their attention away from Vicksburg. It was a fairly tenuous assertion, but by this point in the war Lee had such enormous prestige that his opinions were hard to ignore. When Lee briefed his plan to invade Northern territory to President Davis and his cabinet on May 15, 1863, Davis concurred.

LEE ON THE MOVE

On June 3, Lee started moving his 89,000 men north from Fredericksburg, Virginia. Major General Joseph Hooker, commander of the Army of the Potomac, was still stinging from his defeat at Chancellorsville, and he proceeded cautiously. Eventually he suggested to

GETTYSBURG

Date	July 1–3, 1863
Location	Adams County, Pennsylvania
Result	Union victory

Strength

| Union: Army of the Potomac (85,500) | Confederate: Army of Northern Virginia (89,000) |

Casualties and losses

23,049	28,063
3,155 killed	3,903 killed
14,529 wounded	18,735 wounded
5,365 missing	5,425 captured

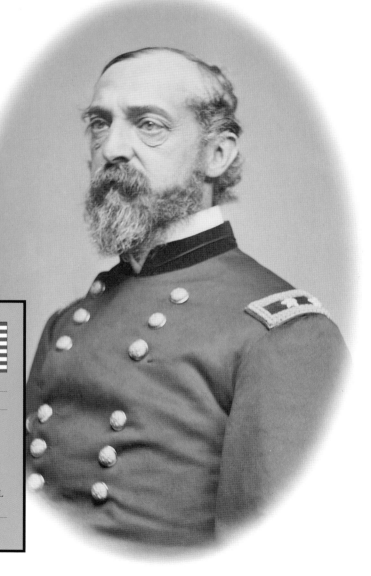

GEORGE G. MEADE

RANK: MAJOR GENERAL

BORN: 1815

EDUCATED: UNITED STATES MILITARY ACADEMY

MILITARY CAREER

VETERAN OF MEXICAN WAR

COMMANDED EXTENSIVELY IN VIRGINIA AND MARYLAND

ASSUMED COMMAND OF THE ARMY OF THE POTOMAC AFTER
CHANCELLORSVILLE AND MAINTAINED OPERATIONAL CONTROL
OF IT UNDER GRANT DURING THE 1864 VIRGINIA CAMPAIGN

DIED: 1872

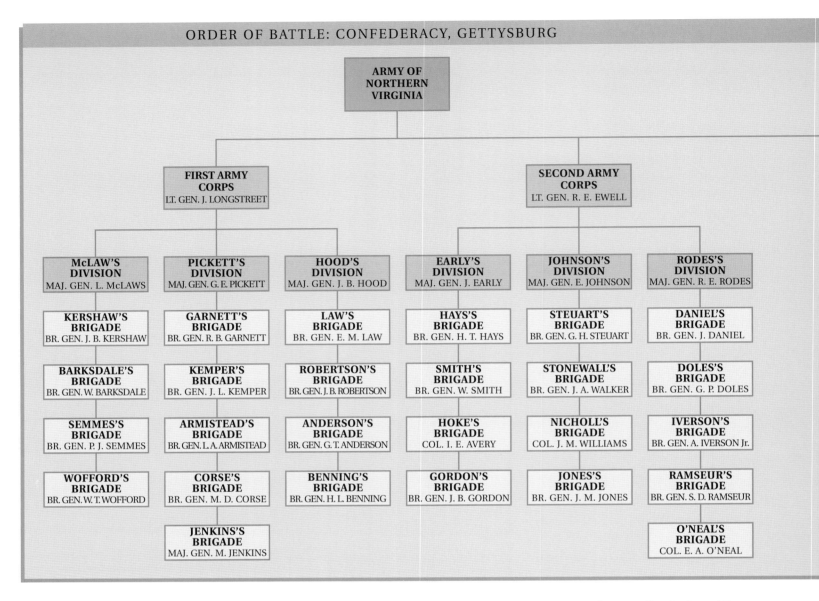

ORDER OF BATTLE: CONFEDERACY, GETTYSBURG

ARMY OF NORTHERN VIRGINIA

FIRST ARMY CORPS
LT. GEN. J. LONGSTREET

SECOND ARMY CORPS
LT. GEN. R. E. EWELL

McLAW'S DIVISION MAJ. GEN. L. McLAWS	PICKETT'S DIVISION MAJ. GEN. G. E. PICKETT	HOOD'S DIVISION MAJ. GEN. J. B. HOOD	EARLY'S DIVISION MAJ. GEN. J. EARLY	JOHNSON'S DIVISION MAJ. GEN. E. JOHNSON	RODES'S DIVISION MAJ. GEN. R. E. RODES
KERSHAW'S BRIGADE BR. GEN. J. B. KERSHAW	GARNETT'S BRIGADE BR. GEN. R. B. GARNETT	LAW'S BRIGADE BR. GEN. E. M. LAW	HAYS'S BRIGADE BR. GEN. H. T. HAYS	STEUART'S BRIGADE BR. GEN. G. H. STEUART	DANIEL'S BRIGADE BR. GEN. J. DANIEL
BARKSDALE'S BRIGADE BR. GEN. W. BARKSDALE	KEMPER'S BRIGADE BR. GEN. J. L. KEMPER	ROBERTSON'S BRIGADE BR. GEN. J. B. ROBERTSON	SMITH'S BRIGADE BR. GEN. W. SMITH	STONEWALL'S BRIGADE BR. GEN. J. A. WALKER	DOLES'S BRIGADE BR. GEN. G. P. DOLES
SEMMES'S BRIGADE BR. GEN. P. J. SEMMES	ARMISTEAD'S BRIGADE BR. GEN. L. A. ARMISTEAD	ANDERSON'S BRIGADE BR. GEN. G. T. ANDERSON	HOKE'S BRIGADE COL. I. E. AVERY	NICHOLL'S BRIGADE COL. J. M. WILLIAMS	IVERSON'S BRIGADE BR. GEN. A. IVERSON Jr.
WOFFORD'S BRIGADE BR. GEN. W. T. WOFFORD	CORSE'S BRIGADE BR. GEN. M. D. CORSE	BENNING'S BRIGADE BR. GEN. H. L. BENNING	GORDON'S BRIGADE BR. GEN. J. B. GORDON	JONES'S BRIGADE BR. GEN. J. M. JONES	RAMSEUR'S BRIGADE BR. GEN. S. D. RAMSEUR
	JENKINS'S BRIGADE MAJ. GEN. M. JENKINS				O'NEAL'S BRIGADE COL. E. A. O'NEAL

Below: General George Meade (seated, center) poses for a photograph with his staff, 1863.

President Lincoln that, now that Lee was gone, the Federals could take Richmond. Lincoln responded, "I think Lee's army, and not Richmond, is your true objective point."

As Hooker timidly shadowed Lee on a parallel route, Lincoln tried to press Hooker to strike. Hoping to spur some action, Lincoln asked Hooker where Lee's army was, to which Hooker replied, "The advance is at fords of the Potomac and the rear at Culpepper Court House." That represented a distance of seventy

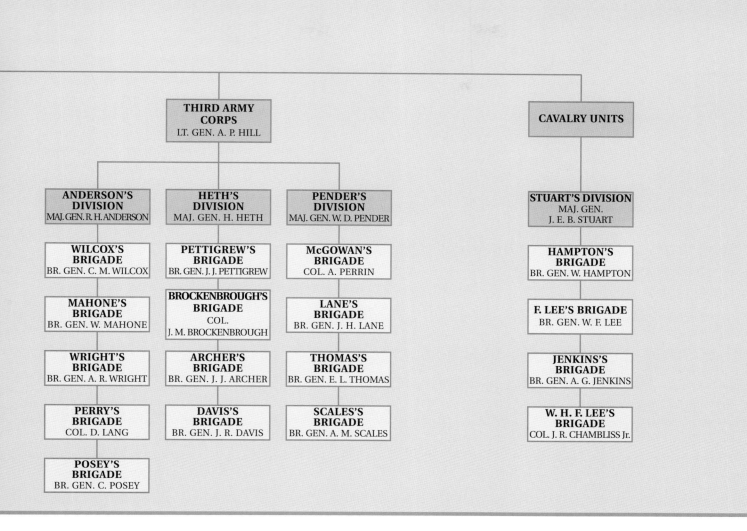

THIRD ARMY CORPS
LT. GEN. A. P. HILL

CAVALRY UNITS

ANDERSON'S DIVISION
MAJ. GEN. R. H. ANDERSON

HETH'S DIVISION
MAJ. GEN. H. HETH

PENDER'S DIVISION
MAJ. GEN. W. D. PENDER

STUART'S DIVISION
MAJ. GEN. J. E. B. STUART

WILCOX'S BRIGADE
BR. GEN. C. M. WILCOX

PETTIGREW'S BRIGADE
BR. GEN. J. J. PETTIGREW

McGOWAN'S BRIGADE
COL. A. PERRIN

HAMPTON'S BRIGADE
BR. GEN. W. HAMPTON

MAHONE'S BRIGADE
BR. GEN. W. MAHONE

BROCKENBROUGH'S BRIGADE
COL. J. M. BROCKENBROUGH

LANE'S BRIGADE
BR. GEN. J. H. LANE

F. LEE'S BRIGADE
BR. GEN. W. F. LEE

WRIGHT'S BRIGADE
BR. GEN. A. R. WRIGHT

ARCHER'S BRIGADE
BR. GEN. J. J. ARCHER

THOMAS'S BRIGADE
BR. GEN. E. L. THOMAS

JENKINS'S BRIGADE
BR. GEN. A. G. JENKINS

PERRY'S BRIGADE
COL. D. LANG

DAVIS'S BRIGADE
BR. GEN. J. R. DAVIS

SCALES'S BRIGADE
BR. GEN. A. M. SCALES

W. H. F. LEE'S BRIGADE
COL. J. R. CHAMBLISS Jr.

POSEY'S BRIGADE
BR. GEN. C. POSEY

miles, and Lincoln, even without formal military schooling, saw an opportunity. "If the head of the animal is at the fords of the Potomac and the tail at Culpepper Court House, it must be very thin somewhere," Lincoln advised Hooker. "Why don't you strike it?"

Lincoln's prodding had some effect on Hooker, and by June 28 Hooker had concentrated his army near Frederick, Maryland. At this point, Hooker was closer to Lee than the extreme ends of the Confederate column were to each other. To make matters more dangerous for Lee, he had no idea where Hooker was.

STUART OUT OF REACH
Lee had made the mistake of giving his skilled but flamboyant cavalryman Major General Jeb Stuart broad latitude in supporting the Confederate advance north. Stuart had used this discretion to leave only a small part of his force screening Lee and lead the rest of his men on a broad sweep around Hooker's rear in hopes of wreaking havoc similar to that he had inflicted against Major General George McClellan during the Peninsula Campaign. Stuart had expected to be out of contact with Lee for just thirty-six hours. Instead, Stuart had been forced to loop much farther east than he had anticipated and would not rejoin Lee for a full week. In the meantime, Lee would be without his prized intelligence asset and thus be painfully unaware of Federal troop dispositions. It would prove to be a costly mistake for Lee.

Hooker finally began to develop a plan to strike the extended Confederate line of communication. He ordered his Twelfth Corps to move to Harpers Ferry,

Below: A Union cavalryman from Rush's Lancers, Sixth Pennsylvania Cavalry. The lance was going out of fashion in the 1860s, though some units still carried it.

Above: This house on Chambersburg Pike served as General Robert E. Lee's headquarters during the Gettysburg Campaign. On June 21, Lee issued Order No. 72, forbidding the seizure or theft of private property. With the exception of some minor infractions, the Confederates obeyed the order and respected civilian property.

Opposite: A section of the Gettysburg Cyclorama, painted in 1883 by French artist Paul Phillippoteaux (1845–1923), depicting Pickett's Charge on the final day of the battle.

combine with other forces there, and attack Lee's rear. When Major General Henry Halleck, whom Hooker had increasingly felt was interfering with the Army of the Potomac, countermanded this order, Hooker asked to be relieved. Lincoln had long since grown frustrated with Hooker and was eager to take this opportunity to replace him with little political repercussion. On June 28, Major General George Meade, former commander of the Fifth Corps, assumed command of the Army of the Potomac.

Throughout the Federal march north, Meade had complained of being uninformed by Hooker. Upon learning that he was now commander of the Army of the Potomac, Meade was hardly happy. "Why me? Why not Reynolds?" Meade complained. "I don't know the Army's position. I don't know its plans. I don't know if it has any plans." Realizing further protest was futile, Meade acquiesced, saying, "Well, I've been tried and condemned without a hearing and I suppose I shall have to go to the execution." It was an inauspicious beginning for the fifth commander of the Army of the Potomac.

DAY ONE: CONFEDERATE ADVANTAGE

Lee advanced north virtually unopposed, and once in Pennsylvania, the Army of Northern Virginia began to enjoy the

bounty of the countryside. A few communities were forced to pay cash ransoms, but for the most part Lee kept a firm hand on his men, insisting Confederate money or receipts be issued for anything taken. Lee was thus far accomplishing his purpose of relieving the Virginia countryside, but, thanks to Stuart's misguided absence, Lee was still ignorant of the enemy's disposition.

What Lee finally learned of the Federal army came from a mysterious spy named Harrison. On June 28, Harrison had informed Longstreet, who had passed the news to Lee, that Meade had replaced Hooker and that the Army of the Potomac was in Maryland. This information was a great surprise to Lee, who had assumed Stuart would have advised him if the Federal army was in pursuit. Lee now had to concentrate his forces to meet the approaching Federal threat.

By June 30 Lee had gathered most of his army in the area of Chambersburg, Cashtown, and Heidelersburg. In the meantime, Meade was pushing his army north, staying to the east of Lee's army in order to protect Washington and Baltimore. Meade employed marching objectives to set a blistering pace for each of his corps. Not knowing exactly where Lee's army was, Meade also kept his corps within supporting distance of one another so that no matter which corps encountered Lee first, Meade could quickly bring to bear the full weight of his army.

Meade considered the seven-corps configuration of the Army of the Potomac too unwieldy for such vigorous pursuit, so he placed Major General John Reynolds, the First Corps' commander, in charge of a wing consisting of the First, Second, and Eleventh corps and a cavalry division. On June 30, Meade advised Reynolds that reports of Lee's current dispositions and the existing road network suggested Lee would concentrate his forces near the small town of Gettysburg. Reynolds thus sent Brigadier General John Buford and two cavalry brigades toward Gettysburg to find Lee.

While Buford was scouting toward Gettysburg, he encountered the brigade of Brigadier General James Pettigrew, who had marched to Gettysburg that morning in order to secure some shoes (which were reported to be in the town) for his men. Pettigrew, not wanting to bring on a general engagement without orders, withdrew to Cashtown and described the incident to his division commander, Major General Henry Heth. While the two men were talking, A. P. Hill rode up and joined the discussion. Hill stated that the Federal cavalry was probably just an outpost, and Heth agreed. Heth asked permission to return to Gettysburg the next day to get the shoes, and Hill authorized the mission. In the meantime, Buford had recognized the importance of Gettysburg as a road junction and organized his small force to defend it.

At about 5:00 a.m. on July 1, Heth left Cashtown with four brigades of infantry. Three hours later, he ran into Buford's dismounted cavalry on McPherson's Ridge. Heth deployed two of his brigades on line, expecting to push quickly through what he thought was only a small Federal reconnaissance force. Instead, Buford resisted vigorously and halted the Confederate advance. Buford quickly requested reinforcements.

Reynolds, Buford's corps commander, was soon on the scene, and the two men observed the developing situation from the cupola of the Lutheran Theological Seminary on the western edge of Gettysburg. Reynolds asked Buford if he thought he could hold on with his cavalry until the First Corps could arrive, and Buford said he thought he could. At 10:00 a.m., Major General James Wadsworth arrived with his division. Brigadier General John Robinson was close behind. Buford's men then withdrew behind the infantry, and the Federals enjoyed early success, badly damaging two of Heth's brigades. Then, as Reynolds was checking to see if more

Above: A Confederate infantryman of the First Texas Brigade lunges forward with his bayonet-tipped musket. Troops of the First Texas were heavily engaged in the capture of the Devil's Den at Gettysburg on July 2, 1863. Bayonet charges were rare during the Civil War. According to one study, of the approximately 250,000 wounded treated in Federal hospitals during the war, only 922 were victims of bayonets or sabers.

Above: Arriving during the battle, Meade positioned his headquarters in this farmhouse, sufficiently close to the action that stray artillery rounds narrowly missed the general and his staff during the battle.

Opposite: The otherwise calm Pennsylvania countryside was rocked by three days of savage fighting around the town of Gettysburg.

troops were arriving, he was struck by Confederate fire and killed.

Reynolds's death momentarily broke the Federal momentum, but soon Major General Oliver Howard arrived with his Eleventh Corps and took command. Confederate troops were rushing to the sound of the guns, and Ewell had his corps moving south from Carlisle and Heidelersburg to the action. Howard sent a desperate request to Major Generals Daniel Sickles and Henry Slocum to bring their Third and Twelfth corps forward. "General Reynolds is killed," wrote Howard. "For God's sake, come up."

SECURING CEMETERY HILL
Howard had earlier seen the importance of Cemetery Hill on the north end of Cemetery Ridge. The hill dominated the approaches to Gettysburg and would be the key to any defensive effort. Howard therefore dispatched Brigadier General

Adolph von Steinwehr's division to occupy the position.

Howard's foresight in deciding to secure Cemetery Hill was fortuitous because the Confederate attack was threatening the Federal flank by 3:00 p.m. Outnumbered, Howard ordered his troops back to a new defensive line built around Steinwehr's position. At first the movement was orderly, but as the Federals surged through Gettysburg, the retreat became a little more rapid. Upon arriving at Steinwehr's position, however, the Federals regained their composure, and when the Second Corps under Major General Winfield Scott Hancock arrived to take charge of the sector, order was restored.

By now Lee was on the scene. He sent word to Ewell "to carry the hill occupied by the enemy [Cemetery Hill], if he found it practicable, but to avoid a general engagement until the arrival of the other divisions of the army." It was the type of discretionary order that Jackson would have energetically executed, but Ewell, new to corps command, hesitated. As Ewell waited for the arrival of Major General Edward Johnson's division, the Federals strengthened their defense. By the time Johnson arrived, it was too late to attack. Ewell ordered his corps to rest for the night.

The opening day of the battle was a Confederate victory, but it also led to a serious difference of opinion between Lee and Longstreet. Longstreet was largely a defensive-minded general, and he had long held concerns about Lee's invasion of the North. The invasion would work, Longstreet argued, only if once the Army of Northern Virginia crossed into Northern territory, Lee took up a strong defensive position that the Federals would be compelled to attack. With such an advantage, the Confederates might gain another inexpensive victory like at Fredericksburg. Summing up his views, Longstreet wrote, "The plan of defensive tactics gave some hope of success, and, in fact, I assured General Lee that the First Corps would receive and defend the battle if he would guard our flanks, leaving the

other corps to gather the fruits of success. The First Corps was as solid as a rock—a great rock. It was not to be broken of good position by direct assault, and was steady enough to work and wait for its chosen battle." For Longstreet, the overriding vision, both of the campaign and his corps, was clearly defensive. Lee disagreed.

As Lee had been waiting for Ewell to attack, Longstreet had ridden up. Lee told Longstreet he had ordered Ewell to seize Cemetery Hill and added that if Meade was still on the field the next day, Lee was going to attack. This strategy shocked Longstreet, who reiterated his thoughts on how the campaign should be fought. He recommended the Confederates move south and east across Meade's line of communications, find a strong defensive position, and force Meade into a costly attack. Longstreet was surprised when Lee remained insistent upon attacking. Longstreet later wrote that he told Lee, "We could not call the enemy to position better suited to our plans. All that we have to do is to file around his left and secure good ground between him and his capital." He claimed that upon starting the campaign

> **"BULLETS HISSING, HUMMING, AND WHISTLING, EVERYWHERE; CANNON ROARING, ALL CRASH ON CRASH, AND PEAL ON PEAL; SMOKE, DUST, SPLINTERS, BLOOD; WRECK AND CARNAGE INDESCRIBABLE . . . EVERY MAN'S SHIRT SOAKED WITH SWEAT, AND MANY OF THEM SOPPED WITH BLOOD FROM WOUNDS . . . SLEEVES ROLLED UP, FACES BLACKENED."**

DESCRIPTION OF THE FIRST DAY OF ACTION AT GETTYSBURG BY UNION CANNONEER AUGUSTUS BUELL, FROM *THE CANNONEER*, 1890

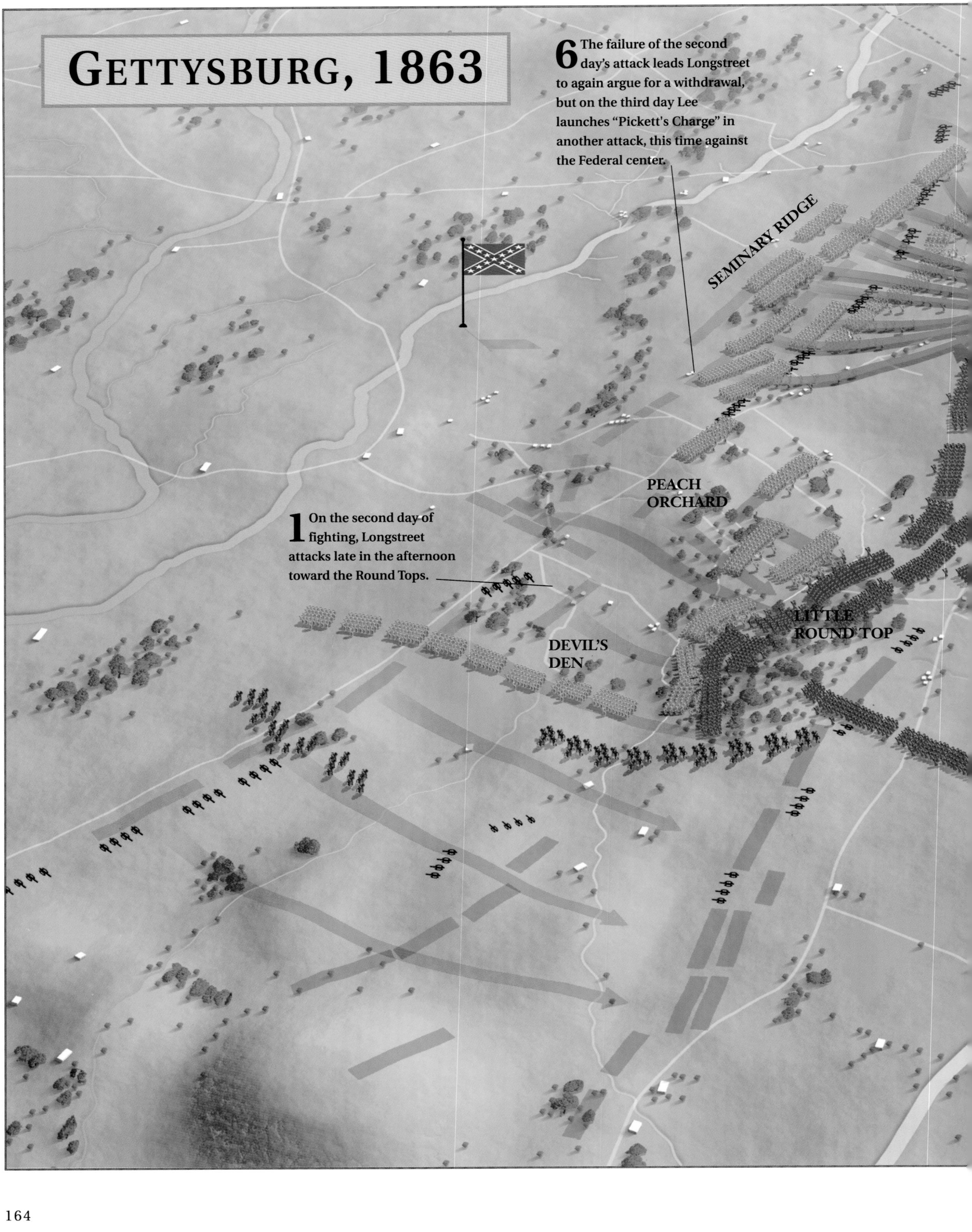

GETTYSBURG, 1863

6 The failure of the second day's attack leads Longstreet to again argue for a withdrawal, but on the third day Lee launches "Pickett's Charge" in another attack, this time against the Federal center.

SEMINARY RIDGE

PEACH ORCHARD

1 On the second day of fighting, Longstreet attacks late in the afternoon toward the Round Tops.

LITTLE ROUND TOP

DEVIL'S DEN

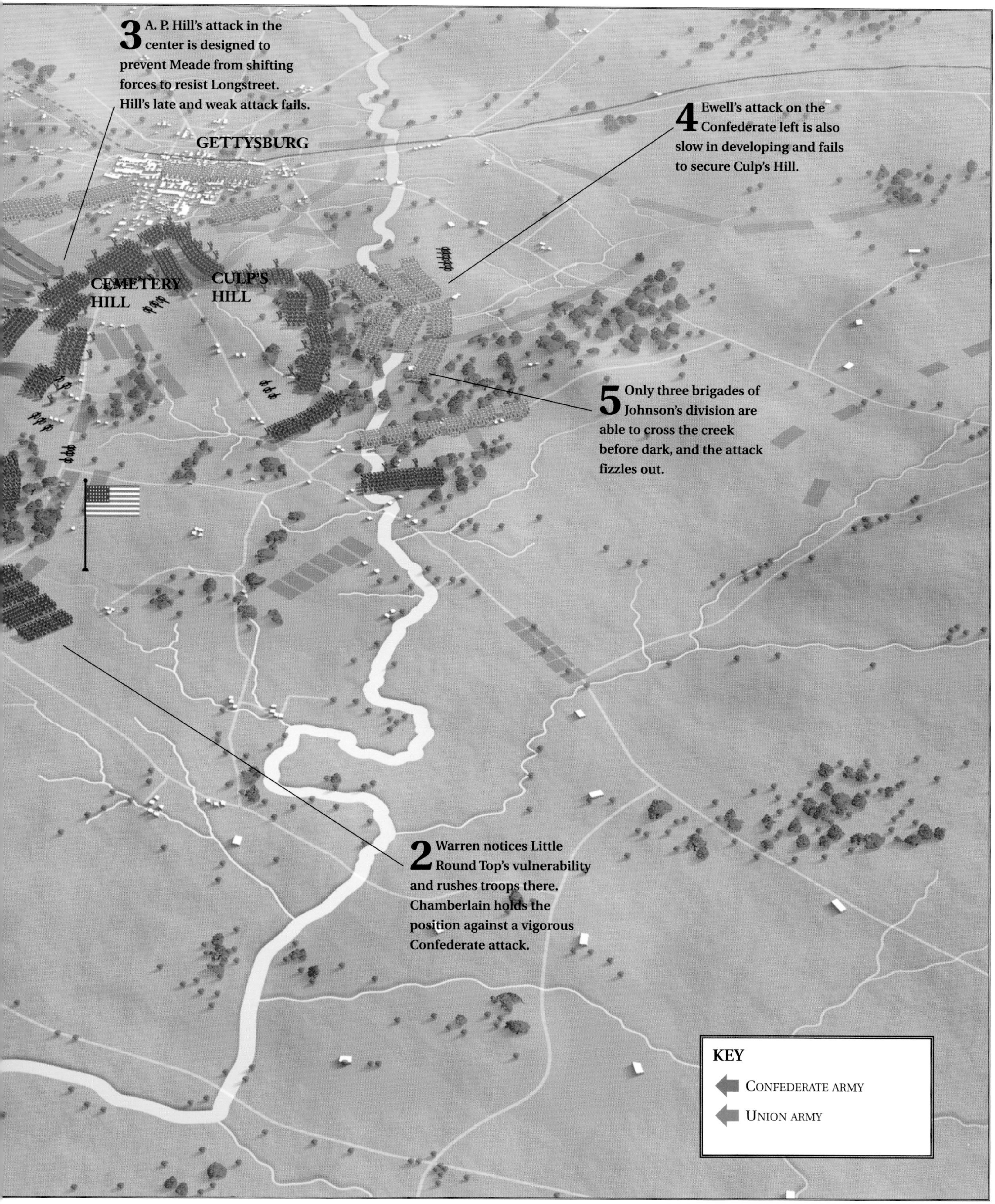

3 A. P. Hill's attack in the center is designed to prevent Meade from shifting forces to resist Longstreet. Hill's late and weak attack fails.

GETTYSBURG

4 Ewell's attack on the Confederate left is also slow in developing and fails to secure Culp's Hill.

CEMETERY HILL

CULP'S HILL

5 Only three brigades of Johnson's division are able to cross the creek before dark, and the attack fizzles out.

2 Warren notices Little Round Top's vulnerability and rushes troops there. Chamberlain holds the position against a vigorous Confederate attack.

KEY	
	CONFEDERATE ARMY
	UNION ARMY

Lee shared these views, but Longstreet had obviously misread Lee's intentions.

DAY TWO: STATUS QUO MAINTAINED

Instead of pursuing the defensive strategy Longstreet favored, Lee wanted to resume the attack as soon as possible on July 2. He initially ordered Ewell to attack Cemetery Hill and Culp's Hill on the Federal right, but Ewell expressed reservations. Lee instead instructed Longstreet to make the main attack against the left of the Federal line in the vicinity of Little Round Top and Big Round Top. Longstreet repeated his arguments against an attack, but Lee was not persuaded. In spite of his objections, Longstreet prepared to carry out his orders.

Meade was active throughout the night of July 1–2. By now most of his 85,500 men were present and he had formed them into the shape of a fishhook, with the tip being at Culp's Hill, the hook curving around Cemetery Ridge, and the eye at the two Round Tops. Although Big Round Top was the taller of the two hills, Little Round Top had been recently cleared of timber, and therefore it had better observation and fields of fire. It would prove to be the key to the second day's fighting. Lee's men wrapped around the outside of the Federal fishhook, with Ewell in the north, Hill in the center, and Longstreet in the south. Such a configuration gave

Below: Entitled *Come on You Wolverines!*, this modern painting depicts General George Armstrong Custer (1839–76) leading the Michigan Brigade in a charge at the Battle of Gettysburg on July 3, 1863.

Meade key advantages in terms of observation and fields of fire as well as central position.

After the war was over, supporters of Lee and Longstreet would argue about whether or not Lee had ordered the second day's attack to begin at daylight. This argument notwithstanding, the fact remains that the attack did not occur early in the morning, and Lee became increasingly impatient throughout the day. In fact, the attack did not begin until 4:30 in the afternoon, and by then the Federals had the opportunity to recover from a serious error in which Sickles had failed to cover the key Little Round Top with his Third Corps. The vulnerability was not discovered until 3:00 p.m., when Meade and his chief engineer, General Gouverneur Warren, reconnoitered the Third Corps' lines.

Observing the void, Warren said, "Here is where our line should be," but Meade only replied, "It is too late now," and rode off. Wanting to get a better look at the terrain, Warren rode to the crest of Little Round Top. From that vantage point he could see the Confederates forming to attack the undefended position. Realizing the critical nature of the situation, Warren rushed into action and hurried Brigadier General Strong Vincent and his brigade to the scene. Colonel Joshua Chamberlain's Twentieth Maine, the advanced regiment of Vincent's brigade, arrived just in time to repulse the attack of Colonel William Oates's Fifteenth Alabama. Had the Confederates been able to gain Little Round Top, they could have rolled up the Federal flank along Cemetery Ridge. Chamberlain saved the day for the Federals and won the Medal of Honor for his heroic actions.

On the other end of the line, Ewell finally heard the sound of Longstreet's guns and launched what Lee intended to be a diversionary attack in support of Longstreet's main effort. After an ineffective artillery barrage, Ewell launched uncoordinated attacks on both Cemetery Hill and Culp's Hill that were easily repulsed. Neither Longstreet nor Ewell had met any success, and the second day's fighting at Gettysburg ended in a stalemate. Earlier in the afternoon, as Longstreet had been slowly moving his men into position to attack, the long-lost Stuart returned from his pointless ride. Lee was initially furious, telling Stuart, "I have not heard a word from you for days, and you are the eyes and ears of my army." Then Lee softened, telling Stuart, "We will not discuss this matter further. Help me fight these people." By then, however, it was too late for Stuart's strung-out column to join the fight. The second day of the battle was marked by frustration on many fronts for Lee, as he could not get his subordinates to behave as he wished.

DAY THREE: FEDERAL VICTORY

In spite of the disappointment Lee must have felt over the second day's failure,

"WHEN NEWS OF THE SURRENDER FIRST REACHED OUR LINES, OUR MEN COMMENCED FIRING A SALUTE OF A HUNDRED GUNS IN HONOR OF THE VICTORY. I AT ONCE SENT WORD, HOWEVER, TO HAVE IT STOPPED. THE CONFEDERATES WERE NOW OUR PRISONERS, AND WE DID NOT WANT TO EXULT OVER THEIR DOWNFALL."

ULYSSES S. GRANT, APRIL 9, 1865, *PERSONAL MEMOIRS OF U. S. GRANT*

Below: George Pickett's (1825–75) gallant but ill-fated charge at Gettysburg is one of the war's most romanticized events. In many ways, this was the last hurrah for the Confederacy. Afterward, the tide had fully turned in favor of the North.

he remained confident in his overall success. Casualties had been heavy on both sides, but the second day had hit the Federals especially hard. In fact, 65 percent of Meade's total losses at Gettysburg occurred on July 2. Having struck the Federal right the first day and the left the second, Lee now resolved to attack the Federal center. He had Major General George Pickett's still-fresh division available for this purpose, and Stuart's newly arrived cavalry could strike Meade's rear while Pickett attacked the front.

Learning of this plan, Longstreet continued his objections to Lee's strategy. When Lee told Longstreet 15,000 men would make the attack, Longstreet replied that such a number of men could not be found. Still, Lee pressed on with his plan. Longstreet, however, was becoming increasingly despondent about the idea. He later wrote, "That day at Gettysburg was one of the saddest of my life."

In contrast to Longstreet, Pickett relished in the glory of the planned attack. The highlight of Pickett's Mexican War service had been carrying the

Eighth Infantry's colors over the ramparts to victory at Chapultepec. Now Pickett was full of optimism and could not help but recall this past glory.

When Colonel Birkett Fry reported to work out some details of the attack, he found Pickett "to be in excellent spirits, and after a cordial greeting and a pleasant reference to our having been in work of that kind at Chapultepec, expressed great confidence in the ability of our troops to drive the enemy." Pickett was as eager as Longstreet was sanguine to begin the attack.

As the time for the attack neared, Longstreet could barely order its commencement. As Colonel E. Porter Alexander, Longstreet's artillery chief, prepared for a 172-gun preassault bombardment, he received a note from Longstreet requesting Alexander to determine whether or not the artillery had done enough damage to make the attack viable. Alexander replied that he would not be able to assess the results to that degree of accuracy, but added that if there was an alternative to Pickett's Charge, it ought to be explored.

Alexander began his bombardment at 1:00 p.m. It was a ferocious cannonade, but most of the rounds sailed over the heads of Brigadier General John Gibbons's division, who held positions on Cemetery Ridge. To make matters worse for the Confederates, Alexander was quickly running out of ammunition. After about thirty minutes, he sent Pickett a note, telling him that now was the best time to attack.

With his command staged in the woods on Seminary Ridge, Pickett rode to Longstreet and asked, "General, shall I advance?" The reluctant Longstreet could not bring himself to do more than merely nod his head. With that

Above: With Big Round Top looming in the distance, these breastworks fortified Little Round Top.

Above: After Pickett's death, his wife Sallie championed an idealized account of Pickett as the perfect Confederate officer.

"PICKETT'S LINES BEING NEARER, THE IMPACT WAS HEAVIEST UPON THEM. MOST OF THE FIELD OFFICERS WERE KILLED OR WOUNDED . . . GENERAL ARMISTEAD, OF THE SECOND LINE, SPREAD HIS STEPS TO SUPPLY THE PACES OF FALLEN COMRADES. HIS COLORS CUT DOWN, WITH A VOLLEY AGAINST THE BRISTLING LINE OF BAYONETS, HE PUT HIS CAP ON HIS SWORD TO GUIDE THE STORM. THE ENEMY'S MASSING, ENVELOPING NUMBERS HELD THE STRUGGLE UNTIL THE NOBLE ARMISTEAD FELL BESIDE THE WHEELS OF THE ENEMY'S BATTERY."

LIEUTENANT GENERAL JAMES LONGSTREET, DISCUSSING THE END OF PICKETT'S CHARGE

unenthusiastic gesture, Pickett was off.

Pickett's men met a galling fire from the Federal artillery, and gaps soon appeared in the Confederate line. Still the Confederates advanced. Eventually their right and left flanks were broken, with only the center remaining. The attack there consisted of a brigade of five Virginia regiments led by Brigadier General Lewis Armistead. Their objective was a low stone wall on the western slope of Cemetery Ridge that was defended by Major General Winfield Scott Hancock—Armistead's dear friend from the "Old Army"—and his Second Corps.

At one point, 150 Confederates poured over the wall and momentarily broke the Federal line, but the defenders recovered, rushed forward fresh artillery, and opened fire less than ten yards from Armistead and his men. As Federals closed in from all sides, Armistead reached a captured Federal cannon, put his hand on it, and was shot. It was the high-water mark of the Confederacy, but Armistead's isolated men could not sustain their attack. Pickett's Charge had failed, and the scattered remnants of his command staggered back across the field. The attack had caused 54 percent losses to the Confederates. One survivor wrote, "It was a second Fredericksburg . . . only the wrong way." The results were a powerful testimony to the impact of modern weapons and the futility of frontal assaults across open terrain. To the east, Stuart's cavalry attack was also

checked. As Pickett's beaten men fell back, Lee said, "It's all my fault."

LINCOLN'S FRUSTRATION

Meade had won the Battle of Gettysburg, but now the question became what to do with the victory. Both sides had been badly hurt, with Lee suffering 28,063 losses and Meade 23,040, and the two armies now lay facing each other, nursing their wounds. Meade too was personally exhausted. After the battle, a newspaper reporter found him "stooping and weary," and his biographer described him as "a picture of sorry discomfort." Meade was of no mind to exploit his victory, and Lee began withdrawing back into Virginia.

Lincoln, however, had other ideas. He sent Meade instructions that "the opportunity to attack [Lee's] divided forces should not be lost. The President is urgent and anxious that your army should move against [Lee] by forced marches." While lavishing praise on Grant for his July 4 victory at Vicksburg, Lincoln withheld such accolades from Meade, whose work he considered yet unfinished. It was not time to celebrate until Lee's army had been defeated.

In the end, however, Meade offered only a halfhearted attempt to pursue Lee that was of no consequence. Once again the Confederate commander had escaped to fight another day, and Lincoln was beside himself. He wrote Meade, "I do not believe you appreciate the magnitude of the misfortune involved in

Lee's escape. He was within your easy grasp, and to have closed upon him would, in connection with our other late successes, have ended the war. As it is, the war will be prolonged indefinitely."

THE GETTYSBURG ADDRESS

The battle had left Gettysburg, a town of just 2,400 people, with a serious problem. Decaying bodies of soldiers and horses littered the battlefield and had to be taken care of. The solution came in the creation of a national cemetery that would provide a dignified resting place for the dead as well as a commemoration of the battle. The cemetery was dedicated on November 19, 1863.

Edward Everett, a highly noted orator and former secretary of state and governor of Massachusetts, was to be the main speaker. Almost as an afterthought, President Lincoln was invited to participate in the ceremony as well. Some 15,000 people attended the event and were treated to a two-hour speech by Everett. Lincoln followed with a speech of two or three minutes. At the time, the public response to Everett's remarks was very enthusiastic, and Lincoln's speech was barely noticed. Yet as time has

Above: At the top of this painting, Confederate infantry breach a wall defended by Federal soldiers. Farm walls and fences provided valuable protection for Civil War soldiers. Behind such cover, the defenders' rifle fire could rip holes in frontal attacks.

Opposite: President Lincoln traveled to Gettysburg to help dedicate the national cemetery there. His Gettysburg Address of November 19, 1863, is one of the classic speeches in American history.

ORDER OF BATTLE: UNITED STATES (UNION), GETTYSBURG

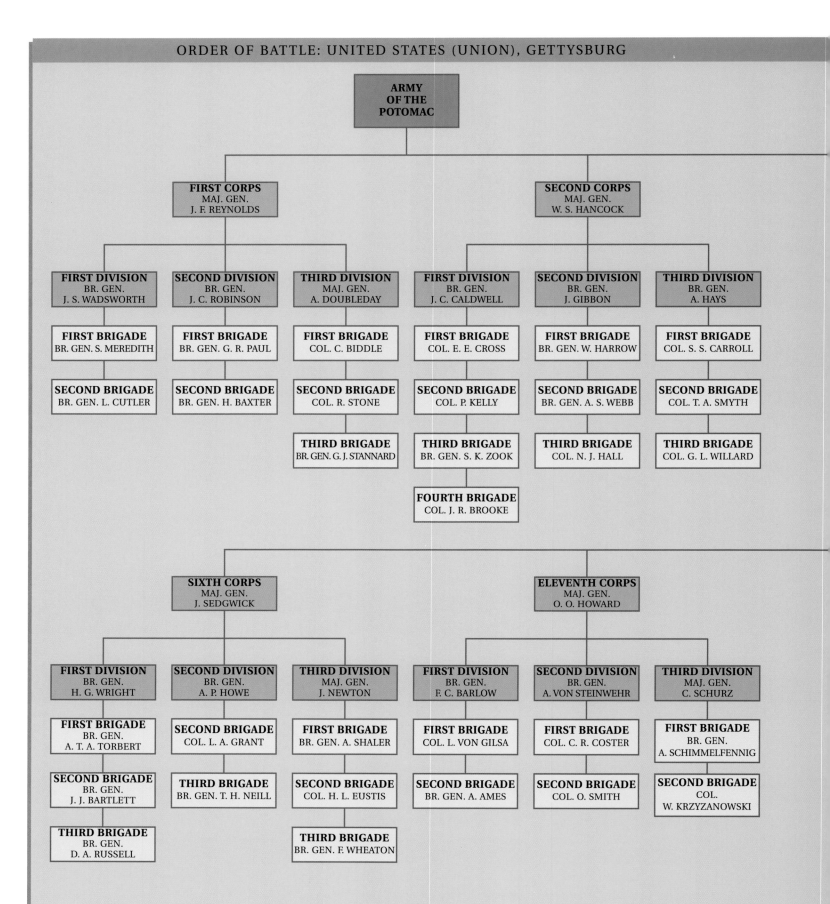

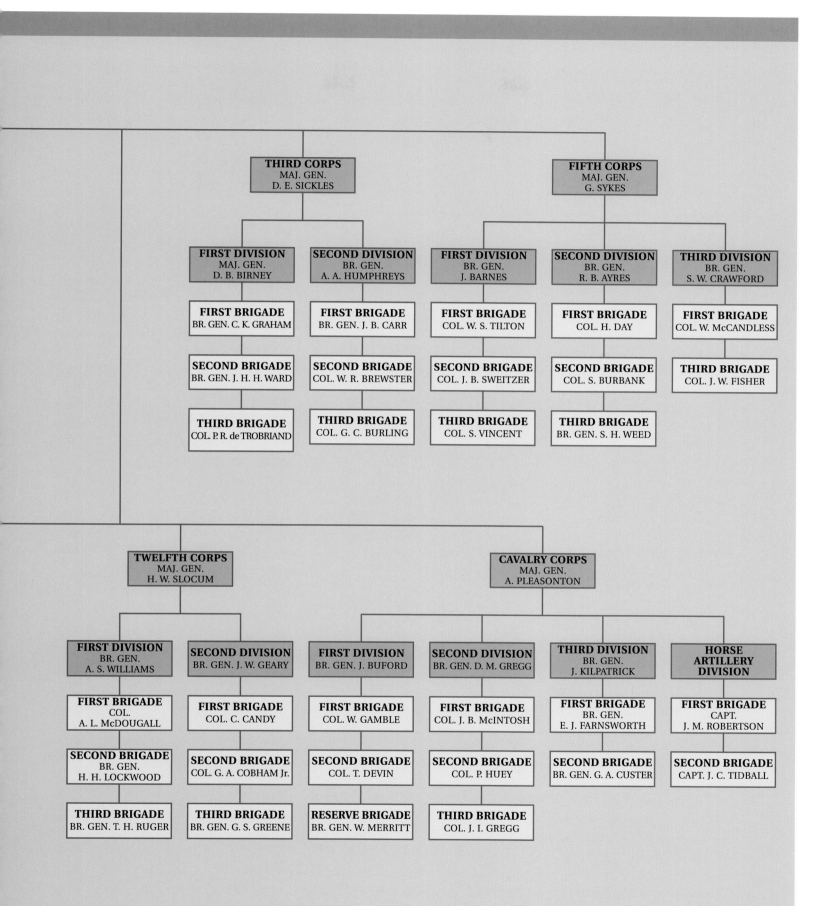

THIRD CORPS
MAJ. GEN.
D. E. SICKLES

FIFTH CORPS
MAJ. GEN.
G. SYKES

FIRST DIVISION
MAJ. GEN.
D. B. BIRNEY

SECOND DIVISION
BR. GEN.
A. A. HUMPHREYS

FIRST DIVISION
BR. GEN.
J. BARNES

SECOND DIVISION
BR. GEN.
R. B. AYRES

THIRD DIVISION
BR. GEN.
S. W. CRAWFORD

FIRST BRIGADE
BR. GEN. C. K. GRAHAM

FIRST BRIGADE
BR. GEN. J. B. CARR

FIRST BRIGADE
COL. W. S. TILTON

FIRST BRIGADE
COL. H. DAY

FIRST BRIGADE
COL. W. McCANDLESS

SECOND BRIGADE
BR. GEN. J. H. H. WARD

SECOND BRIGADE
COL. W. R. BREWSTER

SECOND BRIGADE
COL. J. B. SWEITZER

SECOND BRIGADE
COL. S. BURBANK

THIRD BRIGADE
COL. J. W. FISHER

THIRD BRIGADE
COL. P. R. de TROBRIAND

THIRD BRIGADE
COL. G. C. BURLING

THIRD BRIGADE
COL. S. VINCENT

THIRD BRIGADE
BR. GEN. S. H. WEED

TWELFTH CORPS
MAJ. GEN.
H. W. SLOCUM

CAVALRY CORPS
MAJ. GEN.
A. PLEASONTON

FIRST DIVISION
BR. GEN.
A. S. WILLIAMS

SECOND DIVISION
BR. GEN. J. W. GEARY

FIRST DIVISION
BR. GEN. J. BUFORD

SECOND DIVISION
BR. GEN. D. M. GREGG

THIRD DIVISION
BR. GEN.
J. KILPATRICK

**HORSE
ARTILLERY
DIVISION**

FIRST BRIGADE
COL.
A. L. McDOUGALL

FIRST BRIGADE
COL. C. CANDY

FIRST BRIGADE
COL. W. GAMBLE

FIRST BRIGADE
COL. J. B. McINTOSH

FIRST BRIGADE
BR. GEN.
E. J. FARNSWORTH

FIRST BRIGADE
CAPT.
J. M. ROBERTSON

SECOND BRIGADE
BR. GEN.
H. H. LOCKWOOD

SECOND BRIGADE
COL. G. A. COBHAM Jr.

SECOND BRIGADE
COL. T. DEVIN

SECOND BRIGADE
COL. P. HUEY

SECOND BRIGADE
BR. GEN. G. A. CUSTER

SECOND BRIGADE
CAPT. J. C. TIDBALL

THIRD BRIGADE
BR. GEN. T. H. RUGER

THIRD BRIGADE
BR. GEN. G. S. GREENE

RESERVE BRIGADE
BR. GEN. W. MERRITT

THIRD BRIGADE
COL. J. I. GREGG

passed, Lincoln's "Four score and seven years ago" speech has been indelibly etched in the American consciousness.

When examining Lee's generalship at Gettysburg, his failure to supervise effectively his lieutenants bears some examination. While working with

Jackson, Lee was able to give the broad discretionary orders with which he was comfortable, but Lee did not have this luxury with his other corps commanders, and he failed to adjust his leadership style accordingly. His vague order to Ewell to take Cemetery Hill "if practicable" on the first day of the battle is the prime example. Jackson would have understood that Lee wanted that key piece of terrain secured and would have acted to that end. Ewell did not interpret the order in the same way and elected to not pursue the opportunity.

Lee's dealings with Longstreet also showed a lack of proper supervision. Lee knew Longstreet had reservations about the entire offensive and specifically about continuing the battle the second day. Nonetheless, Lee did nothing to ensure Longstreet acted aggressively, and the result was an unacceptably slow initiation of the attack. With Jackson, Lee could reason and persuade, but with Longstreet, Lee had to be firm and resolute. While Longstreet obeyed Lee's orders, he did so grudgingly and with a heavy heart. Lee failed to bring his subordinate's will in line with his own.

Finally, Lee failed to control Stuart.

LEE'S LEADERSHIP

Gettysburg was clearly the low point of Lee's career. The initial decision to invade the North was misguided, and based largely on Lee's overconfidence in his men and underestimation of his enemy. Especially on the heels of the great victory at Chancellorsville, Lee was convinced that the Army of Northern Virginia could win by attacking. Outnumbered and forfeiting to Meade the defender's advantage, Lee's offensive strategy was not appropriate for the situation.

In contrast, Longstreet, from the campaign's initial planning stages, urged Lee to combine the strategic offensive with defensive tactics. Even after July 1, Lee still had alternatives that were in keeping with Longstreet's ideas. Lee could have withdrawn southward, taking all the supplies he had gathered with him, and accomplished his important objective of providing relief to war-torn Virginia. Lee, however, continued to seek victory through decisive battle. Steeped in the Napoleonic tradition, Lee sought a strategy of annihilation that was simply beyond the capability of the Confederacy's limited resources to obtain.

In addition to these strategic criticisms, Lee is often faulted for insisting upon invading Pennsylvania at a time when Confederate forces may have better been used to assist Pemberton at Vicksburg. This argument criticizes Lee for not possessing a grand strategic view of the entire Confederacy. Lee was in fact very Virginia-centric, but it must be remembered that such was his position. He was the commander of the Army of Northern Virginia, not the general-in-chief of all the Confederate armies. By the time Lee was made general-in-chief in January 1865, the war was all but over. The decision to invade Gettysburg may have been an incorrect one, but it is also incorrect to fault Lee for the failure of the Confederacy to have a holistic strategy. That responsibility more appropriately rested with President Jefferson Davis.

By this point in the war, Lee had become dependent on Stuart's reliable information about the enemy. In Stuart's absence, Lee had no satisfactory knowledge of the Army of the Potomac and could not act with his usual precision and initiative.

Lee appears to have never fully understood that he had to adjust his leadership style to the new situation. In retrospect, he lamented, "If I had Stonewall Jackson at Gettysburg, I would have won that fight." A more accurate and realistic appraisal would have been to supervise the subordinates he did have in a way that met both their needs and the needs of the situation.

UNION VICTORY

In spite of the incomplete victory, Meade had succeeded in inflicting more than 20,000 casualties on the Army of Northern Virginia, a number amounting to one-third of Lee's total strength. These losses forever blunted Lee's offensive capability, and set the stage for Lieutenant General Ulysses S. Grant to use unrelenting pressure to grind the Army of Northern Virginia into submission. But up to that point, Meade

MEADE'S LEADERSHIP

Great generals must be audacious—they must take calculated risks in order to achieve spectacular results. Meade lacked this important characteristic of generalship. After Gettysburg, Meade acted as if his mission was accomplished. Some observers comment that he appeared to have "escorted" Lee out of the North rather than pursuing him, bent on his destruction. Watching Meade's halfhearted effort, President Lincoln complained, "I'll be hanged if I could think of anything but an old woman trying to shoo her geese across a creek." Nonetheless, Meade had many defenders on his staff, including his engineer, Major General Gouverneur Warren, and his artilleryman, Brigadier General Henry Hunt. Still, many historians share Lincoln's view that after Gettysburg Meade lost an opportunity to end the war.

To be fair to Meade, any analyses of his actions must be done not from the comfortable view of the detached observer but from the much more tenuous position that was Meade's perspective. Meade commanded an army that was battered by its victory. The men were tired from days of marching and fighting. Dead and wounded soldiers and damaged and discarded equipment filled the battlefield and had to be recovered. Many veteran soldiers, as well as key leaders such as John Reynolds and Winfield Scott Hancock, had been killed or wounded.

One can only imagine the psychological state of Meade. Historian Bruce Catton paints a vivid picture: "Meade was on the road with his troops, an infinitely weary man with dust on his uniform and his gray beard, feeling responsibility as a paralyzing weight. He had been one of the few men who could have lost the war irretrievably in one day, and he had managed to avoid the mistakes that would have lost it. He would continue to avoid mistakes, even if he had to miss opportunity . . . Meade could see all the things that might go wrong." Under such circumstances, Meade can be forgiven for playing it safe. He had assumed command under extremely traumatic circumstances and turned back the great Robert E. Lee from Northern soil. That, Meade thought, was enough.

had done what none of his predecessors had done. He had truly beaten Lee. Moreover, Meade had stood in the gap at a time when, if he had failed, the Union cause may have very likely been lost. Eclipsed in history by Grant's much greater fame, Meade nonetheless did his duty when his country needed him to.

Left: The decaying bodies of the battle left the small town of Gettysburg with a serious problem. The establishment of a national cemetery provided for a dignified resting place for the dead.

GRANT VS. LEE

SPOTSYLVANIA COURT HOUSE, 1864

The Battle of Spotsylvania Court House was part of Lieutenant General Ulysses S. Grant's Virginia Campaign. On the Federal side, Major General George Meade commanded the Army of the Potomac, but Grant accompanied Meade throughout the campaign and provided the overall strategy and direction. On the Confederate side, General Robert E. Lee led the Army of Northern Virginia.

Many battles in the Virginia Campaign, including Spotsylvania, were tactical victories for Lee, but that was of little consequence. Grant's grand strategy was to keep the pressure on Lee and grind down his force, knowing that the North could replace its losses while the South could not. The campaign showed both Lee's excellence as a bold tactician fighting against the odds and Grant's mastery of strategy and maneuver. The campaign concluded with Lee's surrender at Appomattox on April 9, 1865.

PRELIMINARIES

When Lieutenant General Ulysses S. Grant became general-in-chief on March 12, 1864, he brought a new perspective to the Federal war effort. For the first

---

ULYSSES S. GRANT

RANK: LIEUTENANT GENERAL

BORN: 1822

EDUCATED: UNITED STATES MILITARY ACADEMY

MILITARY CAREER

VETERAN OF MEXICAN WAR

RESIGNED FROM THE ARMY IN 1854

COMMANDED AT FORT DONELSON, SHILOH, AND VICKSBURG

FINISHED WAR AS A LIEUTENANT GENERAL AND GENERAL-IN-
  CHIEF OF THE ARMIES

DIED: 1885

time, the Federals would treat the war as a whole, pressing the Confederates on all sides simultaneously rather than allowing them to reinforce first one threatened area and then another. To this end, Grant devised a cohesive strategy for 1864 to attack the Confederates from all directions. Major General Franz Sigel would advance up the Shenandoah Valley. Major General Benjamin Butler would conduct an amphibious operation in the area of Richmond and Petersburg. Major General Nathaniel Banks would march on Mobile, Alabama, and shut down the Confederacy's last major port on the Gulf of Mexico. Major General William T. Sherman would attack the Confederate war-making abilities in the Deep South. Major General George Meade would focus on General Robert E. Lee and his Army of Northern Virginia. "Lee's army is your objective point," Grant told Meade. "Wherever Lee goes, there you will go also." The synergy of all these operations would isolate Lee and lead to the destruction of the Army of Northern Virginia. President Lincoln summarized the strategy in typically homespun fashion by saying, "Those not skinning can hold a leg."

THE WILDERNESS REVISITED

All these operations were designed to jump off simultaneously in May, and on May 4 Grant crossed the Rapidan River into an area of Virginia called the Wilderness, home of the earlier battle between Lee and Major General Joseph Hooker at Chancellorsville. As both sides prepared for battle, the numbers clearly favored the Federals. Including his cavalry, Grant had a force of more than 118,000 men, while Lee could muster fewer than 62,000. One Federal general on the scene figured that if Grant's force could have been deployed properly, it would have covered a front of twenty-one miles, two ranks deep, with a third of its strength held in reserve. Under the same conditions, Lee could cover a total of only twelve miles.

Of more importance than the mere size of the force was its composition. In the key areas of firepower and maneuverability, Grant boasted 274 guns manned by 9,945 artillerymen, as well as Major General Phil Sheridan's crack command of 11,839 cavalrymen. On the other hand, Lee had only 224 guns manned by roughly 4,800 artillerymen and Major General Jeb Stuart's

SPOTSYLVANIA COURT HOUSE

Date	May 8–20, 1864
Location	Spotsylvania County, Virginia
Result	Inconclusive (Union offensive continued)

Strength

| Union: Army of the Potomac (100,000) | Confederate: Army of Northern Virginia (52,000) |

Casualties and losses

| 18,000 (approximate) | 12,000 (approximate) |

ROBERT E. LEE

RANK: GENERAL

BORN: 1807

EDUCATED: UNITED STATES MILITARY ACADEMY

MILITARY CAREER

VETERAN OF MEXICAN WAR

SUPERINTENDENT OF THE UNITED STATES MILITARY ACADEMY

MILITARY ADVISER TO JEFFERSON DAVIS

LED ARMY OF NORTHERN VIRGINIA FROM 1862 UNTIL THE CONCLUSION OF THE WAR

DIED: 1870

Above: A sergeant of Sheridan's Cavalry Corps. The Confederacy initially enjoyed a tremendous advantage in terms of cavalry thanks to commanders such as Jeb Stuart. By 1864, however, the much-improved Federal cavalry was a force to be reckoned with.

cavalry of just 8,000. In order to win, Lee would have to overcome these discrepancies. He would achieve this by selecting a battlefield on which restrictive terrain would mitigate his small numbers and negate Grant's firepower advantage.

The original timber of the Wilderness had been cut down long ago, and a tangled second growth of stunted pines, vines, scrub brush, and creepers had grown up in its place. What few roads there were often led to dead ends in the middle of nowhere and were not accurately mapped. The ground itself was compartmentalized by irregular ridges and crisscrossed by numerous streams that cut shallow ravines. In many places, these streams followed serpentine routes that created brush-covered swamps. Civil War correspondent William Swinton wrote that it was "impossible to conceive a field worse adapted to the movements of a grand army." One historian deemed the Wilderness "the last place on earth for armies to fight."

But now this otherwise desolate and inhospitable place was just what Lee needed. The thick vegetation neutralized the mobility of the Federal cavalry and limited the effectiveness of the artillery by rendering observed fire nearly impossible. The dense woods would prevent Grant from massing his superior numbers, and the broken ground would make command and control difficult. By picking his position carefully, Lee was able to make the otherwise indifferent terrain work to the advantage of his smaller and lighter force.

After crossing the Rapidan, Grant had hoped to avoid Hooker's mistake at Chancellorsville and clear the dangerous Wilderness as soon as he could. Instead, he was delayed as he waited for his supply train to catch up with his army. Grant and Lee were now in close proximity to each other, but neither knew exactly where the other was. This situation changed on May 5 when the Federals made contact with Lieutenant General Dick Ewell's corps. Mistakenly thinking they had bumped into a smaller element, the Federals launched a hasty frontal attack. Ewell's lead division fell back at first, but then Brigadier General John Gordon launched a counterattack that overwhelmed both Federal flanks. Having halted the Federal advance, Ewell dug in and held his ground until Lieutenant Generals A. P. Hill and James Longstreet could arrive with their corps.

"THESE ARE MY BRAVE TEXANS"

Both Grant and Lee had offensive plans for May 6, and the fighting resumed at 5:00 a.m. Again the Federals gained the initial advantage, partially collapsing Hill's line, but as the battle wore on, the restrictive terrain caused Grant's units to dissolve into smaller and smaller groups. Using an unfinished railroad cut that provided a covered approach to the Federal southern flank, Longstreet was able to stabilize the line with an attack that began at 11:00 a.m. As Longstreet's corps reached the field, Lee rode to meet them and greeted Brigadier General John Gregg's Texas Brigade, saying, "Ah! These are my brave Texans. I know you, and I know that you can and will keep those people back!" Lee then prepared to personally lead the first counterattacking units, but passionate cries of "Lee to the rear" dissuaded him.

Gregg's men met stiff resistance, and within ten minutes half of the Texans had become casualties. However, additional brigades arrived and drove the Federals back. Then, just before dark, Gordon attacked the Federal right. A panicked officer reported to Grant with news of the attack and the prediction that all was now lost. "I'm tired of hearing about what Lee is going to do," Grant muttered. "Some of you always seem to think he is suddenly going to turn a double somersault and land in our rear and on both our flanks at the same time. Go back to your command and try to think about what we are going to do ourselves, instead of what Lee is going to do." Grant had brought a new resolve and moral courage to the Army of the Potomac, and his confidence proved warranted. While Gordon's attack initially gained ground, it could not be sustained. Darkness and the arrival of Federal

Left: Grant's 1864 campaign in Virginia began with two days of costly fighting in the Wilderness. Many wounded on both sides died horrible deaths when the trees and thick underbrush caught fire. The dense terrain of the Wilderness helped offset Grant's numerical advantage.

reinforcements halted the Confederate effort, and both sides dug new lines during the night.

The heavy fighting throughout the day had ignited many brush fires in the thick undergrowth of the Wilderness, and at several points shooting had stopped by mutual consent as both sides worked together to rescue wounded soldiers from the flames. Cries for help and water pierced the air over the battlefield. Most, however, went unanswered. During the night of May 7–8, around 200 men suffocated or burned to death, and by morning, the smell of charred and decaying flesh hung everywhere.

In the end, the Wilderness was a lopsided tactical victory for the Confederates, with Grant suffering 17,000 casualties compared to 10,000 for Lee. More important, however, was what happened next. In the past, such a beating would have caused the Army of the Potomac to retreat and lick its wounds. With Grant now in command,

Below: During periods of rest, soldiers would "stack arms," a way to ground weapons in a uniform and organized manner to prevent damage and provide easy access.

Above: Dick Ewell was promoted to corps command after Stonewall Jackson's death.

those days were over. Instead of retreating, Grant would keep the pressure on Lee by simply disengaging and continuing the effort to get around Lee's flank.

Grant's soldiers soon became aware of exactly what type of man their new commander was. Late on May 7, Grant rode at the head of the army and approached a road junction in the Wilderness. A left turn would mean the usual withdrawal toward the fords of the Rapidan and Rappahannock rivers. To the right was the road to Richmond via Spotsylvania Court House. As the Federal columns approached, Grant pointed to the right. The soldiers cheered. They knew that things were different now. "Our spirits rose," remembered one veteran. "That night we were happy."

Earlier, Grant had met a reporter returning to Washington to file his story and said, "If you see the president, tell him, from me, that whatever happens, there will be no turning back." Even after a tactical defeat, Grant would press forward, using the powerful Federal resources to grind away at Lee. In that sense, the Battle of the Wilderness marked the beginning of the end for the Army of Northern Virginia, and with it, the Confederacy.

SPOTSYLVANIA COURT HOUSE

After the Wilderness, Lee understood Grant had just two options—he could either advance or he could retreat. Many, like Gordon, believed that after such a one-sided defeat Grant would opt to retreat. With his now-characteristic ability to understand his opponent, Lee disagreed, telling Gordon, "Grant is not going to retreat. He will move his army to Spotsylvania." Surprised, Gordon

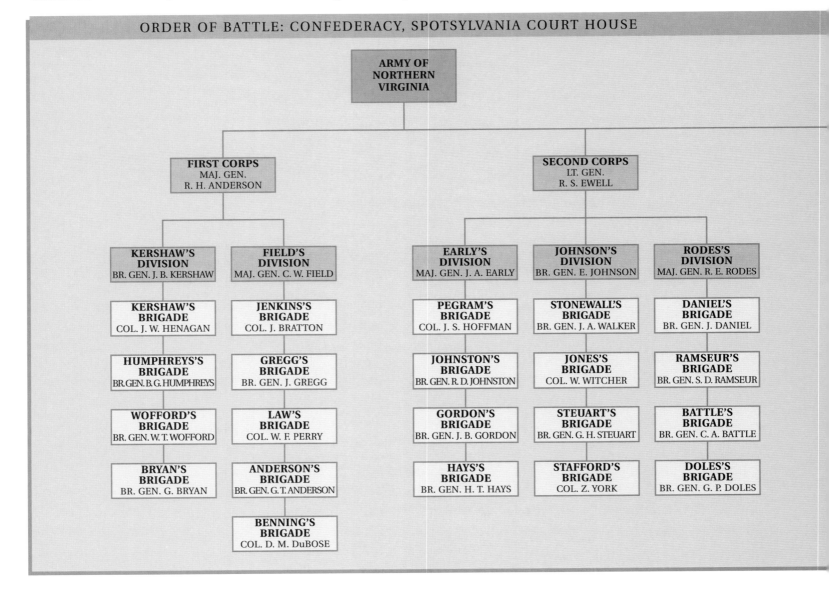

ORDER OF BATTLE: CONFEDERACY, SPOTSYLVANIA COURT HOUSE

asked Lee if there was any evidence that the Federals were moving in that direction. "Not at all, not at all," Lee said, "but that is the next point at which the armies will meet. Spotsylvania is now General Grant's best strategic point."

Lee based this conclusion on careful analysis of the reports he had received throughout his command. Major General Jubal Early, on the extreme left of the Confederate line, reported that the Federal troops had abandoned their positions opposite his division. The same thing had occurred in front of parts of Brigadier General Edward Johnson's command. Likewise, Ewell had reported that the Federals were dismantling their pontoon bridges at Germanna. From these telltale observations, Lee concluded that Grant had severed his line of communications via Germanna

and would not retreat back across the Rapidan River. With this course of action discounted, Lee then had to determine in which direction Grant would advance. Again Grant had two choices. He could move either eastward toward Fredericksburg or southeastward toward Spotsylvania Court House.

As Lee contemplated these two possibilities, he discovered there was much more to recommend Spotsylvania Court House to Grant. First of all was the matter of distance. If Grant intended an advance on Richmond, the direct road to Spotsylvania Court House was less than half as long as the Fredericksburg route. Second, Spotsylvania Court House was key terrain for anyone desiring to control Hanover Junction. Two major railroads met there, and if Grant intended to drive Lee back on Richmond by cutting off his supplies, Grant would almost certainly

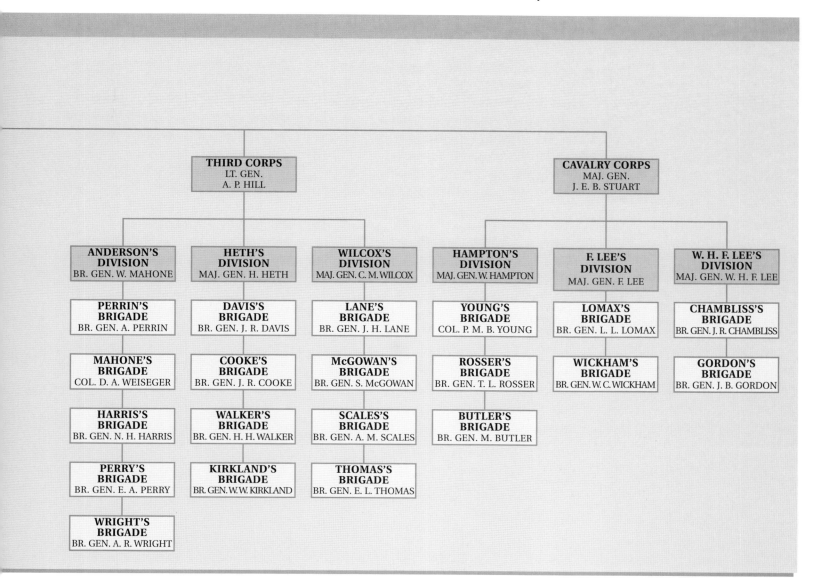

Above: Union troops attack across the Ni River, May 7, 1864. Union troops used pontoon bridges to assault Confederate defensive positions.

try to seize the junction. While Lee's reasoning seemed to recommend Spotsylvania Court House as Grant's objective, reports from the field were conflicting. Cavalry scouts had seen heavy wagon traffic in the Fredericksburg direction. On the other hand, Stuart was also reporting that a strong Federal force had occupied Todd's Tavern, midway between Grant's present position and Spotsylvania Court House.

In the end, Lee relied on his analysis and began hedging his bets toward Spotsylvania Court House. He sent Brigadier General William Pendleton to

cut a road southward through the woods from the Plank Road to the highway running from Orange Court House to Spotsylvania. This precaution would give the Confederates an inner line in the event of a race to Spotsylvania. Lee also advised Stuart to reconnoiter the roads in the direction of Spotsylvania.

REPOSITIONED ARTILLERY PROVIDES A CLUE

With these steps in motion, Lee continued to closely monitor every intelligence report of Grant's probable movements. All day long, the evidence

Right: Known as "Hancock the Superb," Winfield Scott Hancock (1824–86) was one of Grant's most capable commanders. It was Hancock's corps that Grant selected to attack the Mule Shoe using Emory Upton's new tactics.

mounted in support of a move toward Spotsylvania Court House, and in the afternoon came the decisive indicator. At 4:00, Lee received a report from a staff officer who had been observing the area from the attic of a deserted house that served as the headquarters of Hill's Third Corps. With the aid of a powerful marine glass, the officer had seen a number of heavy artillery pieces, which had previously been held in reserve, now being moved. They were headed south down Brock Road, in the direction of the Confederates' right flank and ultimately Spotsylvania.

No Federal infantry had yet begun to move, but the repositioning of the artillery was all Lee needed to reach his conclusion and to dispatch his First Corps under Major General Richard Anderson along Pendleton's newly cut road. Lee quickly dispatched two of his staff officers to instruct the cavalry to hold Spotsylvania Court House. As they rode, one said to the other, "How in God's name does the old man know General Grant is moving to Spotsylvania Court House?" The answer lay in Lee's detailed and critical study of intelligence reports, which both eliminated certain Federal courses and suggested the likelihood of others. The race to Spotsylvania Court House was on and, thanks to their commander's awareness, analysis, and intuition, the Confederates had a head start.

THE "MULE SHOE"

Throughout May 8, the two armies flowed into the Spotsylvania area and built corresponding lines of earthworks east and west of Brock Road. On May 9 and 10, Grant probed both of Lee's flanks but could not find any vulnerability. Lee held back. Unlike at the Wilderness, where he had counterattacked extensively, at Spotsylvania Lee fought almost entirely from behind his entrenchments. While Grant viewed this as an indication of weakness, he nonetheless found it difficult to crack the Confederate line.

Grant, however, was encouraged by a possibility he saw in an imaginative attack by just twelve regiments led by Colonel Emory Upton. Upton was an up-and-coming visionary. Just twenty-four years of age, he was fewer than three years out of West Point. The Confederate line had ended up including a huge salient, or bulge, pointing north in the direction of the Federals. Its shape gave rise to this part of the battlefield being nicknamed the "Mule Shoe." On May 10, Upton struck this Mule Shoe, but instead of attacking on line across a broad front, he had approached in column formation, and, in order to maintain momentum, he had ordered his men not to fire as they advanced. Upton ensured this discipline would be maintained by having all but his first rank advance with uncapped muskets. His idea was to shatter a small segment of the Confederate line and then have a second wave of attackers pour through and divest the flanks and rear.

The attack enjoyed remarkable initial success. As Upton's men emerged from the cover of a thick wood, it was just a matter of minutes before they closed with a startled brigade of Georgians, seized four guns and a second line of works, and almost reached the McCoull House in the center of the Mule Shoe. There, Confederate artillery at the top of the salient halted the Federal advance. Plans had called for Upton to be reinforced by Brigadier General Gershom Mott's division, but Mott was halted by Confederate artillery fire. Without this support, Upton was unable to hold his gains and was compelled to pull back.

> ## "IT LOOKED AS IF THE HEAVENS WERE TRYING TO WASH UP THE BLOOD AS FAST AS THE CIVILIZED BARBARIANS WERE SPILLING IT."
>
> CONFEDERATE ARTILLERYMAN, ON THE HEAVY RAINS DURING THE WILDERNESS CAMPAIGN

Below: Much battlefield photography of the Civil War recorded dead bodies, an approach that made many viewers feel the horrors of war in a previously unimagined way.

ORDER OF BATTLE: UNITED STATES (UNION), SPOTSYLVANIA COURT HOUSE

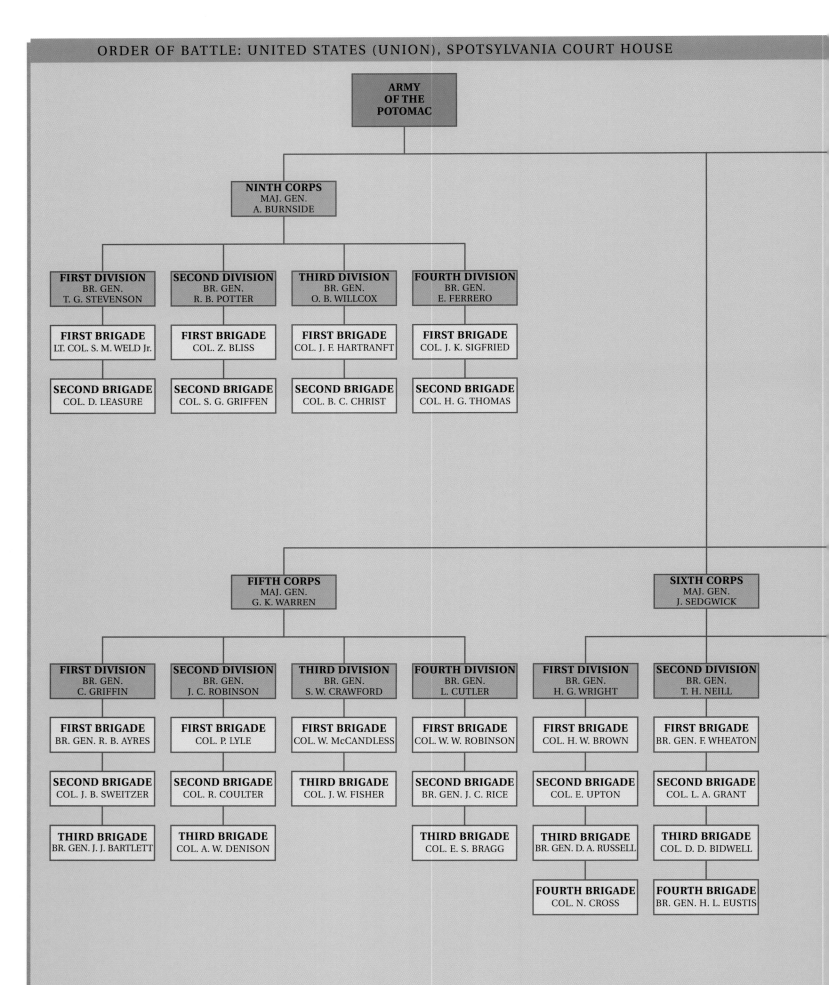

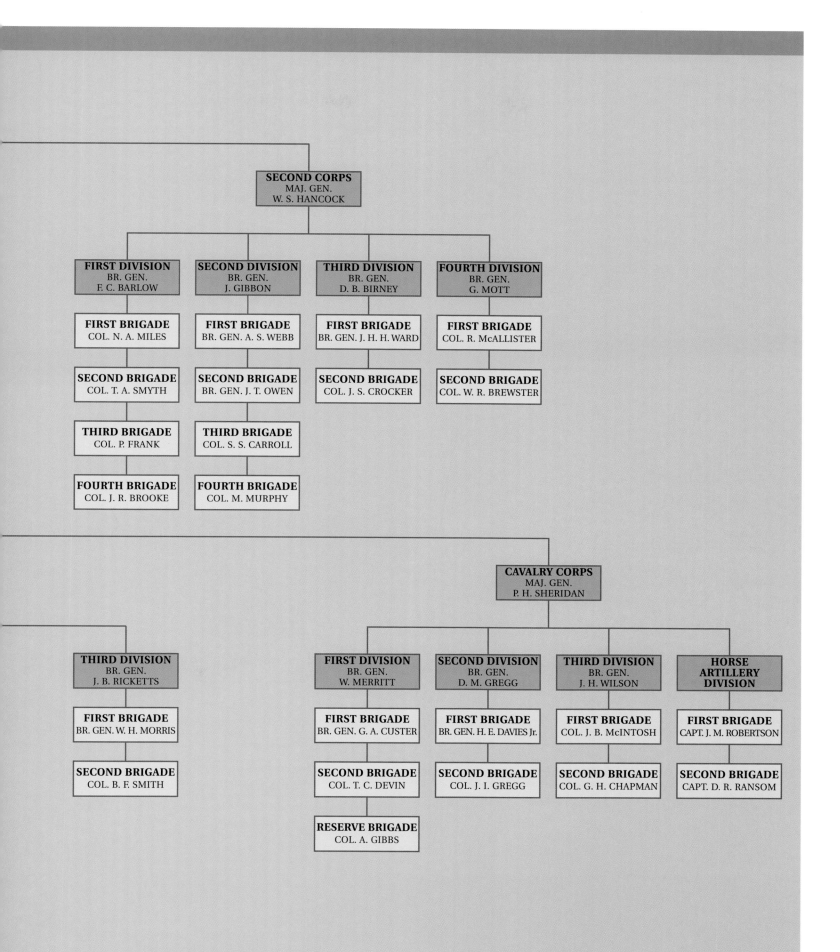

SECOND CORPS
MAJ. GEN.
W. S. HANCOCK

FIRST DIVISION
BR. GEN.
F. C. BARLOW

SECOND DIVISION
BR. GEN.
J. GIBBON

THIRD DIVISION
BR. GEN.
D. B. BIRNEY

FOURTH DIVISION
BR. GEN.
G. MOTT

FIRST BRIGADE
COL. N. A. MILES

FIRST BRIGADE
BR. GEN. A. S. WEBB

FIRST BRIGADE
BR. GEN. J. H. H. WARD

FIRST BRIGADE
COL. R. McALLISTER

SECOND BRIGADE
COL. T. A. SMYTH

SECOND BRIGADE
BR. GEN. J. T. OWEN

SECOND BRIGADE
COL. J. S. CROCKER

SECOND BRIGADE
COL. W. R. BREWSTER

THIRD BRIGADE
COL. P. FRANK

THIRD BRIGADE
COL. S. S. CARROLL

FOURTH BRIGADE
COL. J. R. BROOKE

FOURTH BRIGADE
COL. M. MURPHY

CAVALRY CORPS
MAJ. GEN.
P. H. SHERIDAN

THIRD DIVISION
BR. GEN.
J. B. RICKETTS

FIRST DIVISION
BR. GEN.
W. MERRITT

SECOND DIVISION
BR. GEN.
D. M. GREGG

THIRD DIVISION
BR. GEN.
J. H. WILSON

**HORSE
ARTILLERY
DIVISION**

FIRST BRIGADE
BR. GEN. W. H. MORRIS

FIRST BRIGADE
BR. GEN. G. A. CUSTER

FIRST BRIGADE
BR. GEN. H. E. DAVIES Jr.

FIRST BRIGADE
COL. J. B. McINTOSH

FIRST BRIGADE
CAPT. J. M. ROBERTSON

SECOND BRIGADE
COL. B. F. SMITH

SECOND BRIGADE
COL. T. C. DEVIN

SECOND BRIGADE
COL. J. I. GREGG

SECOND BRIGADE
COL. G. H. CHAPMAN

SECOND BRIGADE
CAPT. D. R. RANSOM

RESERVE BRIGADE
COL. A. GIBBS

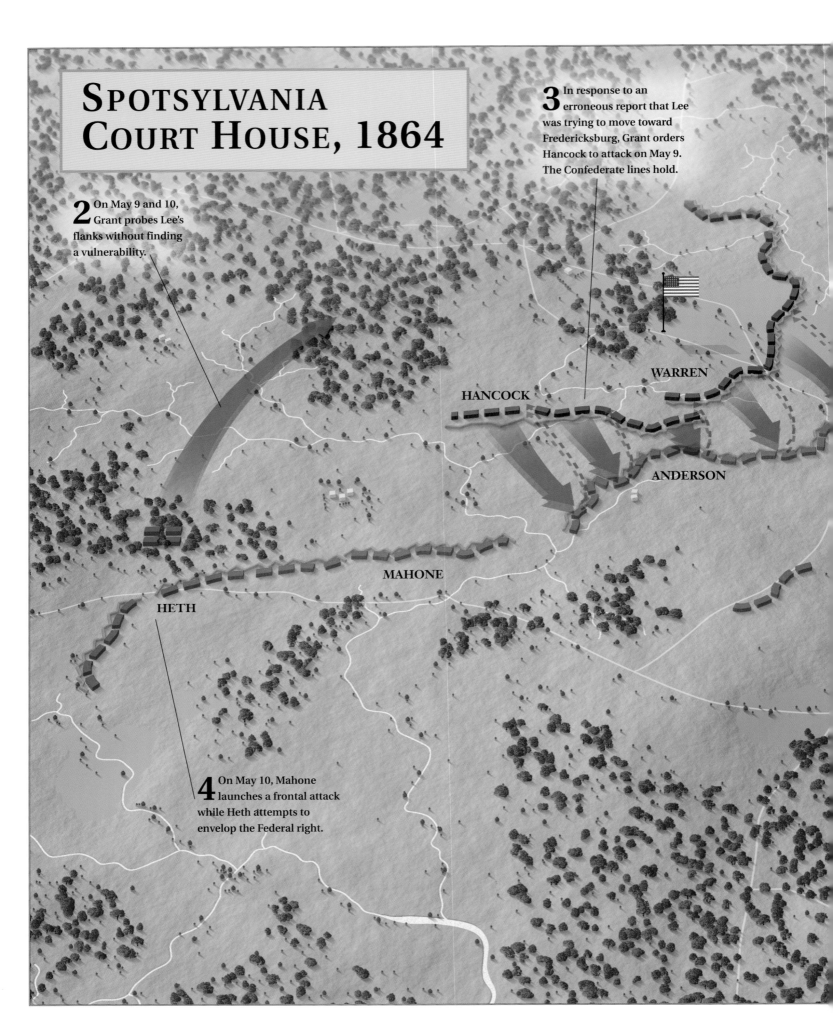

SPOTSYLVANIA COURT HOUSE, 1864

2 On May 9 and 10, Grant probes Lee's flanks without finding a vulnerability.

3 In response to an erroneous report that Lee was trying to move toward Fredericksburg, Grant orders Hancock to attack on May 9. The Confederate lines hold.

HANCOCK

WARREN

ANDERSON

MAHONE

HETH

4 On May 10, Mahone launches a frontal attack while Heth attempts to envelop the Federal right.

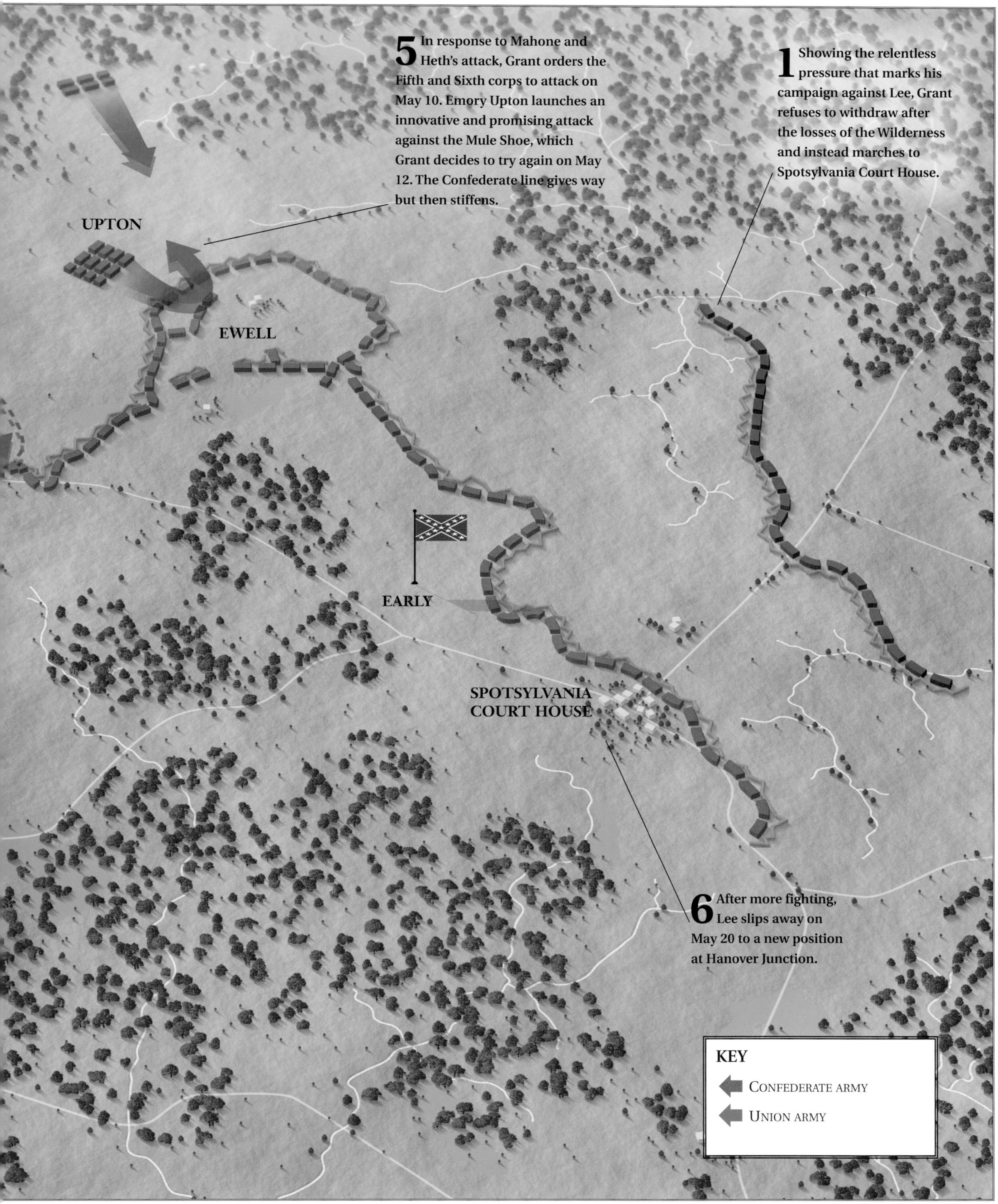

5 In response to Mahone and Heth's attack, Grant orders the Fifth and Sixth corps to attack on May 10. Emory Upton launches an innovative and promising attack against the Mule Shoe, which Grant decides to try again on May 12. The Confederate line gives way but then stiffens.

1 Showing the relentless pressure that marks his campaign against Lee, Grant refuses to withdraw after the losses of the Wilderness and instead marches to Spotsylvania Court House.

UPTON

EWELL

EARLY

SPOTSYLVANIA COURT HOUSE

6 After more fighting, Lee slips away on May 20 to a new position at Hanover Junction.

KEY

◀ CONFEDERATE ARMY

◀ UNION ARMY

Above: The Battle of Cold Harbor, June 1–12, 1864. By 1864, the tremendous Federal advantage in manpower allowed Grant to aggressively pressure Lee, knowing that the Federals could replace casualties and the Confederates could not.

Although Upton was ultimately repulsed, the new tactic impressed Grant, and he decided to try it again. This time, Grant would throw Major General Winfield Scott Hancock's entire Second Corps against the Mule Shoe. On May 12 at 4:30 a.m., a massed attack of 20,000 Federals advanced, and in just fifteen minutes they were pouring through gaps in the Confederate lines. Hancock captured 4,000 Confederate prisoners.

In a desperate attempt to rescue the situation, Lee ordered Gordon to counterattack and seemed prepared to lead the charge himself. Amid shouts of "General Lee to the rear," Gordon's men gathered around Lee's horse Traveller and led him to safety. Then at 5:30 a.m., Gordon ordered the charge. By now Hancock's attack was losing momentum as the Federal brigades became intermingled in an unmanageable mob. One soldier noted that officers "were giving orders to a dozen different organizations," and in the confusion the Federals fell back. In desperate hand-to-hand fighting, the Confederates

succeeded in completing a new line of entrenchments across the base of the salient. For nearly twenty hours, the fighting continued almost unabated in what may have been the most ferociously sustained combat of the entire war. The hotly contested area became known as the "Bloody Angle," and the firing was so intense that musket balls cut down an oak tree twenty-two inches in diameter. There was more inconclusive fighting on May 18 and 19, but the Confederate line held. In a pattern that would foreshadow World War I, the defenders had proved it was possible to repair a breach in a fortified line faster than the attackers could exploit it.

LOSSES

Federal losses at Spotsylvania included Major General John Sedgwick, the popular commander of the Sixth Corps, and, in a related battle at Yellow Tavern, the famed Confederate cavalryman Major General Jeb Stuart was also killed. Fighting mostly behind the protection of entrenchments, Lee suffered 12,000 casualties compared to Grant's 18,000. Having survived this close call, Lee withdrew on May 20 to a new position at Hanover Junction.

THE COMPLETION OF THE CAMPAIGN

By this point it had become obvious that Grant was going to get little help from the secondary efforts in Virginia. A hastily assembled Confederate force that included cadets from the Virginia Military Institute defeated Sigel in the Shenandoah Valley at the Battle of New Market. To make matters worse, after landing on the peninsula formed by the James and Appomattox rivers, Butler's attack had stalled, and he was now bottled up by a Confederate force led by General Pierre Gustave Toutant Beauregard. Instead of helping Grant isolate Lee by keeping the Confederate forces occupied, these operations were having the opposite effect. With Sigel defeated and Butler isolated, Lee was able to receive 8,500 reinforcements from the forces that had opposed the two Federal operations.

Lee was aware that he had to avoid a siege of Richmond in order to keep the Confederacy alive. He also knew that his inferior numbers made it impossible to defeat Grant in open battle. Instead, Lee would have to fight behind entrenchments to preserve his force, hoping that Grant would make an error that would allow Lee to attack.

Lee found the opportunity he was waiting for at Hanover Junction. He had placed his army in an inverted V configuration, with its point on the North Anna River at Ox Ford, a crossing site held by the Confederates. Lieutenant General A. P. Hill's Third Corps held the left leg of the V on the Little River. The right leg was on a bend of the North Anna River as it flowed to the Pamunkey River. Major General Richard Anderson's First Corps and Lieutenant General Richard Ewell's Second Corps manned these positions. The idea was to draw Grant to divide his force by crossing the river in two places, Jericho Mill and the Telegraph Road bridge, which were on opposite sides of the V. By also blocking

Grant's crossing of the river at Ox Ford, Lee hoped to split Grant's force in three places. Lee could then use interior lines to hold one side of the V with a small force and mass the rest of his army against one of the isolated parts of Grant's command.

Lee had been forced to abandon the bridges at Jericho Mill and Telegraph Road in earlier fighting, and when Grant advanced, he assumed the Confederates had retreated to Richmond. He ordered a pursuit, but instead of finding fleeing Confederates, on May 24 Grant's men ran into Lee's stout defense. It was not until evening that Grant realized what he was up against. Lee's plan was unfolding perfectly.

GRANT SLIPS AWAY

Unfortunately for the Confederacy, Lee had become seriously ill and was unable to personally direct the battle. Confined to his tent, Lee could only declare, "We must strike them a blow, we must never allow them to pass again." However, without a capable subordinate like Stonewall Jackson to carry out Lee's intent, the opportunity slipped away. Grant ordered his army to entrench, and

Below: Using the tool shown attached to the barrel of this cannon, Civil War artillerymen had to swab the piece after each firing to prevent stray sparks from prematurely igniting the next load.

Above: The conditions of battle usually precluded adherence to conventional rituals for burial. Burial often consisted of simply covering bodies with dirt or placing the dead in common graves.

the Federals and Confederates spent the next two days skirmishing. Of the 68,000 Federal soldiers committed over the course of the fighting, 2,623 became casualties. Lee lost 2,517 of his 53,000 men. Grant had been coaxed into Lee's trap, but he managed to slip away and press on with his superior numbers.

Grant resumed his relentless pressure on May 27 by crossing the Pamunkey and then turning northwest and west to threaten Lee's railroad. Grant moved to Totopotomoy Creek, where Lee blocked him again. After that engagement, both forces began moving to the vital road junction at Cold Harbor. Lee dispatched Major General Fitzhugh Lee's cavalry division to secure the crossroads and hold it until infantry could arrive. Grant also recognized the importance of the location and sent Major General Phil Sheridan on the same mission. These lead elements of the opposing armies clashed on May 31 and continued to struggle for the next two days. The main Federal assault came on June 3.

By this time, the Army of the Potomac numbered 108,000 men against Lee's 59,000. Grant had planned a general assault for June 2, but it had been delayed until the next day. Lee's men

used the time wisely, digging strong trenches and carefully emplacing their weapons to achieve interlocking fields of fire. The Federal soldiers knew exactly what awaited them. As they prepared for the attack, many wrote their names and addresses on slips of paper and pinned them on the backs of their coats. These precursors to dog tags would be used to identify dead bodies and help in notifying loved ones back home.

WANTON SLAUGHTER

Grant gave no instructions about the specifics of the attack, leaving those decisions to the individual corps commanders. There had been no substantive reconnaissance of the Confederate lines, and the defenders had so expertly blended their trenches with the natural folds in the ground that the Federals lacked a true picture of the objective. Major General William Smith, commander of the Eighteenth Corps, complained of "the utter absence of any military plan." Nonetheless, at 4:30 a.m. on June 3, the buglers sounded the advance and 50,000 infantrymen of the Second, Sixth, and Eighteenth corps began moving toward the Confederate defenses several hundred yards away.

The Confederate officers had trouble enforcing their men to hold fire against such a tempting target, but when the order to fire was given, the results were devastating. "It seemed almost like murder to fire," said one Confederate. The cohesiveness of the Federal line broke under such withering discharge, and the battle took on the nature of a series of isolated individual struggles.

Murderous enfilading fire from the Confederate zigzag trenches tore the attack to pieces. By 5:30 a.m., all three Federal corps that made the attack were hugging the ground just trying to stay alive. Grant remained remarkably aloof during the attack. Not until around noon did he ride out to the corps headquarters and learn the attack was a failure. Between 5,600 and 7,000 Federals had become casualties, most in the first fifteen minutes of the attack. Lee lost fewer than 1,500. Amid all the carnage, the Federal Fifth Corps had not attacked at all and the Ninth Corps did little besides create a small diversion. One Confederate concluded that Cold Harbor was "perhaps the easiest victory ever granted to the Confederate arms by the folly of the Federals commanders."

Federals were quick to criticize the attack as well. One captain called it "the greatest and most inexcusable slaughter of the whole war." Upton wrote his sister that he was "disgusted with the generalship displayed; our men have, in many instances, been foolishly and wantonly sacrificed." Even Grant himself confessed, "I regret this assault more than any one I ever ordered." Yet he did not obsess about the catastrophe—instead, he began to plan his next move.

By now Grant was running out of maneuvering room and could see no prospect at all of breaking through to Richmond. He instead chose to follow a course he had begun to consider back at Spotsylvania. Grant would shift the Army of the Potomac south of the James River and use it as his line of supply for an advance on Petersburg.

Petersburg lay about twenty miles south of Richmond. It was a shipping port as well as a rail center, and many of the supplies headed for both Richmond and Lee's army passed through there. Lee understood the gravity of the situation, explaining to Lieutenant General Jubal Early, "We must destroy this army of Grant's before he gets to the James River. If he gets there, it will become a siege, and then it will be a mere question of time."

MASTERY OF SIEGE LOGISTICS

Still, Grant was able to get the jump on Lee. Between June 12 and 16, Grant crossed the James River, and it took Lee several days to ascertain exactly what Grant was doing. When the Federals first reached Petersburg, only a skeleton Confederate force was defending the city. However, the Federals failed to press their advantage and capture the prize, and the Confederates then were able to strengthen their lines. Grant launched an uncoordinated attack with his entire army on June 18 but was repulsed.

By then Lee had arrived, bringing reinforcements. The next day, Grant began a siege.

During the siege, Grant displayed the same mastery of logistics he had demonstrated at Vicksburg, building up a huge logistical base at City Point. From this location, Grant had outstanding rail and water communications that kept his force well supplied. The scope of the operation was phenomenal. The port facilities consisted of eight wharves spread over eight acres with 100,000 square feet of warehouses. More than twenty-two miles of railroad ran from the wharves to directly behind the Federal lines. These tracks transported more than 500,000 tons of supplies, including fresh meat and more than 100,000 loaves of fresh bread daily, directly to the combat units during the siege. A massive repair shop maintained the force of more than 5,000 wagons and the 60,000 animals necessary to support Grant's army.

Above: Cannon, mortars, and cannonballs sit in the harbor at City Point. The massive Federal logistics advantage allowed Grant to grow stronger as Lee became weaker.

"THEY COULDN'T HIT AN ELEPHANT AT THIS DISTANCE."

UNION MAJOR GENERAL
JOHN SEDGWICK (1813–64),
MOMENTS BEFORE BEING SHOT
DEAD BY A CONFEDERATE
SNIPER AT SPOTSYLVANIA

Hospitals built at City Point were capable of treating 15,000 wounded, with medical care unsurpassed in a field environment. A highly efficient transmission system allowed Grant to communicate not only with Washington but also with Federal forces anywhere in the country. The result of this massive Federal logistical apparatus was that as Lee weakened inside Petersburg, Grant grew stronger outside.

LINCOLN FIGHTS AN ELECTION

While Grant was comfortable with his position at Petersburg, the seemingly stalemated situation caused problems for President Lincoln, who was facing a serious challenge in the 1864 election. Grant's lack of forward movement in Virginia appeared to be just another indication that the war would continue to drag on. To make matters worse, Early conducted a raid through the Shenandoah Valley in June that caused panic in Washington. Fortunately for the president, Major General William T. Sherman's capture of Atlanta reversed the pessimistic situation, and Lincoln rode the new wave of enthusiasm to electoral victory.

With this fortuitous outcome still in the future, Grant did what he could to keep the pressure on Lee. On July 30, Federal soldiers detonated four tons of black powder in a mine they had dug under the Confederate position. The explosion created a hole 175 feet long, 60 feet wide, and 30 feet deep. For at least 600 feet on either side of the crater, the Confederate line had been reduced to havoc. However, this initial Federal advantage of surprise gave way to mismanagement and delay, and the Confederates were able to recover. Now the Federals were largely trapped in the crater. In the Battle of the Crater, the Federals lost about 5,300 soldiers in what Grant described as "the saddest affair I have witnessed in the war. Such opportunity for carrying fortifications I have never seen and do not expect again to have." By contrast, Confederate losses were just 1,032. Grant was more successful on August 18 when Major

General Gouverneur Warren seized the Weldon Railroad, Lee's connection to Weldon and Wilmington, North Carolina. On August 25, Lee won a victory at Reams Station, twelve miles south of Petersburg, but he was still unable to use the Weldon Railroad

Right: This painting shows Confederate forces under Major General William Mahone (1826–95) counterattacking Union troops (foreground) at the Battle of the Crater, Petersburg, July 30, 1864. Union troops became trapped in the crater and were massacred in what Mahone later described as a "turkey shoot." The Battle of the Crater was one of the Civil War's greatest tactical blunders.

farther north than Stony Creek Depot, sixteen miles south of Petersburg. From there, supplies had to be moved by laborious wagonloads.

As the siege continued, Grant kept extending his lines to the west. He was never able to get around Lee, but he

forced Lee to stretch his lines to the breaking point. The scales clearly tipped in the Federals' favor in March 1865 when Major General Phil Sheridan and most of his cavalry joined Grant from the Shenandoah Valley. Grant gave Sheridan an infantry corps and told him

LEE'S LEADERSHIP

Lee was at heart an offensive-minded general who sought victory through a decisive battle in the Napoleonic tradition. One of his officers claimed Lee's "very name is audacity." Yet in the face of sparse Confederate resources, especially after the losses of Gettysburg, such a strategy proved problematic. In the Virginia Campaign, Lee was forced to go on the defensive, although he always looked for an offensive opportunity. The combination of absorbing Grant's relentless attacks even in victories such as Spotsylvania as well as Lee's own limited offensive forays bled Lee's army dry. Some observers criticize Lee for destroying his army by his aggressive tactics, but by the time of the Virginia Campaign, Lee undoubtedly felt he had to produce a major victory to keep the Confederate hopes alive.

Making the best of what little he had, Lee showed excellent tactical skill. His ability to understand and use the terrain and his ability to analyze intelligence to anticipate Grant's moves were amazing. Once derided as the "King of Spades" for his use of entrenchments early in the war, Lee showed in Virginia the power of the defense, repulsing Federal attacks at Cold Harbor and elsewhere. However, his attempt at a flexible defense ultimately failed as he ran out of manpower, space in which to maneuver, and capable lieutenants.

Assessments of Lee's generalship have swayed like a pendulum. Early hagiographic biographers such as Douglas Southall Freeman and Clifford Dowdey idolized Lee. Revisionists then came along and blamed Lee for the Confederacy's defeat. In the final analysis, Lee simply did not have the resources to fight the way he wanted to and the way he did, but that should hardly constitute an indictment on his generalship. Lee came closer to bringing victory to the Confederate cause than any other Southern general, and under the circumstances it is hard to imagine anyone else doing any better. As one observer noted, if Lee "had been a Union general, his moral courage and audacity would have won the war." But the Confederacy simply did not have the manpower to support Lee's vision. Instead, it was Ulysses S. Grant who was able to mold an offensive strategy around the vast Federal resources and gain ultimate victory.

to break Lee's western flank. In the ensuing Battle of Five Forks on April 1, Sheridan succeeded in doing just what Grant had hoped for. Grant then ordered a general attack all along the Petersburg front. Faced with this threat, Lee was forced to abandon Petersburg, and the city fell on April 3. The siege of Petersburg had lasted nine and a half months and was spread over 176 square miles. It had involved six major battles, eleven engagements, and numerous other contacts. Throughout it all, Grant's men suffered 42,000 casualties compared to 28,000 for Lee. However, as was the case throughout the Virginia Campaign, Grant could replace his casualties and Lee could not. Grant had earlier said, "The key to taking Richmond is Petersburg." He was right. Federal troops entered Richmond the day after Petersburg fell.

Lee's only alternative now was to try to get his 50,000-man army into central North Carolina to join with General Joseph Johnston's 20,000 men then opposing Sherman's advance north from Savannah, Georgia. Grant anticipated this move and used his cavalry to prevent Lee from turning south, and instead forced Lee to the west.

Lee was fast running out of provisions for his army. He made a desperate run to reach a supply dump at Lynchburg, but on April 6, Federal cavalry caught up with Lee's rear guard and destroyed it. On April 8, Sheridan got ahead of Lee and cut off the Confederate retreat. Lee knew further resistance was futile and on April 9, he requested a conference with Grant. The two met at Appomattox Court House, where Lee surrendered the Army of Northern Virginia.

WAR OF ATTRITION

In the process of using his numerical advantage at Spotsylvania, Grant would gain a reputation as being a butcher who sacrificed his men with repeated attacks against Lee's strong defenses and eventually won only because of superior numbers. In reality, Grant understood that the quickest way to end the war was to defeat Lee's army, and the quickest way to defeat Lee's army was to attack it. Grant knew that suffering losses to achieve the object of the war was preferable to suffering losses merely to perpetuate the stalemate. Such a strategic understanding saved lives in the long run.

Grant could pursue such a strategy of attrition because of his characteristic persistence. He had refused to give up after the disastrous first day at Shiloh. He had not been deterred at Vicksburg in spite of all his failed attempts over the winter of 1862–63. In Virginia, he would likewise continue to persist. On May 11, Grant wired Major General Henry Halleck from Spotsylvania that he intended "to fight it out on this line if it takes all summer." It would take even longer than that, but Grant had made his point. He would continue the relentless pressure of his Virginia Campaign at Hanover Junction, Cold Harbor, and Petersburg and ultimately lead the Army of the Potomac to victory.

THE GREATEST GENERAL?

One of the Civil War's most enduring debates is over the relative greatness of Generals Lee and Grant. The traditional conclusion that Lee was the superior tactician and Grant was the superior strategist has come under recent scrutiny, but has largely stood the test of time. Grant took stock of his resources and used them in a way that accomplished his strategic objective. Along the way, he suffered large numbers of casualties, but that does not diminish the magnitude of his strategic accomplishments. Grant persistently demonstrated masterful integration of logistics and maneuver.

Lee fought expertly with the limited resources he had, repeatedly thwarting Grant on the tactical battlefield. The fact that Lee ultimately succumbed to Grant's relentless pounding likewise should not be interpreted as an indictment against Lee's generalship. Both men were the best their armies had to offer, and their head-to-head confrontation in the Virginia Campaign is one of military history's most impressive showcases of generalship.

GRANT'S LEADERSHIP

Grant's success in the Virginia Campaign was largely a function of his strategic acumen, his characteristic persistence, and his logistical expertise. In Grant, President Lincoln finally found a partner who shared his strategic vision. "Since [the Peninsula Campaign]," Lincoln explained, "I have constantly desired the Army of the Potomac to make Lee's army and not Richmond, its objective point." Grant agreed, instructing Meade, "Wherever Lee goes, there you will go also."

But Grant also understood that the strength of the defense and other factors present in the Civil War had made the annihilation of an army in a single battle a near impossibility. Therefore, Grant chose to pursue a strategy of attrition, which sought to reduce the effectiveness of the enemy by loss of personnel and materiel. Grant would accomplish this end by keeping Lee under constant pressure.

A large part of Grant's genius was an ability to look beyond individual battles and see the campaign as a whole. Grant entertained no hope of destroying Lee in a single, decisive Napoleonic battle. Instead, in the words of one scholar, Grant "extended the concept of the battle until the battle became literally synonymous with the whole campaign: he would fight all the time, every day." Grant understood that at this point in the war, the numbers clearly favored the Federals. Grant could replace his casualties while Lee could not, making it possible for Grant to continually pound away, knowing that his superior resources would allow his army to survive while Lee's disintegrated. Grant's strategy of attrition was so relentless and so dominating that it bordered on being a strategy of annihilation.

SHERMAN VS. JOHNSTON

KENNESAW MOUNTAIN, 1864

The Battle of Kennesaw Mountain was fought between Major General William Tecumseh Sherman's Military Division of the Mississippi and General Joe Johnston's Army of Tennessee. The battle was part of the larger Atlanta Campaign, which advanced from Dalton, Georgia, to the outskirts of Atlanta.

Along the way, Sherman and Johnston engaged in a duel in which the former repeatedly tried to maneuver around Johnston's flank while Johnston skillfully thwarted Sherman's attempts by pulling back to one entrenched position after the other. Only on one occasion, at Kennesaw Mountain on June 27, 1864, did Sherman forego his usual flank maneuver and launch a frontal attack. The results were catastrophic for the Federals, but they did not dissuade Sherman from his ultimate goal. He

---

WILLIAM T. SHERMAN

RANK: MAJOR GENERAL

BORN: 1820

EDUCATED: UNITED STATES MILITARY ACADEMY

MILITARY CAREER

VETERAN OF MEXICAN WAR

DEVELOPED A GREAT PARTNERSHIP WITH GRANT AT SHILOH

FINISHED THE WAR WITH HIS VICTORIOUS MARCH TO THE SEA
  AND CAROLINAS CAMPAIGN

DIED: 1891

continued his steady advance to Atlanta and finally took possession of the key city on September 2.

PRELIMINARIES

This Atlanta Campaign was a part of Lieutenant General Ulysses S. Grant's coordinated strategy for the spring of 1864, which involved simultaneous advances designed to press the Confederacy on all fronts. Previously, the disjointed Federal effort had allowed the Confederates to shift forces from one threatened position to another. Now Grant planned to use his own campaign in Virginia, in which Major General George Meade would maintain constant pressure on General Robert E. Lee's Army of Northern Virginia, together with Sherman's Atlanta Campaign against Johnston's Army of Tennessee, to overwhelm the Confederates.

The Atlanta Campaign was preceded by Grant's defeat of General Braxton Bragg in the Chattanooga Campaign. After the victory, Grant was called to Washington to assume command of the overall Federal effort and Sherman succeeded him as commander in the western theater. For his part, Bragg retreated twenty-five miles south of Chattanooga to Dalton, Georgia, and dug in his forces. Bragg's poor performance in Kentucky and at Chickamauga had already caused him to lose credibility throughout much of the Confederacy. There had even been a petition signed by such high-ranking officers as James Longstreet, Simon Buckner, Patrick Cleburne, D. H. Hill, Leonidas Polk, and William Preston requesting that President Jefferson Davis remove Bragg from command. After Chattanooga, the public outcry had become so strong that Bragg succumbed to the pressure and asked to be relieved. Davis replaced Bragg with General Joe Johnston, a seasoned general but a man with whom Davis had had strained relations since the very beginning of the war. Johnston was a defensive fighter by nature, and the fact that he began the campaign with only 62,000 men compared to Sherman's 100,000 reinforced this tendency.

Sherman, on the other hand, thrived on the offensive. By this point in the war he had developed an extremely close relationship with Grant, and Sherman fully understood what the new general-in-chief wanted him to do.

KENNESAW MOUNTAIN

Date	June 27, 1864
Location	Kennesaw, Georgia
Result	Confederate victory

Strength

Union: Army of the Tennessee, Army of the Cumberland, Army of the Ohio (100,000)	Confederate: Army Army of Tennessee (62,000)

Casualties and losses

3,000 (approximate)	1,000 (approximate)

JOSEPH E. JOHNSTON

RANK: GENERAL

BORN: 1807

EDUCATED: UNITED STATES MILITARY ACADEMY

MILITARY CAREER

VETERAN OF MEXICAN WAR

WON JOINT VICTORY WITH BEAUREGARD AT FIRST MANASSAS

WOUNDED AT SEVEN PINES AND SUCCEEDED BY ROBERT E. LEE

SURRENDERED APRIL 26, 1865, IN NORTH CAROLINA

DIED: 1891

Above: Union troops prepare to engage the advancing Confederates at Resaca, May 13, 1864. While a powerful offensive weapon in the Mexican War, artillery was used most effectively on the defense in the Civil War because of the impact of the rifle.

Grant's instructions were "to move against Johnston's army, to break it up, and to get into the interior of the enemy's country as far as you can, inflicting all the damage you can against their war resources." Sherman was exactly the right man for such a task.

Grant and Sherman were thoroughly modern generals who understood maneuver, logistics, and the importance of the support of the population. Atlanta was a vital supply, manufacturing, and communications center second only to Richmond in its industrial importance to the Confederacy. Thus far it had escaped the ravages of war. By capturing Atlanta,

Sherman would not only interrupt supplies that were helping keep Lee's Army of Northern Virginia in the field, he also would be taking the war to the Confederate people. Furthermore, capturing Atlanta would not only dishearten the Confederate population, it would also silence those peace advocates in the North who considered the war to be hopelessly deadlocked with no end to the fighting in sight. With Grant seemingly going nowhere against Lee in Virginia, President Lincoln faced a tough challenge in the 1864 election from a Democratic peace platform. If Sherman could capture Atlanta, it would

have as much political importance as it would military.

Sherman began his march on May 7, just a few days after Grant and Meade began their offensive against Lee in Virginia. Finding Johnston's Dalton defenses too strong, Sherman sent Major General James McPherson's Army of the Tennessee to turn the Confederates from the west while Major General George Thomas's Army of the Cumberland advanced frontally along the Western and Atlantic Railroad. Fighting took place around Rocky Face Ridge on May 5–9, but Johnston fell back without becoming decisively engaged.

Johnston's force was then bolstered by the arrival of Lieutenant General Leonidas Polk's corps and took up strong defensive positions at Resaca, where fighting occurred on May 13–16. As Sherman threatened envelopment from the west, Johnston again withdrew. In this now relatively open country, Sherman chose to advance on a broad front. In the process, his corps were not in close supporting distance of each other, and this situation gave the usually defensive-minded Johnston an opportunity to go on the offensive at Cassville. Major General John Schofield's small Army of the Ohio, augmented by

Above: A flag bearer from Polk's Brigade. The Confederate battle flag emerged after First Manassas as a means of ending confusion caused by similarities in appearance between the first national flag of the Confederacy and the Federal Stars and Stripes.

Above: John Bell Hood (1831–79) was an aggressive fighter who succeeded Johnston in command after Johnston's repeated withdrawals had frustrated President Davis.

Major General Joe Hooker's corps, was on the road from Adairsville to Cassville while McPherson's army was marching about five miles west of Adairsville. Most of Thomas's army was on a road that went from Adairsville ten miles south to Kingston before veering east to Cassville. Johnston had plans to concentrate his 74,000 men at Cassville and ambush the fewer than 35,000 Federals under Schofield and Hooker. Ideally, the other two Federal armies could then be defeated piecemeal as they rushed to Schofield's aid.

It was a promising opportunity, but the normally aggressive Lieutenant General John Bell Hood mistakenly assumed a small Federal cavalry detachment was a much larger force and faced east as a precaution rather than west as called for in the attack plan. The ensuing delay foiled Johnston's initial plan, and then on May 19, Hood and Polk convinced Johnston their lines were too vulnerable to enfilade fire and Johnston again withdrew.

Johnston then occupied positions at Allatoona Pass, which Sherman considered too formidable to attack. Instead, Sherman rested his army for three days and then undertook another turning movement at Dallas. Fighting

Right: Leonidas Polk was killed by a well-aimed artillery shot while conducting reconnaissance on Pine Mountain.

occurred there on May 25–27 and Johnston retired to Kennesaw Mountain.

KENNESAW MOUNTAIN

In this new position, Johnston formed a defensive front ten miles long that took in three mountains—Brush Mountain on the right, Pine Mountain in the middle, and Lost Mountain on the left. Two miles behind these three stood Kennesaw Mountain, the strongest part of the Confederate line.

Kennesaw Mountain is actually a ridge that slants from northeast to southwest for two miles, with three distinct summits separated by saddles, or low areas, in between. Big Kennesaw, at the northeastern end of the ridge, is the highest peak, rising nearly 700 feet

above the adjacent valley. Little Kennesaw is in the middle of the ridge and boasts a bald top 400 feet above its base. To the southwest lies Pigeon Hill, a 200-foot rise above the low ground at the foot of its slopes.

The position at Kennesaw not only gave Johnston a commanding view of the area, it also gave him control of the Western and Atlantic Railroad, which skirted its base. Furthermore, it allowed Johnston to block Sherman's approach to the Chattahoochee, the last broad river north of Atlanta. These advantages made Kennesaw Mountain the most formidable natural defensive position between Chattanooga and Atlanta. Sherman summed up the situation when he wrote to Washington, "The whole

Above: Entitled *Thunder on Little Kennesaw*, this modern painting shows Lumsden's Alabama Battery defending Little Kennesaw Mountain against Sherman's attack while incendiary devices stream overhead. Johnston's retrograde during the Atlanta Campaign was facilitated by strong breastworks that afforded the Confederates excellent protection.

Above: By the time of the Atlanta Campaign, Sherman had two war horses—Sam and Lexington. His favorite was Lexington, which he rode into Atlanta.

close contact and the fighting incessant, with a good deal of artillery. As fast as we gain one position the enemy has another all ready . . . Kennesaw . . . is the key to the whole country."

On June 10, Sherman began probing Johnston's position, but nearly two weeks of constant rains slowed progress. The Pine Mountain position gave the Confederates an excellent view of Federal movements, but it was also so far forward of the Confederate line that it was vulnerable to a quick Federal strike. On June 14, Johnston, accompanied by Lieutenant General William Hardee, whose corps had a brigade occupying the position, rode forward on Pine Mountain to assess the risk. Polk joined the reconnaissance party in order to get a look at Sherman's positions.

Johnston quickly ascertained that the position was too exposed and ordered Hardee to pull his forces back by nightfall. Having made that decision, Johnston stopped to take another look at

countryside is one vast fort, and Johnston must have at least fifty miles of connected trenches with abatis and finished batteries . . . Our lines are now in

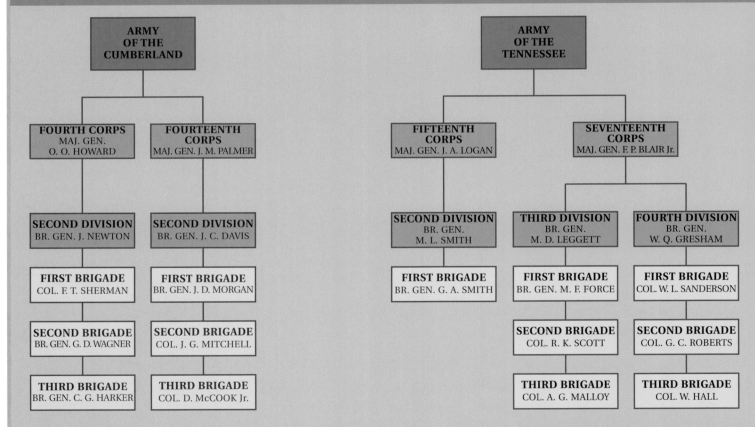

ORDER OF BATTLE: UNITED STATES (UNION), KENNESAW MOUNTAIN

ARMY OF THE CUMBERLAND

- **FOURTH CORPS** — MAJ. GEN. O. O. HOWARD
  - **SECOND DIVISION** — BR. GEN. J. NEWTON
    - **FIRST BRIGADE** — COL. F. T. SHERMAN
    - **SECOND BRIGADE** — BR. GEN. G. D. WAGNER
    - **THIRD BRIGADE** — BR. GEN. C. G. HARKER
- **FOURTEENTH CORPS** — MAJ. GEN. J. M. PALMER
  - **SECOND DIVISION** — BR. GEN. J. C. DAVIS
    - **FIRST BRIGADE** — BR. GEN. J. D. MORGAN
    - **SECOND BRIGADE** — COL. J. G. MITCHELL
    - **THIRD BRIGADE** — COL. D. McCOOK Jr.

ARMY OF THE TENNESSEE

- **FIFTEENTH CORPS** — MAJ. GEN. J. A. LOGAN
  - **SECOND DIVISION** — BR. GEN. M. L. SMITH
    - **FIRST BRIGADE** — BR. GEN. G. A. SMITH
- **SEVENTEENTH CORPS** — MAJ. GEN. F. P. BLAIR Jr.
  - **THIRD DIVISION** — BR. GEN. M. D. LEGGETT
    - **FIRST BRIGADE** — BR. GEN. M. F. FORCE
    - **SECOND BRIGADE** — COL. R. K. SCOTT
    - **THIRD BRIGADE** — COL. A. G. MALLOY
  - **FOURTH DIVISION** — BR. GEN. W. Q. GRESHAM
    - **FIRST BRIGADE** — COL. W. L. SANDERSON
    - **SECOND BRIGADE** — COL. G. C. ROBERTS
    - **THIRD BRIGADE** — COL. W. HALL

the Federal positions, ignoring warnings that Sherman's artillery had the exact range to the hill. Indeed, Captain Hubert Dilger and his Battery One of the First Ohio Light Artillery had spotted the tempting target of generals, and moments later opened fire. Johnston and Hardee scurried to safety, but the

Above: The combination of the protection of the breastwork and the range and accuracy of the rifle proved deadly for attackers during the Civil War.

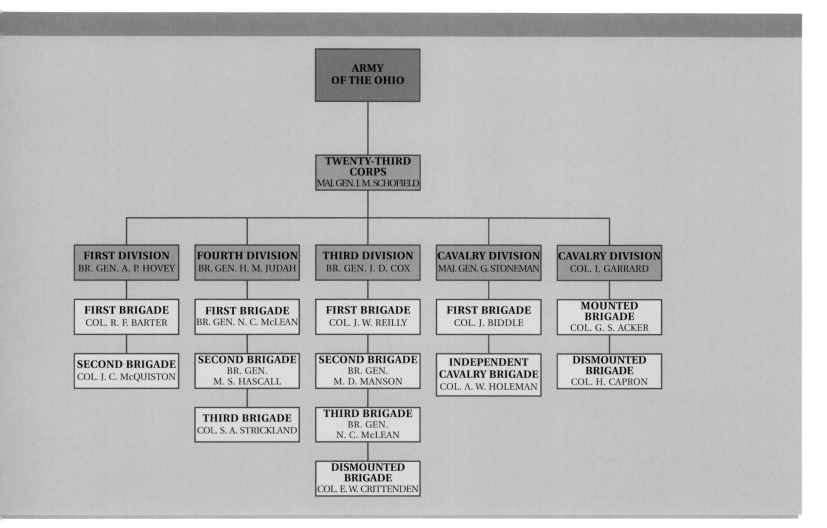

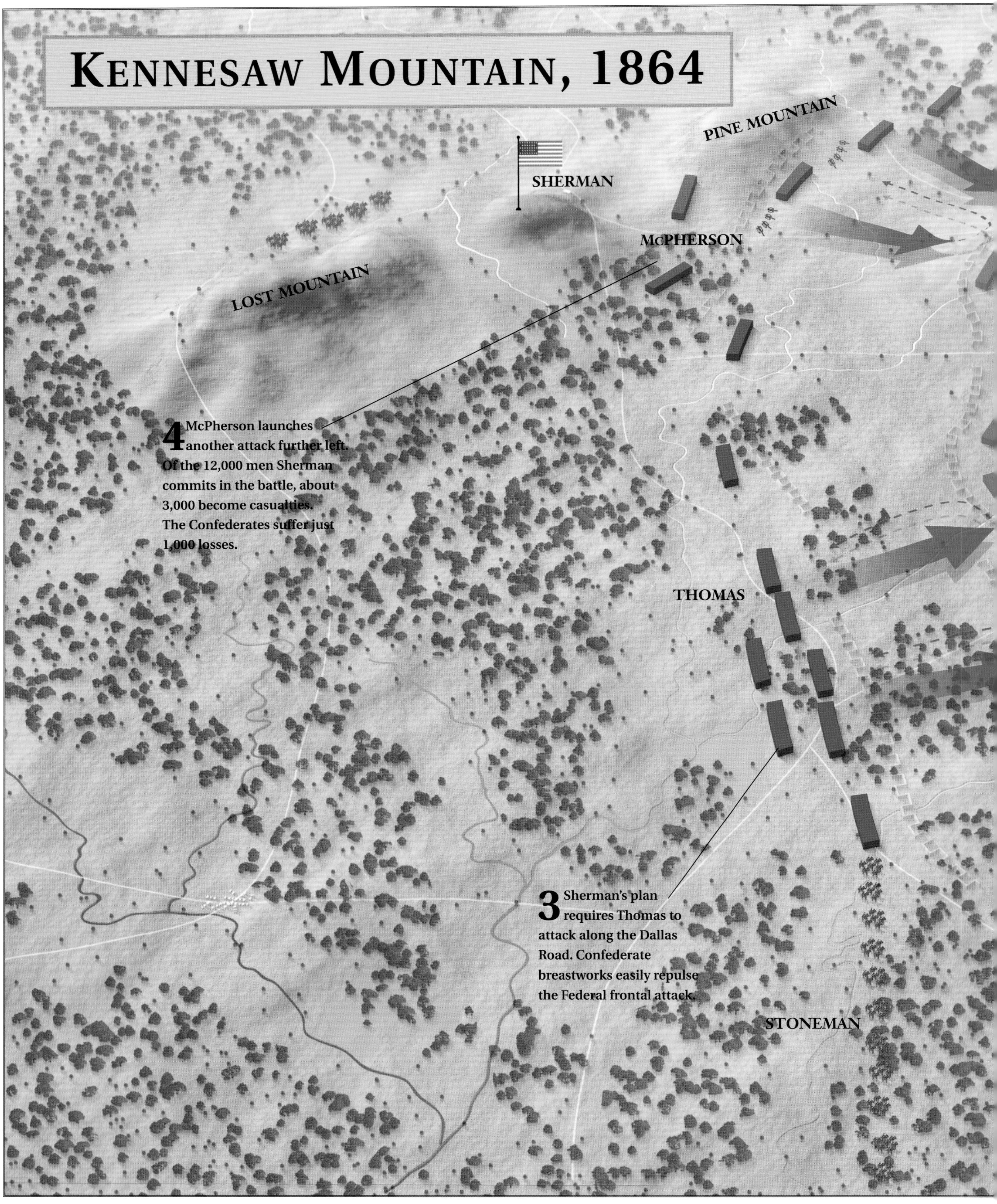

KENNESAW MOUNTAIN, 1864

PINE MOUNTAIN

SHERMAN

McPHERSON

LOST MOUNTAIN

4 McPherson launches another attack further left. Of the 12,000 men Sherman commits in the battle, about 3,000 become casualties. The Confederates suffer just 1,000 losses.

THOMAS

3 Sherman's plan requires Thomas to attack along the Dallas Road. Confederate breastworks easily repulse the Federal frontal attack.

STONEMAN

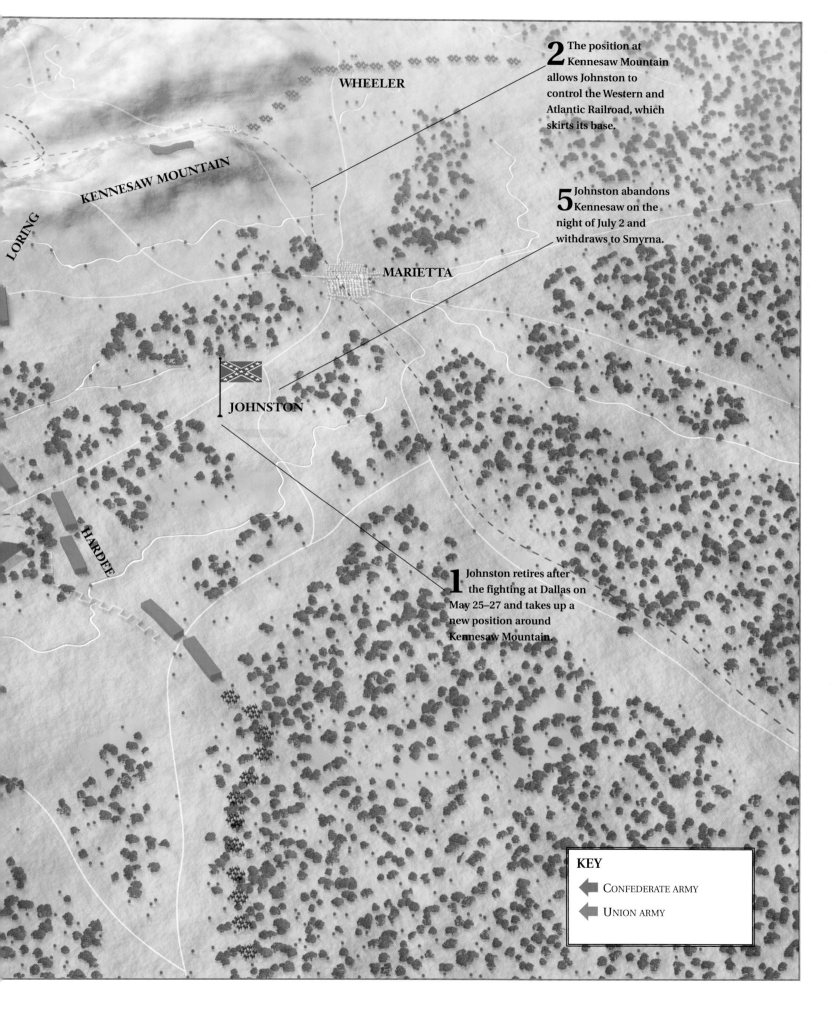

WHEELER

2 The position at Kennesaw Mountain allows Johnston to control the Western and Atlantic Railroad, which skirts its base.

KENNESAW MOUNTAIN

LORING

5 Johnston abandons Kennesaw on the night of July 2 and withdraws to Smyrna.

MARIETTA

JOHNSTON

HARDEE

1 Johnston retires after the fighting at Dallas on May 25–27 and takes up a new position around Kennesaw Mountain.

KEY

CONFEDERATE ARMY

UNION ARMY

Above: Three Federal assaults brought Sherman's men within ninety feet of the Confederate lines at Kennesaw Mountain, but the defense held. His frontal attack thwarted, Sherman resumed his turning movements after Kennesaw.

popular Polk was killed by Dilger's famously accurate fire. Johnston pulled his troops off of Pine Mountain the next day, and the Federals occupied the abandoned position. Upon arrival they found a sign that read, "You damned Yankee sons of bitches have killed our old Gen. Polk."

On the night of June 17–18, Johnston withdrew from Lost Mountain and Brush Mountain because of another threatened envelopment and consolidated his position on Kennesaw Mountain. Polk's division, temporarily being led by Major General William Loring, assumed an entrenched position on Kennesaw's northern rim. Hood was on the right, blocking the railroad, and Hardee was on the left with a line that began at the western edge of Kennesaw and then turned south across the Dallas–Marietta road, lying at right angles to the rest of the Confederate position. Visitors from Atlanta rode up to observe the developments, but the excursions came to an end after a few civilians were killed.

BREASTWORK CONSTRUCTION
IN ACTION

Throughout the campaign, Johnston pulled back to positions that had previously been reconnoitered by his engineers. By this point in the war, his men had the breastwork construction

process down to a science. First trees were felled and trimmed and the logs rolled in line to form a revetment usually four feet high. The logs were then banked with earth from a ditch dug to their front. The earth formed a sloping parapet about seven to ten feet at the top and three feet at ground level. On top of the revetment, skids supported a line of head logs punctuated by horizontal loopholes three inches wide, through which the men could fire while still being protected. In front of these breastworks the men felled trees and bushes toward the enemy to form elaborate chevaux-de-frise and abatis. The defenses went up so quickly that one Federal soldier surmised that the Confederates must carry their breastworks with them. Sherman himself complained, "The enemy can build parapets faster than we can march."

In addition to the protection of breastworks, defenders also greatly benefited from the technological advances of the rifled musket and the minié ball. The old smoothbore muskets had a range of 100–200 yards, but the new rifles were effective from 400–600 yards. Infantry firepower was further enhanced by the minié ball, a cylindro-conoidal bullet that was slightly smaller in diameter than the rifle barrel and thus could be easily dropped down the barrel. One end, however, was hollow, and when the rifle was fired, expanding gas widened the sides of this hollow end so that the bullet would grip the rifling and create the spinning effect needed for accuracy. These developments greatly increased the power of the defense relative to the offense, as defenders could now deliver accurate long-range fire from behind the protection of their breastworks and decimate frontal attacks.

As well as these advantages, Johnston had chosen excellent terrain from which to defend. Sherman noted, "On the 20th Johnston's position was unusually strong. Kennesaw Mountain was his salient; his two flanks were refused and covered by parapets and by Noonday and Nose's Creeks." Another Federal commented, "If the Rebs cannot hold such a country as this, they cannot hold anything." Yet in spite of the strength of the Confederate position, Sherman elected to deviate from his pattern of turning movements and instead attempted a frontal assault at Kennesaw.

SHERMAN'S RATIONALE

There were several reasons behind Sherman's decision. First, he thought he had found a point where the Confederate line was weak and a breakthrough was possible. The recent rains that had reduced his mobility also frustrated him. The only alternative to attacking was to delay, an idea that was anathema to Sherman. Furthermore, another flanking movement would move Sherman yet farther away from the railroad that he knew was his critical means of logistical support. Perhaps most significant in Sherman's mind was that an attack was important to maintaining the offensive spirit of his troops, whom he believed "had settled down to the belief that

flanking alone was my game." Sherman complained, "A fresh furrow in a plowed field will stop a whole column, and all begin to entrench." An attack would also disrupt the fairly predictable pattern that Johnston had settled into of withdrawing before becoming decisively engaged.

Whatever the proximate cause, Sherman's decision to attack Kennesaw Mountain was not made without due consideration. On June 13, Sherman had told Major General Henry Halleck in Washington, "We cannot risk the heavy loss of an assault at this distance from our base." Three weeks later, Sherman reversed his assessment and told Halleck, "I am now inclined to feign on both flanks and assault the center. It may cost us dear, but the results would surpass any attempt to pass around." A brief encounter between Hood and Schofield at Kolb's Farm on June 22 further convinced Sherman

Below: The Confederates set up palisades and chevaux-de-frise to defend the approaches to Atlanta. The area around the defenses has also been flattened or stripped bare, allowing open fields of fire for the defenders.

Opposite: The popular and capable James McPherson (1828–64) was one of the casualties of the Atlanta Campaign. Fort McPherson in Atlanta was later named in his honor.

that Kennesaw could not be bypassed with a march to Marietta or Smyrna. By June 23, Sherman was again thinking about a frontal assault. He had weighed his options and decided on what he considered to be the best possible course of action.

Thus, Sherman ordered Schofield and his Army of the Ohio to extend the Federal right in order to compel Johnston to lengthen and thin his lines. The original plan was for Schofield to attack still further to the right, but when Sherman realized the strength of the Confederate defenses in that sector, he canceled that attack and had Schofield focus on a demonstration. McPherson would demonstrate on the other end of the Confederate line by sending cavalry and infantry to bluff an attack that was threatening the approach road to Marietta from the north. These wide flank demonstrations were designed to divert Confederate attention from the

main attack in the center. This effort would actually be a two-pronged assault with Thomas's Army of the Cumberland striking along the Dallas Road at an exact point of Thomas's own choosing. McPherson's Army of the Tennessee would make a secondary attack on the southwestern end of the Kennesaw ridge at Pigeon Hill.

Sherman's plan committed only about one-fifth of his force to immediate battle, with the remainder standing ready to exploit success. He instructed his troops, "Each attacking column will endeavor to break a single point in the enemy's line, and make a secure lodgment beyond, and be prepared for following it up toward Marietta and the railroad in case of success."

"HELL HAS BROKEN LOOSE IN GEORGIA!"

There was little finesse in the attack. Early on June 27, Sherman initiated a

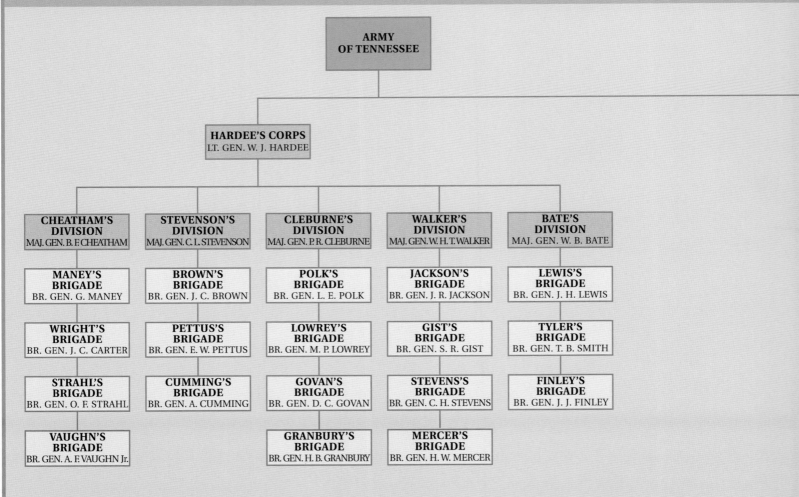

ORDER OF BATTLE: CONFEDERACY, KENNESAW MOUNTAIN

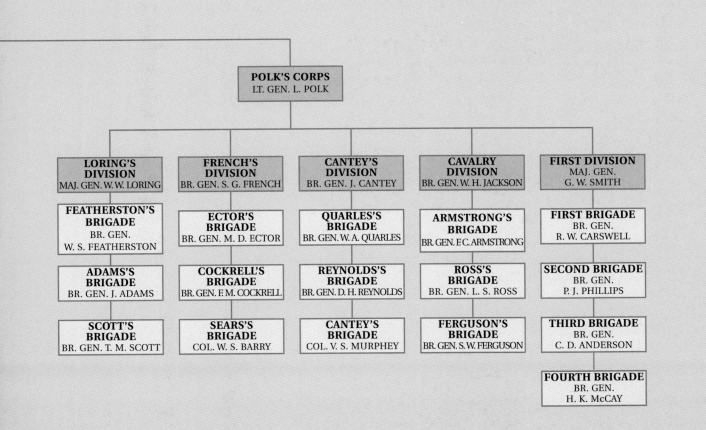

"furious cannonade" of about 200 guns against the Confederate position. One defender exclaimed, "Hell has broke loose in Georgia, sure enough!" About 8:00 a.m., the artillery stopped firing, and some 5,500 Federal soldiers advanced through the dense and rugged terrain. Almost immediately, they came under heavy fire. Their leaders had little specific information of the lay of the land or the nature of the Confederate positions. To make matters worse, the cover provided by the woods ended well before the Federals reached the Confederate lines, and the defenders enjoyed excellent fields of fire. One historian describes it as "a no-man's-land bristling with abatis."

In some places, the Federal attackers had success against the Confederate outposts, but they could not get close to the main defenses before encountering a murderous fire. "The air seemed filled with bullets," recalled one survivor. Another said, "It was almost sure death to take your face out of the dust." One Confederate explained that, in order to kill the enemy, "all that was necessary was to load and shoot." Elsewhere, defenders rolled large boulders down and threw rocks at the attackers. In some places, the combatants fought hand to hand using their rifles as clubs and pummeling each other with their fists. All told, the Federals launched three separate assaults and got nowhere. In the early afternoon, Sherman asked Thomas, "Do you think you can carry any part of the enemy's line today?" Thomas replied, "We have already lost heavily today without gaining any material advantage. One or two more such assaults will use up this army."

Sherman had had enough. Of the 12,000 men he had committed to battle on June 27, he had lost about 3,000. The Confederates lost fewer than 1,000. For the next five days, some Federals held their ground within thirty yards of the Confederate positions, but there was no further fighting. On June 30, the armies negotiated a truce to bury the dead that by that time had been lying for three days in the hot Georgia sun.

But in spite of the disproportionate casualties at Kennesaw, the much larger Federal force was able to absorb its losses, and Sherman still had the railroad to keep his army supplied. He waited for the roads to dry, and on July 1 he resumed his efforts to turn the Confederate line. Ever vigilant for such a development, Johnston abandoned Kennesaw with great stealth on the night of July 2 and withdrew to a prepared position at Smyrna, having been quite satisfied to have stalled Sherman for two weeks, defeated his attack, and inflicted disproportionate losses.

THE FALL OF ATLANTA

Johnston's new line was built along the Chattahoochee River, which represented the last major obstacle between Sherman and Atlanta. In fighting on July 4–9, Sherman again turned the Confederates, and Johnston withdrew to Peach Tree Creek. By this time, President Davis was exasperated by Johnston's failure to make a stand. Davis replaced Johnston with John Bell Hood, a man with a marked reputation as a fighter.

Many observers questioned President Davis's decision. Sherman wrote that by this act, "the Confederate Government rendered us most valuable service." Grant also felt that replacing Johnston was a mistake, believing that "Johnston [had] acted very wisely: he husbanded his men and saved as much of his territory as he could, without fighting decisive battles in which all might be lost . . . I know that both Sherman and I were rejoiced when we heard of the change. Hood was certainly a brave, gallant soldier and not destitute of ability; but unfortunately his policy was to fight the enemy wherever he saw him, without thinking much of the consequences of defeat." Even General Robert E. Lee had advised Davis, "Hood is a bold fighter. I am doubtful as to other qualities necessary."

THE CONFEDERATES WITHDRAW TO ATLANTA

If Davis wanted offensive action, he was not to be disappointed. As Sherman closed in on Atlanta from the north and east, Hood ordered an attack to begin at

Opposite: Parts of Atlanta were damaged by Union artillery fire before the city was captured. Atlanta was a critical transportation and production center in the Confederacy. Sherman's victory there helped ensure Lincoln's reelection.

1:00 p.m. on July 20. The target was Thomas's army, which had secured a shallow bridgehead across Peach Tree Creek and was now unsupported by Sherman's other armies. Thomas was nicknamed "the Rock of Chickamauga" for his ability to hold ground even when isolated, and he would live up to this reputation at Peach Tree Creek. The Confederates launched a series of assaults until 6:00 p.m., but ultimately were forced to withdraw to the defenses of Atlanta. Hood had suffered 2,500 casualties, compared to about 1,600 for the Federals.

As Hood pulled back, Sherman mistakenly thought the Confederates were abandoning Atlanta and sent McPherson in pursuit to the south and east. Hood sent his cavalry under Major General Joseph Wheeler and Hardee's corps on a fifteen-mile night march to strike McPherson's exposed southern flank. In the fighting on July 22, the popular and capable McPherson was killed, but the Confederate attack was defeated. Both Sherman and Grant held McPherson in the highest regard. When Grant learned of McPherson's death, an

Below: A Union artillery battery waits behind defensive fortifications near Atlanta. Civil War soldiers experienced the stress, danger, and excitement of close combat as well as the boredom and monotony of waiting for the next action.

observer said Grant's "mouth twitched and his eyes shut . . . then the tears came and one followed the other down his bronzed cheeks as he sat there without a word or comment." In another lopsided battle, Hood suffered 8,500 casualties, compared to just 3,700 for Sherman.

By July 25, Sherman had invested Atlanta from the north and east. Hood still had an open railroad to the south, which Sherman unsuccessfully tried to sever with two raids between July 26 and July 31 and the Battle of Ezra Church on July 28. Nevertheless Hood,

sensing that eventually his lines of communications would be completely cut, finally evacuated Atlanta on September 1, and the Federals moved in to occupy the city the next morning. The Atlanta Campaign was over.

The results of the Atlanta Campaign were critical to the continuation of the Federal war effort. With the Northern population growing tired of the war and George McClellan campaigning as a peace candidate for president in 1864, Lincoln feared he would lose the election. On August 23, he went so far as to have his cabinet members endorse a "blind memorandum" in which he wrote, "This morning, as for some days past, it seems exceedingly probable that this Administration will not be re-elected. Then it will be my duty to so co-operate with the President elect, as to save the Union between the election and the inauguration; as he will have secured his election on such ground that he can not possibly save it afterwards." Sherman's capture of Atlanta reversed this trend and showed the North was clearly winning the war. This attitude carried over to the polls and Lincoln was reelected easily. The fate of the Confederacy was now sealed, as Lincoln would continue to prosecute the war to a Union victory. If Lincoln had lost, a negotiated settlement would have been a probable outcome. The Atlanta Campaign demonstrates the close interaction between military and political developments and was critical to the war's outcome.

OFFENSIVE–DEFENSIVE TACTICS

Johnston's limitations as a strategist prevented him from thinking in offensive terms. Yet his defensive tactics could still have been incorporated into a broader Confederate strategy. Realizing the Confederacy's inability to defend itself at its borders, President Davis had early in the war articulated an "offensive–defensive" formula through which the Confederate forces would permit a Federal penetration to develop, determine its axis of advance, wait for the right time and place, and then

"A GRAND AND AWFUL SPECTACLE IS PRESENTED TO THE BEHOLDER IN THIS BEAUTIFUL CITY, NOW IN FLAMES. BY ORDER, THE CHIEF ENGINEER HAD DESTROYED BY POWDER AND FIRE ALL THE STORE-HOUSES, DEPOT BUILDINGS AND MACHINE-SHOPS. THE HEAVEN IS ONE EXPANSE OF LURID FIRE; THE AIR IS FILLED WITH FLYING, BURNING CINDERS; BUILDINGS COVERING TWO HUNDRED ACRES ARE IN RUINS OR IN FLAMES; EVERY INSTANT THERE IS THE SHARP DETONATION OR THE SMOTHERED BOOMING SOUND OF EXPLODING SHELLS AND POWDER CONCEALED IN THE BUILDINGS."

AN AIDE TO WILLIAM T. SHERMAN, ON THE BURNING OF ATLANTA, NOVEMBER 15, 1864

counterattack. Such an approach would have been very appropriate in the Atlanta Campaign because, as Sherman advanced farther into Georgia against Johnston's delay, the Federal lines of communications lengthened and became vulnerable to attack.

To hit this target, Lieutenant General Stephen D. Lee, commander of the Confederate Department of Alabama, Mississippi, and East Louisiana, had available nearly 14,000 cavalrymen led

by the dangerous Lieutenant General Nathan Bedford Forrest. On eleven occasions between May and July 1864, Johnston sent requests to Davis, Lee, or Bragg that Forrest's cavalry be used to strike Sherman's supply line. Each time, Johnston's request was refused for the general reason that Forrest was already committed to operations in Mississippi.

Even though Forrest succeeded in gaining a series of tactical victories against Federal forces in Mississippi, the fact that Forrest was contained in this much lower-priority area must be considered a strategic advantage for the Federals. In this way, the Confederacy's ineffective department command system placed Forrest's cavalry resources beyond Johnston's reach, and the lack of unity of effort precluded the Confederates from introducing the necessary offensive component to complement Johnston's defense.

JOHNSTON'S LEADERSHIP

Johnston had been relieved from command because of his defensive strategy, but the failure of Hood's offensive-minded approach seemed to vindicate Johnston to many. Even Grant lent his support for Johnston, writing, "For my own part, I think Johnston's tactics were right. Anything that could have prolonged the war a year beyond the time that it did finally close would probably have exhausted the North to such an extent that they might have abandoned the contest and agreed to a separation." The logic behind such thinking was that the overall Confederate strategy was one of exhaustion. The South did not have to defeat the North on the battlefield but merely had to keep the war going long enough for the Federals to tire of it and acquiesce to Southern independence. Several historians have favorably compared Johnston's efforts against Sherman to Lee's delay against Grant in Virginia.

There is, however, an important difference. While Johnston was a master of the defense, fully showing he understood the power of the rifle and breastworks at Kennesaw, he was nearly devoid of any offensive spirit. In fact, Johnston's detractors point out that there is really no evidence to show Johnston ever intended to fight for Atlanta. Instead, he may have planned merely to continue retreating to Macon or some other location.

Such an approach to strategy conflicts with the long-standing principle of war of the offensive. Military strategists consider offensive action to be the key to decisive results and the essence of successful operations. Defense operations alone can normally not obtain a decision, so army forces defend only until they gain sufficient strength to attack. Johnston did not share this perspective and seems to have considered the defense to be an end unto itself.

MAINTAINING SUPPLY LINES

While focusing on disrupting the Confederate logistical effort, Sherman also understood the need to protect his own supply lines. He had gained valuable experience operating deep within enemy territory during his Meridian Campaign in February, but unlike at Meridian, the push to Atlanta was not a raid in which Sherman would be gone for a definitive period of time and return to his secure base. In the Atlanta Campaign, Sherman was pressing straight ahead and had no intention of turning back. The ability to support his force would be critical. Supplying his 100,000 men would require 1,300 tons of supplies a day, most of which would be brought forward by rail, and Sherman confided to his brother that "my long and single line of railroad to my rear, of limited capacity, is the delicate point of my game."

What concerned Sherman most was the serious threat Forrest's cavalry posed to the vulnerable Federal logistics. At one point Sherman had vowed to assemble a force designed to "go out and follow Forrest to death, if it costs 10,000 lives and breaks the Treasury. There will never be peace in Tennessee till Forrest is dead." For the time being, however, Sherman had to rely on 5,000 infantrymen and 3,300 cavalrymen under the command of Brigadier General Samuel Sturgis.

A GENERAL GROWING IN SKILL

On June 1, Sturgis began carrying out instructions to launch "a threatening movement from Memphis," southeast into Mississippi, to prevent Forrest "from swinging over my [Sherman's] communications in North Georgia or Middle Tennessee." On that same day, Forrest had left Tupelo, Mississippi, with 2,200 men to attack Sherman's supply line below Nashville. Forrest advanced as far as north Alabama, and on June 3 he was preparing to cross the Tennessee River when he received word to return to Mississippi. Stephen Lee was unwilling to accept the threat posed by Sturgis within Lee's department. Thus, Forrest's valuable asset was diverted from its important mission in order to defend Tupelo and Corinth. Forrest eventually routed the much larger Federal force, but Sherman correctly credits Sturgis for accomplishing his chief object, which had been "to hold Forrest there [in Mississippi] and keep him off our [rail]road."

Sherman was one of the few Civil War generals who grew in skill during the conflict, and Kennesaw Mountain played an important part in his development as a modern commander. Sherman refined his mastery of strategy and logistics, but he also continued to progress in his understanding of what he would come to call "hard war." On June 29, he wrote his wife, "I begin to regard the death and mangling of a couple of thousand men as a small affair, a kind of morning dash." He continued, "It may be well that we become hardened . . . The worst of war is not yet begun." After Atlanta, Sherman would continue his evolution to becoming the Civil War's principal practitioner of "hard war" with his March to the Sea.

SHERMAN'S LEADERSHIP

Sherman's frontal attack at Kennesaw underscores the fact that his military genius rested not so much in tactics but in the mastery of strategy and logistics. Sherman knew he had been defeated on the tactical battlefield, writing, "Failure as it was, and for which I assume the entire responsibility." Nonetheless, Sherman kept his eye on the bigger strategic picture, adding, "I yet claim it produced good fruits, as it demonstrated to General Johnston that I would assault, and that boldly." Sherman understood that he was in a strategic campaign, and he was willing to absorb a tactical defeat if he felt it served a broader strategic purpose. In this case, that meant showing Johnston that Sherman had more than one course of action available to him. He did not want to become so predictable that Johnston could anticipate Sherman's every move. In the process, he would also impress the defensive-minded Johnston that the campaign would involve deadly fighting and not just the relatively low-cost maneuver that Johnston preferred. Sherman understood the nature of his opponent and was willing to risk a frontal assault in part to gain a psychological advantage on Johnston.

Sherman also understood that his true objective during the Atlanta Campaign was not even Johnston's army but the Confederates' logistical base. Johnston's army merely stood in the way of Sherman's overall goal, which was "to get into the interior of the enemy's country as far as you can, inflicting all the damage you can against their war resources." Atlanta, which Sherman considered to be "too important a place in the hands of the enemy to be left undisturbed, with its magazines, stores, arsenals, workshops, foundries, and more especially its railroads, which converged there from the four great cardinal points," was the real prize of the campaign. Thus, a tactical setback at Kennesaw was of little importance so long as Sherman was able to continue his advance, which is exactly what he did.

BIBLIOGRAPHY

Anderson, Bern. *By Sea and by River: The Naval History of the Civil War.* New York: Knopf, 1962.

Arnold, James. *Grant Wins the War: Decision at Vicksburg.* New York: Wiley, 1997.

Ballard, Michael. *Vicksburg: The Campaign that Opened the Mississippi.* Chapel Hill, NC: University of North Carolina Press, 2003.

Berringer, Richard et al. *Why the South Lost the Civil War.* Athens, GA: University of Georgia Press, 1986.

Castel, Albert. *Decision in the West: The Atlanta Campaign of 1864.* Lawrence, KS: University Press of Kansas, 1992.

Catton, Bruce. *Gettysburg: The Final Fury.* Garden City, NY: Doubleday, 1974.

_____. *Mr. Lincoln's Army.* Garden City, NY: Doubleday, 1962.

Cleaves, Freeman. *Meade of Gettysburg.* Norman, OK: University of Oklahoma Press, 1960.

Coddington, Edwin B. *The Gettysburg Campaign: A Study in Command.* New York: Scribners, 1984.

Connelly, Thomas L. *Army of the Heartland: The Army of Tennessee, 1861–1862.* Baton Rouge, LA: Louisiana State University Press, 1997.

_____. *Autumn of Glory: The Army of Tennessee, 1862–1865.* Baton Rouge, LA: Louisiana State University Press, 2001.

Davis, William C. *Battle at Bull Run: A History of the First Major Campaign of the Civil War.* Mechanicsburg, PA: Stackpole Books, 1995.

Dougherty, Kevin et al. *Battles of the Civil War, 1861–1865.* New York, Barnes and Noble, 2007.

Dowdey, Clifford. *Lee's Last Campaign: The Story of Lee and His Men Against Grant—1864.* Boston: Little, Brown and Company, 1960.

Duffy, James. *Lincoln's Admiral: The Civil War Campaigns of David Farragut.* New York: Castle Books, 2006.

Foote, Shelby. *The Civil War: A Narrative.* Vol. 1, *Fort Sumter to Perryville.* Vol. 2, *Fredericksburg to Meridian.* Vol. 3, *Red River to Appomattox.* New York: Random House, 1986.

Frassanito, William A. *Gettysburg: A Journey in Time.* New York: Scribners, 1975.

Freeman, Douglas S. *Lee's Lieutenants: A Study in Command.* 3 vols. New York: Charles Scribner's Sons, 1942–1944.

_____. *R. E. Lee: A Biography.* 4 vols. New York: Charles Scribner's Sons, 1934.

Furguson, Ernest. *Chancellorsville, 1863: The Souls of the Brave.* New York: Alfred A. Knopf, 1992.

Gallagher, Gary. *The Shenandoah Valley Campaign of 1862.* Chapel Hill, NC: University of North Carolina Press, 2008.

Grant, Ulysses S. *Personal Memoirs of U. S. Grant.* 2 vols. New York: Webster and Company, 1885–1886.

Hallock, Judith and Grady McWhinney. *Braxton Bragg and Confederate Defeat in Two Volumes.* Tuscaloosa, AL: University of Alabama Press, 1991.

Hattaway, Herman and Archer Jones. *How the North Won: A Military History of the Civil War.* Chicago: University of Illinois Press, 1983.

Hearn, Chester. *The Capture of New Orleans, 1862.* Baton Rouge, LA: Louisiana State University Press, 1995.

Jones, Archer. *Civil War Command and Strategy.* New York: The Free Press, 1992.

Jones, Virgil C. *The Civil War at Sea.* 3 vols. New York: Holt, 1960–1962.

McDonogh, James. *Shiloh: In Hell Before Night.* Knoxville, TN: University of Tennessee Press, 1997.

_____. *War in Kentucky: From Shiloh to Perryville.* Knoxville, TN: University of Tennessee Press, 1994.

McMurry, Richard. *Atlanta 1864: Last Chance for the Confederacy.* Lincoln, NE: University of Nebraska Press, 2000.

McPherson, James. *Battle Cry of Freedom: The Civil War Era.* Oxford, UK: Oxford University Press, 1988.

Miller, Edward Stokes. *Civil War Sea Battles.* Mechanicsburg, PA: Stackpole, 1995.

Murfin, James. *The Gleam of Bayonets: The Battle of Antietam and Robert E. Lee's Maryland Campaign.* New York: Thomas Yoseloff, 1965.

Rafuse, Ethan. *McClellan's War: The Failure of Moderation in the Struggle for the Union.* Bloomington, IN: Indiana University Press, 2005.

Rhea, Gordon C. *The Battles for Spotsylvania Court House and the Road to Yellow Tavern.* Baton Rouge, LA: Louisiana State University Press, 1997.

Rhea, Gordon C. *The Battle of the Wilderness, May 5–6, 1864.* Baton Rouge, LA: Louisiana State University Press, 2004.

Robertson, James. *Stonewall Jackson: The Man, the Soldier, the Legend.* New York: MacMillan Publishing USA, 1997.

Sears, Stephen. *Chancellorsville.* New York: Houghton Mifflin Company, 1996.

_____. *George McClellan.* New York: Ticknor and Fields, 1988.

_____. *Gettysburg.* New York: Houghton Mifflin Company, 2003.

_____. *Landscape Turned Red: The Battle of Antietam.* New York: Ticknor and Fields, 1983.

_____. *To the Gates of Richmond.* New York: Houghton Mifflin Company, 1992.

Shea, William and Terrence Winschel. *Vicksburg Is the Key: The Struggle for the Mississippi River.* Lincoln, NE: University of Nebraska Press, 2003.

Smith, Jean Edward. *Grant.* New York: Simon and Schuster, 2001.

Sommers, Richard. *Richmond Redeemed: The Siege at Petersburg.* Garden City, NY: Doubleday, 1981.

Tanner, Robert. *Stonewall in the Valley.* Garden City, NY: Doubleday, 1976.

Tucker, Glenn. *High Tide at Gettysburg.* New York: Smithmark, 1994.

Williams, T. Harry. *Lincoln and His Generals.* New York: Alfred A. Knopf, 1952.

_____. *P. G. T. Beauregard, Napoleon in Gray.* Baton Rouge, LA: Louisiana State University Press, 1955.

Woodworth, Stephen. *Nothing but Victory: The Army of the Tennessee, 1861–1865.* New York: Alfred A. Knopf, 2005.

_____. *Six Armies in Tennessee: The Chickamauga and Chattanooga Campaigns.* Lincoln, NE: University of Nebraska Press, 1998.

INDEX

PICTURE CREDITS

All maps and line illustrations
© Amber Books Ltd.

All images courtesy of the Library of
Congress, except for the following:

Alamy: 114–115 (Jim Lane)
Amber Books: 43, 101 (bottom)
Art-Tech/John Batchelor: 36
Art-Tech/MARS: 161 (bottom)
Cody Images: 47

Corbis: 41 (Bettmann), 107
  (Bettmann), 113 (Bettmann)
Getty Images: 74 (Hulton Archive),
  76–77 (Hulton Archive), 121
  (Hulton Archive)

Photos.com: 153, 171, 176
**Don Troiani/Military and Historical
  Image Bank:** 18–19, 50–51, 82–83
  (bottom), 130–131, 166–167,
  192–193, 201